About the author

Sydney-based journalist and author Murray Engleheart has written millions of words about music over more than four decades, with his work published from Moscow to São Paulo, Japan to New York. From first doing album reviews in a high school magazine in 1974, he has interviewed a virtual who's who of rock and roll from Keith Richards, Lou Reed and Patti Smith to Bob Dylan, John Lee Hooker and David Bowie. His first book was the global best seller *AC/DC Maximum Rock & Roll* with Arnaud Durieux (2006) and his second, *Blood Sweat and Beers: Oz Rock from the Aztecs to Rose Tattoo* (2010).

★

'Radio Birdman live brought loyalty as strong and powerful as their music. Yeah hup!' —Anthony Albanese, Prime Minister of Australia

'Radio Birdman are analogous to dark matter: largely unseen yet profoundly influential. That first record, *Radios Appear*, is immediate danger, defiance and seething fury. For my adolescent self in the mid-1970s, against the then contemporary landscape of Countdown-era bilge, that album was an instruction manual.' —Brad Shepherd, Hoodoo Gurus

'Murray's raw passion somehow doesn't mess with his skill to present the story, the context and the truth. But his passion is what will always beat like a desperate heart.' —Tim Rogers, You Am I and the Hard-Ons

'Radio Birdman are one of the greatest Australian rock 'n' roll bands. Murray has written a riveting and insightful account of their career and the world that shaped them. This book overflows with heart, soul, spirit and passion.' —Stuart Coupe

'An evocative telling of the history of this crucial, influential band mainly in the words of those who were there. I was too young to witness Radio Birdman in full flight at the Oxford Fun House but Murray's writing makes me wish I'd been part of that community.' —Murray Cook

RADIO BIRDMAN

RETALIATE FIRST

MURRAY ENGLEHEART

First published in 2024

Allen & Unwin
Cammeraygal Country
83 Alexander Street
Crows Nest NSW 2065
Australia
Phone: (61 2) 8425 0100
Email: info@allenandunwin.com
Web: www.allenandunwin.com

Allen & Unwin and the author acknowledge the Traditional Owners of the Country on which we live and work. We pay our respects to all Aboriginal and Torres Strait Islander Elders, past and present.

A catalogue record for this book is available from the National Library of Australia

ISBN 978 1 76106 964 2

Page 341: Lyrics from 'Mandraxed Watching Hellcats' with kind permission of Damien Minton

Set in 13/17 pt Adobe Garamond Pro by Midland Typesetters, Australia

10 9 8 7 6 5 4 3 2 1

The paper in this book is FSC® certified. FSC® promotes environmentally responsible, socially beneficial and economically viable management of the world's forests.

For Alley

Charlie

and for Ron S. Peno—Godbless them

'Your image is like a shadow, it's always there behind you!'—**Keith Richards**

'The more energy in the sound, the bigger the sound that gets to you, the more intense the experience is; and the more intense the experience is, the more intense reality is . . . music is equated on that level too, because it does make metabolic changes.'—**The MC5's Rob Tyner (to David Walley in *The Age of Rock 2*)**

'I have my husband, my son, my professional achievements, and I'm a Radio Birdman fan. They all sit right up there. [Radio Birdman] is that important to my identity.'—**Dr Shelley Kay, Exercise Physiologist and Research Fellow in Exercise Oncology at Chris O'Brien Lifehouse, Sydney**

'1977 was the best year to be 17.'—**Bob Short, Radio Birdman Teengenerate**

People Would Have Killed for That Band!

The wine flagon had been thrown through the closed windows of the first floor of Paddington Town Hall with almost superhuman force. It cleared the footpath in a graceful arc, trailed by a galaxy of tinkling glass, and shattered on a car parked on Oxford Street, bathing the vehicle in the last of its alcohol content. There was a near cinematic pause, as if to allow any stunned passers-by to digest what had just detonated before them; then other projectiles—anything that wasn't bolted in place—began to rain down from on high, each incoming heralded by the sound of further smashing glass. Some fervent punters above probably even considered taking a leap of faith themselves to personally enlist in the unscripted fireworks commemorating Radio Birdman's virtual coronation.

The date was 12 December 1977, and without any great flourish of publicity, the ultimate in rank outsiders had pulled around two thousand rabid bodies to the cathedral-like landmark in Sydney's eastern suburbs.

The crowd under its ten-metre ceiling was similar in number to that drawn by AC/DC to the Hordern Pavilion just a few kilometres away after returning from their successful UK and European tour exactly a year earlier.

Just three short years prior, Birdman's personnel of five had often exceeded their audience. From there, armed with microphone stands and an equally steely self-belief, they steered toward the oncoming traffic in the local music industry, horrifying record companies, enraging bouncers, bewildering audiences, with desperate publicans reaching for the power kill switch. Their attack and defence strategy was the same: retaliate first, and second if necessary. No triggering action was ever required.

At Paddington, those hand-to-hand combative labours came to fruition, the scattering of fevered support in their earliest days having coalesced into this vast legion. But while their summit-reaching night at the town hall—which was broadcast on Radio 2JJ—was a triumph, it was a badly lacerated win, with the worship of many cloaked in dark overzealous energies, some even signing on for duty with a smearing of blood on the internal walls of the venue.

At the end of the night, almost every sheet of glass in the building was shattered. The remnants looked like macabre mouths of jagged teeth or ceremonial masks from some lost tribe. They seemed to be grinning down at the carnage as a sea of individuals poured from the building and fanned out across Oxford Street with no regard for the traffic. Any vehicular impact wouldn't be felt for a day or two anyway. They were anaesthetised en masse, in a state of euphoria, the sound of a new world and tinnitus screeching in their ears.

Fast forward a few months and the Radios were still sparking spot fires. At first the comments by the heathens seemed lighthearted, even welcoming.

'The Birdman is here!' one guest declared to all at the backyard gathering in western Sydney, pointing at my band T-shirt.

Any ambiguity was soon ripped away by the more pointed directions provided by another very large attendee.

'Fly the fuck away, little Birdman!' the behemoth growled down with slow deliberate menace, crop-dusting my face from point-blank range.

It escalated from there and retreat soon seemed the best option. My friends and I made a swift exit from the premises, with a booming hail of beer cans beating out a broken rhythm on the body of our departing car.

To be fair, the aggressors recognised something was out of sync, that we were different. And they were right. It was as if the Radio Birdman name alone projected a challenge, a perplexing, unnerving uncertainty, even from my pale, somewhat concave chest.

I had been a Birdman convert for several years by that point. Actually, you could trace my links to their origins back to 1971, and an older cousin who played me a reel-to-reel recording of the Stooges' *Fun House* LP, along with Grand Funk Railroad's *Live Album*. The tape was sequenced in such a manner that the final feedback hum and guttural growl of 'L.A. Blues', which closed side two of *Fun House*, dissipated as the crowd chant that opened Grand Funk's effort faded in.

Cuz also introduced me to Alice Cooper's masterful *Love It to Death* and *Killer* records, their *School Days* compilation, and Iggy and the Stooges' *Raw Power*, sourced through the Australian Record Club.

I didn't hear or see mention of the Stooges again until I saw a piece in late 1975 in *RAM*, a Sydney-based music magazine, about an obscure yet fascinating local group called Radio Birdman. The grainy photo of the band leaped off the page and the musical links being made in relation to the Sydney outfit—the Stooges, as well as two other acts I wasn't as familiar with: the New York Dolls and the MC5—were a joining of previously unconnected dots into a glowing new rock order.

From there, I stumbled across a German copy of the MC5's *Kick Out the Jams* LP in a small pawn shop at Parramatta in western Sydney, of all places. Then, in a neat piece of cosmic symmetry, I took the train into the city to buy Birdman's *Burn My Eye* EP and that night saw Alice Cooper (now a solo act) welcome tens of thousands to his nightmare at the Sydney Showground.

Finding *Radios Appear*—the debut LP by Birdman—months afterwards filed near the Rolling Stones in a record store at a shopping complex again at Parramatta remains a moment impossible to express in any recognised language.

Around that time, I have some memory of an advertisement in *RAM*, with Birdman listed as being on the books of the Harbour Premier agency. This had us feverishly considering making enquiries for our high-school dance. The notion wasn't met with wider enthusiasm and the matter failed to proceed beyond being a marvellous idea for ten seconds.

Miraculously, within twelve months in late 1978 I was attempting to hold my own in the presence of the singer from the band, Rob Younger. No small thrill for someone whose first outfit was called Blitzkrieg in homage to the Radios. I was working in the city, only a few minutes' walk from the second-hand record temples of Martin's, Ashwood's and Lawson's.

Some of my copies of Alice Cooper's *Killer* and *Love It to Death* came from Martin's, bearing the Younger imprint in black texta.

Bumping into the man himself at nearby Phantom Records, where he was working behind the counter, or in the street in that part of town was a common occurrence, and we would talk for ages about records while I pinched myself and my office sent out a search party.

Initially, I struggled to match the warm, witty and engaging individual before me with the highly intimidating performer who had forcibly led Radio Birdman from the front.

The singer was considerably more full and frank in his expression the day I walked into Phantom and he asked to see what records I had bought. With great pride and extreme naivete, I unveiled a freshly purchased copy of *Eureka Birdman*, the Radios' bootleg live album.

For years to come we would have other, not quite as animated engagements about such pertinent world issues as the merits of the Beatles' *Sgt Pepper* album and the degree to which latter-day Sonic Youth could be regarded a pop band.

The creation of this book on the other hand was at times anything but a casual chatty proposition with a personal war for the ages continuing to rage between some Birdman members. The frustration of being caught in the seething crossfire provided some slight measure of what Francis Ford Coppola must have experienced directing *Apocalypse Now*.

Such was, and remains, the enormous depth of feeling within those intimately involved in something as unique and life-changing as Radio Birdman.

But rather than documenting the rolling drama in forensic detail and overshadowing what was created, my hope (even all-too-irregular prayer) is that these pages—through the voices of the band and, critically, their close associates and very early fans—capture something of the fury, bliss and empowerment that were handed down from high atop what was truly the Kingdom of the Birdmen.

Paint It Black, You Devils!

A slightly exotic-looking kid, his dark hair largely obscured by a striped beanie, was among a crowd of 14,000 basking in the glowering presence of the Rolling Stones at Detroit's Olympia Stadium in late November 1969.

Seventeen-year-old Deniz Tek, his girlfriend, Barbara Gubachy, and friend Scot Earle Smith were seated a considerable distance from the front, so when an opportunity to better that position presented itself, Tek didn't hesitate.

Scot Earle Smith: 'The crowd made a mad rush for the stage. We had a tape recorder and it recorded Deniz yelling at me, "Let's go! Let's go!" I was thinking that Barbara wasn't going to rush the stage, and, if we lost her, our ride home was gone. Also, there was a chance of getting thrown out. So I stayed. Very typical of Deniz and me. He takes chances and always comes out ahead.

'Deniz was the most self-assured person I ever met. First to have girlfriends, first to have a car, first to pick up a musical instrument, first to ride trains. He was ahead of the curve. All the time.'

It was two in the morning when the Stones finally appeared and Deniz, Scot and Barbara all had classes the next day at Ann Arbor's Huron High School 70 kilometres west of Detroit. But for Tek, balancing cars, girls, getting high, rock and roll and his final-year studies, although not an effortless endeavour, was certainly proving to be achievable.

Tonight, however, his tutors were the Stones, who now stood, towering well above their actual height, just metres away. Deniz had idolised founding member Brian Jones, who'd died in mysterious circumstances four months earlier, but now the young guitar player gazed up at a new messiah who had been in plain view the whole time.

Deniz Tek: 'Keith! I'd never seen anything so cool in my whole life! The Stones destroyed! It was a life-changing event. It was the ultimate revelation.'

Three days later, the Stones tore through several performances at New York's Madison Square Garden, which would be captured on the *Get Yer Ya-Ya's Out!* record. Their stop in Detroit, however, had momentarily placed the English overlords in a salt-of-the-earth music scene in the state of Michigan whose broader influence, though in most cases negligible at the time, would in years to come echo around the world. In what would be later generally referred to as the 'Detroit scene' there was the soon-to-be ridiculously successful Grand Funk Railroad, along with Brownsville Station, the Rationals (with Scott Morgan), the Up, SRC (led by singer Scott Richardson), the Frost (with guitarist Dick Wagner at the helm), the Amboy Dukes (featuring Ted Nugent), Mitch Ryder and Detroit (including axeman Steve Hunter), and the Bob Seger System. High in that pack were the Stooges—with the wildly interactive and endlessly physically flexible singer, then known as Iggy Stooge—and the MC5.

The collective sound of these acts was the extension of Detroit's blue-collar reputation as a major car manufacturer. Here, Ford, General Motors, Chrysler and Dodge had forged a dynasty early in the twentieth century and created the 'Motor City'.

Their plants were repurposed when World War II began and produced all manner of military hardware from jeeps and tanks, to a mind-boggling number of bullets with Ford, at its peak, producing, as boldly forecast, a B-24 Liberator Bomber every 60 minutes at its 3.5-million-square-foot Willow Run operation.

After the war, the industry shifted back to making automobiles, but a steely militaristic air remained. It was in that post-war period that Deniz Tek's father immigrated to America from Turkey, his adopted surname a perfect family descriptor.

Deniz Tek: 'Following Ataturk's revolution after the first war, Turkish men had to choose family surnames and register them. My grandfather chose "Tek" meaning "singular, or unique".'

Tek Senior met his future wife at the University of Michigan, and Deniz, the eldest of three sons, was given his first name from the Turkish term for 'ocean'.

Detroit's contribution to the war effort was in young Tek's blood from an early age and it ignited what would be a lifelong interest in the armed forces.

Deniz Tek: 'I was born only seven years after the end of World War II. As a child, I was very proud of the fact Detroit made the bombers and tanks that helped crush the Nazis.'

His father was a high achiever and expected excellence in all things from his son.

Deniz Tek: 'He did a Masters and PhD at the University of Michigan, worked as an engineer, and later as a professor. He was fluent in three languages, a genius at mathematics, wrote many textbooks and held hundreds of patents for various inventions.

'My dad conditioned me to accept nothing less than my own best effort. It comes down to genetics and conditioning. My dad was responsible for half the genetics, but most of the conditioning. He was athletic, played high-level soccer initially, and then later tennis. He was intensely competitive. He used to quote Vince Lombardi [NFL head coach and master motivator of the Green Bay Packers in the sixties]: "Winning isn't everything—it's the *only* thing." He would say, "There are two kinds of people—radar-guided, and gyro-guided. Radar-guided people react to what others around them do, say or think. Gyro-guided people do what they are going to do as a result of their inner drive. They are not influenced by others." He insisted that I become a "gyro-guided" person.'

The Tek Way was thus instilled before Deniz had picked up a tennis racquet at the age of five. It flowed over into his schooling and all other pursuits, including art and drawing.

Unsurprisingly, his reading matter, which included Edgar Allan Poe, was well out of the norm for kids his age.

Deniz Tek: 'I was reading higher-level stuff as a child—adult history books and such. I was very interested in military history, and I read all sorts of war biographies, from all sides—Japanese, German, British, American. I liked the aviation element best, but it was all fascinating to me. I wasn't above collecting comic books, but my room was just as full of *National Geographic* magazines as it was comics.'

A new world presented itself when Deniz was given a tiny blue transistor radio. It was quickly glued to local station WKNR, as well as CKLW, which beamed out of Ontario thanks to some major transmission muscle.

But Tek's imagination really soared in May 1961, when Alan Shepard became the first American in space and the dreams of millions took flight.

Deniz Tek: 'Every kid, including me, wanted to be an astronaut. I remember that day vividly. I was way into it!'

Five Years Ahead of His Time

It was an exercise in music as violence and violence as music. The Australian tour by the Who and the Small Faces in January 1968 was the country's first real experience with rock and roll as an aggressive, almost physical force. All the crafted perfection of the singles from both acts was dragged out of camera range, away from any lighting, and badly beaten. For seventeen-year-old Rob Younger, it was an eye-opening class in demonology.

Rob Younger: 'That was a seminal gig in my life. You couldn't understand a fucking thing the Small Faces were playing, but it was great! Steve Marriott with his hair in his eyes and standing pigeon-toed, really just wrenching his guitar and screaming into the mike. It was a revolving stage and one of those crappy old PAs, but at the time it seemed monstrously loud and brutal and wild. And the Who were great! They smashed some gear up and some smoke bombs went off and they threw a couple of drums into the crowd and shit like that.

'I wasn't thinking about starting a group or anything. That was just something that people in bands already did! It didn't occur to me that you could actually decide to do something like that.'

Growing up in Sydney's southern suburbs, a red-haired kid with a not quite slender physique and all the agonising self-consciousness that went with both, Younger was, in addition, a year junior to many of his classmates, a seemingly small disadvantage, but something else to amplify the discomfort in his own skin.

The radio became his guide, an all-knowing saviour, although he didn't ever lodge a formal request for salvation.

Rob Younger: 'I just listened to pop radio because that's what there was and I just loved it.'

A Christmas gift of a record player was a revelation, with Roy Orbison's single 'Working for the Man' his first vinyl purchase and the birth of what would be a lifelong passion for seven inches of compacted, crafted black plastic.

Rob Younger: 'Singles were a dollar or ten shillings and it was two pounds twelve sixpence for an album, so I didn't get an LP for about a year after I got that record player, and it was *Bombora* by the Atlantics. I already had the 45.'

He attended Jannali Boys' High and enjoyed the music of the surf scene that was so hugely popular at the time, although its sun-drenched aspect was a poor fit for fair skin. Nor was he attuned to the culture.

Rob Younger: 'I tried riding a board once. I stood up on the thing, thinking, "Shit, this is easy," then next I know, I've slipped off and the fucking board—they were nine feet long and weighed forty pounds in those days—slammed into the back of my head. I never tried it again. Most surfies I knew to any degree weren't particularly interested in music—surf or otherwise. Not that I was at all cool, above it all. Buying records obsessively somehow reinforced a certain sense of separation from that crowd.'

After school, Rob would get the train to nearby Sutherland and go to Eric Anderson's Electrical Appliances, which had records on a spinning rack, or McDowells at Caringbah.

Rob Younger: 'The radio stations used to publish their Top 40. It was mainly 2SM, 2UW and 2UE, and it was all there for you to grab.'

The Beatles hit the country in June 1964 but Younger's mind was blown in advance.

Rob Younger: 'The Beatles were a fucking revelation! They encouraged other people to start groups, and of course they wrote their own songs so other people did. We owe the Beatles absolutely everything, as far as I'm concerned, musically. We'd have nothing like we have now. We wouldn't have the Stones or the Who or any of those bands. The Beatles made music important. If you weren't there, I'm afraid you can't imagine it.

'I came in with the Stones on the first album or the singles, really. I love that first record. The energy, the sneer, and the tone and the singing—all that.'

At school, Rob's social circle wasn't huge, but tight and like-minded. Chief among his mates was Ray Lonsdale, and Younger spent a lot of time at the Lonsdale family home at Oyster Bay and got to know Ray's young brother, Doug.

Then, when he was fourteen, a student joined Younger's classes who would be pivotal in his life.

The Life of Brian Jones

Living in Detroit meant the magic of the Miracles, the Temptations and the Supremes was virtually absorbed through the skin, but it was a sound a five-hour plane flight away from the Motor City that Deniz Tek really fell for: surf music.

Deniz Tek: 'For me, it was all about the Ventures, the Beach Boys, Jan and Dean, and I have to include the Trashmen also, just for their one earth-shattering monster hit, "Surfin' Bird". There were others, of course—the Chantays with "Pipeline"; [the Tornados'] "Telstar", all the hot-rod tunes by one-off groups like the "GTO" song and "Hey Little Cobra", "Bucket 'T'". But none of these came close to those first four I mentioned.

'The first record I ever bought with my own money was the Beach Boys' "Shut Down" 45. My young mind was blown by this stuff.'

Tek had been on cornet in the school orchestra, but playing guitar like Don Wilson and Bob Bogle in the Ventures was now his goal.

Bob Dylan then stepped within Deniz's earshot with 'Blowin' in the Wind'.

Deniz Tek: 'I can recall everything about the first time I heard it—where I was, the weather, the look of the sky, everything. That raw voice, those lyrics and that attitude! I bought the single with my allowance money. "Don't Think Twice", "Hard Rain" and "Times They Are a-Changin'" affected me similarly.'

However, the impact of the Beatles' appearance on *The Ed Sullivan Show* in February 1964 put almost everything else in the shade.

Deniz Tek: 'Kennedy had been shot in November, and you could feel a big change coming. The Beatles played on *Ed Sullivan* to maybe 30 million viewers? This caused a seismic cultural revolution in America. The look, the sound and the songs. It changed everything. The world was pushed off its axis.

'Millions of kids wanted to play guitars and drums after that. I was already on the path, but it cemented my resolve and pointed a new direction to aim for. All of a sudden, surf music seemed old hat.'

The Fab Four weren't the only jolt that year with James Brown's electrifying television performance on the *T.A.M.I. Show*. Brown's dance moves and the energy and discipline involved, as well as the simple yet exacting precision of his band, fascinated Deniz.

Deniz Tek: 'I had never seen anything like it! JB blew everything else out of the water. I was hooked!'

By that point Tek had conquered his first song on guitar, the Ventures' 'Walk Don't Run', and was taught briefly by Dan Erlewine at Herb David Guitar Studio on State Street in Ann Arbor.

Deniz Tek: 'Dan was the guitar player in the Prime Movers, and Iggy [Pop] was the drummer. I took lessons for about three months, then quit. Dan wanted me to read classical. I just wanted to play rock and roll.'

He was able to do so on the electric guitar and small amp he had received for his birthday, just as Bob Dylan was also making the most of the new power source with *Highway 61 Revisited*.

Deniz Tek: 'There were all sorts of Dylan rumours my friends and I discussed. Like Mr Jones [in 'Ballad of a Thin Man'] was [Rolling Stone] Brian Jones, which didn't really make sense unless, as we suspected, Dylan was *so* ultra-hip he could see Brian in that way!'

Tek was steadying himself from the collective impact of the Beatles, James Brown and Dylan when the Stones made him an offer he and his guitar were utterly helpless to refuse.

Deniz Tek: 'They didn't connect with me in a fundamental way until "Satisfaction" and "Get Off of My Cloud". They were just so cool! The music hit me so hard!'

He had begun a lifetime affair with the Kinks from the moment he heard 'You Really Got Me' and the Who with 'I Can't Explain' and 'My Generation', but the Stones were the gang Deniz really wanted to join, and Keith Richards, particularly his rhythm work, was firmly placed on his list of idols.

Emulating the ice-cool perfected appearance of Stone Brian Jones, and attempting to replicate the chief component of that vision, was, however, a bridge too far.

Deniz Tek: 'One of my biggest traumas of childhood or adolescence was I could never have hair like Brian Jones!'

He made the best of the follicle configuration his genes were able to conjure up, which perfectly suited the garage sounds of the Troggs' 'Wild Thing' and the Kingsmen's 'Louie Louie', while offering assurance it wasn't necessary to be a guitar god to play something that sounded cool.

With that ethos in mind, Deniz and his friend Steve Kambly began toying around together on their guitars in Kambly's basement and bedroom.

Deniz Tek: 'His father was a psychiatrist, and they had some high-quality reel-to-reel tape recorders at their house. I was under the impression that Dr Kambly used these to record psychoanalysis sessions. So we got hold of one of these recorders and set it up in Steve's bedroom and recorded some songs we made up. One was "Man with Golden Helmet". Our lyrics were a clumsy but earnest attempt to write like Bob Dylan.'

Steve Kambly: 'I had an art print of the painting by Rembrandt—though I understand it may have been a work of another unknown artist—taped to the wall in my room.'

Late one afternoon, long after classes had finished, Deniz noticed a van pull into the school grounds. The vehicles' occupants, who would offer a class of a very different manner to Huron High, were local outfit the Rationals. They looked like strange new gods, even while engaged in the menial act of unloading their equipment for the dance that night. Tek's plans for the evening were now set in cement and he attended the school function and witnessed for the first time, face to face, ear to amplifier, a rock band. As the reverberations bounced around the room, he felt his body chemistry change course.

By now, Deniz's own guitar skills were sufficient for him to join a band with classmate Roger Miller, who later founded Mission of Burma. Their stage, for the most part, was nothing more than the basement at the Tek family home, along with a party or two playing the hits of the day, including Deniz singing the Kinks' 'A Well Respected Man'.

Deniz Tek: 'We called ourselves the Inducers, because we thought we were so bad we would induce people to vomit!'

In the background was the release of Hunter S. Thompson's book *Hell's Angels*, which concluded with the author being beaten for overfamiliarity and disrespect.

Heart Full of Dali

The interplanetary twang of Australian surf-music kings the Atlantics at the 2SM 'Stomp' had fascinated twelve-year-old Warwick Gilbert, but a decade later in August 1971, in broad daylight at Randwick Racecourse, he was really transported beyond the stars by Pink Floyd.

Warwick Gilbert: 'There was no light show, just the band creating soundscapes. "Set the Controls for the Heart of the Sun", "Careful with that Axe, Eugene" and "Echoes" pretty much poleaxed me. A shirtless, acid-fried hippie was sitting in a lotus position doing an upper-body interpretive dance to my right, in front of the monster WEM PA speakers, during Floyd's set.'

Life hadn't always been quite so elevating for Gilbert, a quiet, sensitive kid who started drawing before he went to school, where he was bullied on a daily basis and art was his great escape.

Warwick Gilbert: 'I was in my own world and out of step with other kids. I was music obsessed, spent most of my time drawing while listening to music in my room.

'At primary school, I drew Goofy, Donald Duck and Mickey for the other kids on plywood for "fretwork" classes, which they'd cut out and paint. I drew cross-sections of the Earth's crust in chalk on the blackboard for the teachers.'

He was captivated by the art of *Mad* magazine, the animation genius of Tex Avery and Chuck Jones, along with imaginative television and cinema such as *Creature from the Black Lagoon*, *The Blob*, *The Three Stooges*, *The Twilight Zone*, and *Journey to the Centre of the Earth*.

At Sydney Boys High, daily torture by peer continued at a more advanced level and Warwick again put his talents on display during lessons, sometimes creating impressive caricatures of the teachers.

On weekends and during school holidays, he earned pocket money operating a fleshing machine—'the worst job in the known universe'—at a tanning company managed by his father, although his earnings went towards something far more uplifting: records, which he had started buying when he was twelve.

His neighbours were often informed of any new purchases.

Warwick Gilbert: 'I remember buying the Beach Boys' [single] "409" and putting the portable speaker up in the window and playing it to the street at full volume. It [a car] revs up at the start. *Rum! rum! rum!* And then "409! 409!" Really great stuff!'

The family's circumstances changed tragically when Warwick's mother committed suicide. He was thirteen and they moved to the Sutherland Shire area in 1964.

Gilbert enrolled at Jannali Boys' High, where he quickly had a meeting of minds with a fellow student.

Warwick Gilbert: 'There were about three people in the school who were interested in the same music and I hit it off with Rob [Younger] straight away. He was obsessive about the same sorts of things and had the same sort of humour.

'We just hung out and listened to music.'

They had plenty to discuss, with the Beatles, the Who, the Stones, the Beach Boys and countless others on the radio.

Warwick Gilbert: 'I bought the Kinks' "You Really Got Me" and must have played it 50 or 60 times in a row! My father went crazy!'

In late 1965 Gilbert left school, with the magic of TV programs like *The Outer Limits* and *Get Smart* bouncing around in his head and the revolutionary sound of Jeff Beck in the Yardbirds setting his ears ablaze.

Warwick Gilbert: '"Heart Full of Soul" was the single that got me interested in guitar. Before that, it was just plunkety plunk sort of stuff.'

He began fooling around with the cheap acoustic his brother brought home. Soon he conquered Booker T & the MG's' 'Green Onions' and bought himself an electric guitar.

Warwick Gilbert: 'I had a lead made so I could plug it into my father's stereogram when he and my stepmother went out—and I blew it up!'

His dad retained firm ideas regarding his son's future and it certainly didn't involve a career in music.

Warwick Gilbert: 'My stepmother saw I was an artist, so she made sure I got into art school and I have to thank her for that. So I went there for two years and I got hauled out of there by my father and went back to the tannery.'

★

Rob Younger was now a more athletic build, having played Aussie Rules from the age of eleven for Como-Jannali, and at sixteen in his high school team in which he was vice-captain at one point. He was also in the Combined Sydney High Schools representative side. While he took his own sporting participation seriously, he often chose a path of greatest possible resistance when watching the efforts of others—in perhaps a form of sport itself.

Warwick Gilbert: 'I went to a football match with Rob one time where he positioned himself in the midst of the opposing team's supporters and loudly began to hurl insults at their team. We had to get out of there!'

Pegged jeans had become a more viable fashion option and Younger began shaping himself in a manner as far away as possible from the 'squares' he already loathed so deeply.

In 1966, Younger farewelled school at the end of fifth form, although he clearly had the intellectual capacity to achieve much more.

Rob Younger: 'All I gave a shit about was records. What's changed, I wonder?'

White City vs the Black Angel's Death Song

The Hill Auditorium at the University of Michigan wasn't even close to filling its 3500-seat capacity and many of those who did attend stayed only briefly for the pair of performances by Andy Warhol's Exploding Plastic Inevitable with the Velvet Underground. The excessive volume, along with the abrasion of Lou Reed's 'Ostrich' guitar and the scraping electric viola of the warlock-like John Cale, usually had that effect.

The arty black-draped cacophony of the New Yorkers' first effort, *The Velvet Underground & Nico*—a stunning German model and actress—with beautifully macabre songs with, for the times, dark subversive themes such as 'Heroin', 'I'm Waiting for the Man' and 'The Black Angel's Death Song', was enclosed in a sleeve with a peelable banana image on the front of initial copies. The Velvets were a monochromatic speed hit to the 'Summer of Love's LSD rainbow.

Deniz Tek didn't have the opportunity to witness the Velvets nor Jimi Hendrix and the Who when they too appeared in Ann Arbor in 1967. He was on the other side of the planet by then, courtesy of his father, a professor at the University of Michigan, who secured an exchange professorship at the University of New South Wales. His dad had an eye to more than just work.

Deniz Tek: 'He was an extremely keen tennis player and Australia in the sixties was known for tennis. He came to play, basically.

'We were members at White City and I played a lot of tennis that year. I even got to work at the Australian championships, and served as a ball boy at a match between Evonne Goolagong and Rosie Casals.'

Deniz enrolled at Sydney Boys High and became tight with fellow student Steve Jones and, by association, his young brother, Chris. But school brought with it a steep learning curve that had nothing to do with education.

Deniz Tek: 'Having to wear a uniform, and the practice of caning, was all very new and quite bizarre to me. I got bullied for being either a "Yank" or a "wog", and got in several fights. I would occasionally come home bloody and bruised with a ripped uniform. After I took down the biggest of the arseholes, I got left alone.'

Oversighting much of this was a copy of the painting *The Man with the Golden Helmet*, which was long believed to have been the work of Rembrandt during the 1650s.

David Wilson (student): 'It was outside the Classical Languages staff room and there happened to be a tap nearby—in the middle of the building in a hallway—which always struck me as odd.'

While the Masters Apprentices, the Loved Ones and the Easybeats sounded marvellous pouring from the radio, the Doors' 'Light My Fire' was a cascade to somewhere darker and very different. The self-titled LP from which it was lifted was a mix of slithering menace and ethereal poetry, jazz flourishes and baroque stylings. There was the snarling urgency of 'Break On Through', a near-obscene animalised reading of the Howlin' Wolf–popularised 'Back Door Man' (the grunting and growling of singer Jim Morrison could not have been lost on one Jim Osterberg back in Ann Arbor) and the record's closer, more than eleven minutes of unsettling mystic hell titled 'The End'. Like the Velvet Underground, the Doors were a dagger to the temple, with Morrison seeming to want to caress and then put out an eye.

The Tek family returned to Ann Arbor in early January 1968. Deniz quickly snapped up the Doors' first two LPs, along with Pink Floyd's *The Piper at the Gates of Dawn* and Dylan's *John Wesley Harding*, its spare sound reaffirming his faith.

Deniz Tek: 'I saw simplicity could *be* power. "Watchtower"—only three chords!'

The FM radio revolution was now hitting its stride in America, with home-stereo quality sound aided by acts placing greater importance on albums. The local FM airwave gateway was WABX FM, which famously beamed from 'high atop the David Stott Building'. Among bands Tek discovered via the station was the Velvet Underground, who, later that year, would unleash the ear-and-teeth-grinding fury of their second effort, *White Light/White Heat*, with its centrepiece, the seventeen-minute distortion-fest of 'Sister Ray'. The skull tattoo on a near-black background on the front spoke volumes about how radically different the recording was to the flowery peace-and-love times.

Deniz Tek: 'The Velvet Underground! I thought they were dangerous and cool, and therefore attractive and worthy of emulating. I immediately saw an opportunity to learn from them.'

Meanwhile, the Stones retook their rightful place in the Tek pecking order with the *Beggars Banquet* album and sealed the fate of Lennon and McCartney.

Deniz Tek: 'It was pretty much over for the Beatles. The Stones were just getting started.'

As were an outfit called Alice Cooper, fronted by Detroit-born Vince Furnier. The Coopers made the Stones look positively regal, all donning a mix of offbeat op-shop clothing, with perhaps the longest hair on the scene. The outfit had been struggling in their adopted home of LA, where their sound and stage act emptied several venues, including, most famously, a club in Venice, California, called the Cheetah Room.

'When I saw 2000 people walk out on them, I knew I had to manage them,' Shep Gordon told *Newsweek*. 'They exhibited the strongest negative force I'd ever seen.'

Happenings Ten Years Ago

It was the glory days of rail transportation in Sydney, when red-rattler trains whisked the wide eyed from the drab grey of the suburbs to the lights, cornucopia of potential sins and liberating freedom of the city. And for those who managed to jump the last rail ride home, the doors or windows could, conveniently, be opened sufficiently to piss or spew out the night's excesses.

Rob Younger and Warwick Gilbert embarked on this teen rite of passage one Saturday night in 1967 and found themselves at Taylor Square in Darlinghurst at venues like the Oxford Hotel. In years past, it had been 'The Happiest Spot in Town!', with floor shows that featured erotic dancers.

Rob Younger: 'We both got so drunk drinking brown muscat. At the Oxford they had a band called the Starving Wild Dogs. Sounded good, didn't it? In fact, there was also a band in a nearby wine bar called Gut Bucket. We were getting drunk at these places, but we were scared of the Oxford, because it was a biker hangout and these guys were really tough looking.'

Darlinghurst and Taylor Square were vibrant scenes, with such spots as Frenchs Tavern, a wine establishment, and the ultra-hip Martin's Bar, which had a capacity of 50 to 60 people and, like Frenchs, was beer free. Martin's didn't charge an admission fee but access was strictly limited, without argument—by the venue's namesake, Martin Du Barry, a no-nonsense bear of an Englishman in a cap—to members and those who accompanied them. Tchaikovsky's explosive '1812 Overture' signalled closing time at midnight.

The area also had a strong creative community, with arts colleges and a blues and folk scene, along with acts like the wildly popular hippie jug band, the Original Battersea Heroes. At the other end of the scale, there was the amplifier-destroying Missing Links at popular venue Beatle Village, where they took over the Easybeats' slot. Added to all this was a fearsome street gang culture.

Ian Hartley (Sydney's Andy Warhol): 'The Darlinghurst scene was like the New York scene in a way.'

Rob Younger had got his first job—and thus cash to spend on records—straight from school at an ad agency. Here, he first encountered a slice of the real Big Apple via the Velvet Underground. A colleague, a former music writer for Brisbane's *Courier Mail*, had sent away for the December 1966 issue of *Aspen* magazine, which had been put together by the Velvets' godfather, Andy Warhol. It came in a box that looked like it contained breakfast cereal. Included in it were a number of promotional items, one of which was a flexi-disc—the earliest floppy disc in a true sense—the second side comprising a feedback opus titled 'Loop'. It was credited as the Velvet Underground, but thought to be John Cale acting alone.

A single of the Velvets' 'Sunday Morning' and 'Femme Fatale' had been released in Australia that year, but disappeared almost immediately without trace. The album from which it was drawn wouldn't see daylight in Oz for some time.

The Beatles' *Revolver*, on the other hand, was hardly obscure and floored both Gilbert and Younger.

Warwick Gilbert: 'I loved the songs, the tracking order, the cover art and the great picture of the Beatles on the back. I even liked the Parlophone logo! *Revolver* was pure genius, both primal and futuristic.'

It was added to the genius pile of the day that included the Yardbirds' *Roger the Engineer*, Pink Floyd's *Piper at the Gates of Dawn*, Jefferson Airplane's *Surrealistic Pillow*, the Mothers of Invention's *Freak Out!* and the first Jimi Hendrix Experience LP.

By this time, Gilbert was living his vocational dream as an assistant animator at Air Programs International in the Salvation Army Building in Elizabeth Street in the city.

Warwick Gilbert: 'I'd do the drawing between the animator's drawings. We were called inbetweeners.'

The continuing acquisition of records, however, remained a pressing concern.

Warwick Gilbert: 'Rob and I both collected records obsessively. You'd hear something on the radio and catch a train into town from Caringbah and go to Palings or Edels and see if you could find the record. Like "Red Sky at Night" by the Accent. They played it once on the radio, I think, and I thought, "Holy shit!" There were two copies in the racks at Palings and I've still got that one. And I loved the Troggs. The Stones was the basis for everything really. The Beatles and the Beach Boys as well. So that was the level of our interest. We were in that weird zone and only a few people were then.'

After about a year at Air International, Warwick took his talents into advertising with J. Walter Thompson—now global giant VML—while being captivated by *Zap Comix*, the artwork of Robert Crumb on the cover of Big Brother and the Holding Company's *Cheap Thrills*, the gloriously complex visual creativity of Cream's *Disraeli Gears* and *Wheels of Fire* records along with the Doors' debut LP.

Warwick Gilbert: 'I saw the [Doors'] cover and thought, "Jesus! This has got to be good!"'

The artwork on Jefferson Airplane's *After Bathing At Baxter's*—a cartoon of a World War I triplane merged with a house from the Haight-Ashbury district of San Francisco—would have particular significance for Warwick almost a decade later. So would a concert poster for a Jefferson Airplane appearance at the Fillmore West, which featured another stylised aircraft in the shape of an armour-plated balloon.

Rob Younger, meanwhile, had begun toying with the guitar and bought an electric model, but never really took to the instrument. Besides, there was too much wonderful music being created by others.

Rob Younger: 'The sixties was a magic period for pop music, because you could easily make a case for owning ten, twelve, maybe fifteen of the Top 40, no sweat. Can you imagine owning ten singles from the eighties? I'm talking about records of the calibre of [the Who's] "My Generation" and [the Stones'] "Get off of My Cloud" and [the Kinks'] "Waterloo Sunset". It didn't happen. The sixties was the greatest. The Beatles, Dylan, the Stones, etc.—we owe them our lives. They're gods.'

Younger had started growing his hair and began to resemble a deity himself.

Rob Younger: 'It grew to be longer than anyone whose records I was buying.'

Having locks below the collar was, however, a red rag to the violent roaming gangs of cropped-haired Sharps, as Younger found one night at Devonshire Street near Central Station, coming home from a concert.

Rob Younger: 'I was with Warwick and my girlfriend Pauline and there were seven of them, if I recall. They sort of surrounded us but Warwick and Pauline split, and then they surrounded me and threw a couple of punches. One of them kicked me in the stomach and I just split. When I get going, I can get going! They didn't catch me. They were just fucking thugs.'

And some of them played Aussie Rules, so Younger would often find himself facing off against teams from the Sharpie heartland of Melbourne. These were literally bruising encounters that the southern teams usually won.

A 1968 double album of various artists, *Underground*, which featured five songs from the first two Velvet Underground LPs, kicked the listener in the head slightly more subtly. For the hip in Australia, it was the gateway to the Velvets—although, because the band was on the Verve label, some enterprising souls had discovered that their records could be ordered from jazz catalogues.

In early 1970, Rob Younger's world was up-ended when his father died. Then, in a double psychological hammer blow, his mother passed late in the year. After things settled as much as they were likely to, Rob had to find somewhere to live, and the Lonsdales—where he'd been spending a lot of time—took him in.

One Sunday morning before departing, he set up his stereo on the front lawn and pointed the speakers towards the church next door, telegraphing the devil's music direct to the congregation. At top volume, the sound was wildly distorted, increasing the intensity of the messaging. But what appeared to be a localised outpouring was really a full-bodied eruption at the world.

Michigan Muscle

Deniz Tek and his friends had witnessed plenty of concerts at the University of Michigan, as well as the free open-air gigs every Sunday at West Park in the heart of Ann Arbor. They had taken it all in from Ike and Tina Turner, John Mayall and the Band, but nothing like the almighty pairing of the MC5—whom Tek had already experienced—with the Stooges at the University's Union Ballroom in September 1968.

The Stooges were more circus troupe than band, with drummer Scott Asheton keeping time on 55-gallon oil drums and singer Iggy Stooge putting a microphone to various kitchen appliances and playing an amplified Hawaiian guitar. On the other hand, the MC5 were part testosterone and part spiritual crusade. Dramatically introduced by Brother J.C. Crawford, their amplifiers were draped in the American flag, afro-haired singer Rob Tyner was as much James Brown as he was Mick Jagger, while guitarists Wayne Kramer and Fred 'Sonic' Smith jousted on the very edge of high-volume chaos. They were fired by Chuck Berry, as well as the wild explorations of the free jazz of John Coltrane and Archie Shepp. The MC5 were sonic pirates.

Deniz Tek: 'The Stooges were doing mainly performance-art stuff, no well-defined "songs", and were very noisy! The local community didn't get it. They thought it was just crazy guys making noise, pretty much. The MC5 was a finely tuned and brutally effective machine.'

Just over a month later, the MC5 would record their debut album, *Kick Out the Jams*, at two free gigs at Detroit's Grande Ballroom on 30 and 31 October 1968.

Courtesy of their manager John Sinclair, they had their mission statement down pat. Sinclair was a former writer for jazz bible *DownBeat* and a strong advocate of empowerment via 'high energy music'. More importantly, he was also co-founder and Minister of Information of the hard-left-wing White Panther Party, whose platform—with the MC5 as foot soldiers—was outlined in November in the Sinclair-founded *Ann Arbor Sun*: 'Our program is cultural revolution through a total assault on the culture . . . there are a generation of visionary maniac white mother country dope fiend rock and roll freaks who are ready to get down and kick out the jams—ALL THE JAMS . . . We have developed organic high-energy guerrilla bands who are infiltrating the popular culture . . .'

Cops with batons were having none of this.

The Five's Rob Tyner featured on the cover of *Rolling Stone* magazine in January 1969 just prior to the release of the *Kick Out the Jams* LP, which would reach number 30 on the *Billboard* charts. The single of the same name would be in the second spot on the local WKNR radio listings by March, when the band appeared in stylised head-and-shoulders portraits in the first issue of Detroit's *Creem* magazine.

Deniz Tek: 'I heard the single on radio, repeatedly, prior to hearing the whole album. I knew what the impact was going to be. Great change was in the air! It was electric!'

Lillian Roxon, the pioneering female rock writer who'd grown up in Australia, wrote about the album in the *Sydney*

Morning Herald from New York, saying that, of all their contemporaries, the MC5 were 'setting the directions for 1969'—although, like the Velvet Underground, it would be almost a decade before the record was released in Oz.

In Ann Arbor, however, all was right with the world. Deniz Tek had discovered *Zap Comix*, the cartoons of Robert Crumb and the passport to life that was a driver's licence.

Deniz Tek: 'I finally had a car by then—a '67 Pontiac Firebird. Really, it was my mother's car, but I drove it all the time. [Dylan's] "Lay Lady Lay" was on the car radio constantly, and really part of the soundtrack of my life at the time, along with Mason Williams' "Classical Gas", "Jumpin' Jack Flash" and of course the Ventures' "Hawaii Five-0".

'When "Hawaii Five-0" came on the radio it would drive me insane, and I would open up the throttle. Lucky I didn't kill myself and others! I should never have been allowed behind the wheel of that car. I survived it somehow.'

Frank Zappa with the Mothers of Invention had been driving into conservative bystanders in America since 1966, with the aptly titled *Freak Out!* record and, most recently, the sprawling *Uncle Meat*. With savage wit and satire, along with dazzling—at times avant-garde—musical smarts, Zappa was intellectual anarchy and a siren call to a global army of misfits. Fittingly, he added industry outcasts Alice Cooper to his posse and issued their first album, *Pretties for You*, on his ironically named Straight label.

With cover art depicting an overweight businessman smirking at a woman who appeared to have raised her dress revealingly, coupled with songs like '10 Minutes Before the Worm' and 'Earwigs to Eternity', Alice Cooper were the punks trying to wilt the flower-power generation—like Dali doing the Beatles. The record sold poorly.

A considerably larger audience—Deniz Tek among them—watched Neil Armstrong take his historic steps on the moon in July 1969. The final-frontier moment gave Tek more pause than most, but teen life in full bloom beckoned.

The Stooges had morphed into a primal rock unit with their self-titled debut produced by John Cale, no longer of the Velvet Underground. Released in August, and with Iggy Stooge now enacting rites similar to what he'd seen Jim Morrison deliver when the Doors had appeared at the University of Michigan, the arrival of *The Stooges* bookended the wildly opposing events of the Charles Manson murders and the gathering of 300,000 people at the Woodstock festival. The LP featured perfect snapshots of drawling, drooling, adolescent nihilism, such as 'No Fun', 'I Wanna Be Your Dog' and 'Real Cool Time', with a sound as base as the emotions which drove it. However, the ten-minute droning mantra of 'We Will Fall' was a test of character for many listeners.

While *Billboard* magazine curiously gushed that the record 'glitters with . . . sophisticated pop execution' and reported more than once that their label, Elektra, the home of the Doors, would be giving the album a strong push in the marketplace, the Stooges really just wanted to fuck, then burn the place to the ground. The LP made little impact beyond local radio but Deniz Tek ate the songs up, having witnessed their new savagery almost too close up.

Scot Earle Smith: 'There was one fraternity party we went to that had hired the Stooges. As I recall, the band got into a fight pretty quickly with the hosts and it was all over in twenty minutes. They were more like riots than concerts.'

Tek quickly added the sound of Stooge guitarist Ron Asheton to his most-wanted list, along with that of MC5 axemen

Fred Smith and Wayne Kramer, although he was intrigued by more than their actual playing.

Deniz Tek: 'The attitude and the intensity really resonated with me. I saw it as being the core aspect to what they were doing. I knew I had the drive to be able to generate the same kind of values, and I could see that the beat, chords and notes, in a technical sense, didn't matter all that much. It was how you delivered it that counted. So when you play a song in that way, and the song itself is a killer, you have the potential for an unbeatable one-two knockout punch.

'Not being a technically great guitar player or singer, I knew the central values I witnessed would be a weapon that could transcend those limitations. That's all I had, and later the ability to write songs that would carry the fire.'

Tek's Stooges and MC5 awakening was at odds with his own musical situation at the time. He was playing in an outfit called Suzy and the Pimps, an eight- or nine-piece group that did songs like the zany 'Gitarzan', by country singer and comedian Ray Stevens. Deniz's unceremonious dumping was almost a blessing.

All the while the MC5 continued to rise albeit without manager John Sinclair, who had been sentenced to up to ten years' prison in July for possessing two marijuana cigarettes. Despite the recent death of Rolling Stone Brian Jones, the Five remained the cover stars of *Circus* magazine in September 1969.

The Stones tour Deniz had witnessed in late November culminated in a chaotic, hastily arranged, outdoor event at the Altamont Speedway in California on 6 December which attracted several hundred thousand people. There, just over a week after the release of the Stones' *Let It Bleed* LP, the Hells

Angels, who had been hired as security, meted out a particularly savage level of crowd control.

The Angels had been an integral though, for some, uncomfortable part of the San Francisco music scene for a number of years—the cover of the *Cheap Thrills* album by Big Brother and the Holding Company, which featured Janis Joplin, carried an 'approval' by the gang and their winged skull logo.

But there was nothing groovy and romantic about their involvement at Altamont, the mood of which from the outset was closer to end of days than the peace and love of Woodstock just four months earlier.

Meredith Hunter was fatally stabbed by an Angel while three other deaths at the event were tragic accidents unrelated to the bikers.

The subsequent media coverage elevated the Angels' fearsome reputation around the world.

Despite the horror of Altamont, the Stones' now uncomfortably titled *Let It Bleed* sold in a much more accountant-pleasing manner than the Stooges' record. By year's end, the first LP by Iggy and his crew had moved a mere 37,000 copies in the North American market.

This Ain't the Summer of Love

In title alone, *Gimme Shelter* was a signpost to an apocalypse of dread and biblical doom. Fittingly, it served also as the name of the Stones' documentary of the hellish events at Altamont.

It sat comfortably with the darker counterculture cinema of the era, such as *A Clockwork Orange*, *Midnight Cowboy*, *Easy Rider* and Andy Warhol's *Trash*, as well as the swag of biker films that had emerged in the mid-sixties such as *The Wild Angels* and *Hell's Angels '69*. The latter featured actual members of the Oakland chapter, including legendary founder Sonny Barger.

In this generally darker environment, the Stooges' first Australian single, 'I Wanna Be Your Dog', might have expected a decent reception, but, like their LP, it had quickly vanished.

At one major theatre in Sydney, the sound system for the *Gimme Shelter* screenings was upgraded to a then extraordinarily loud 1000 watts. The inclusion of footage from the Stones' Madison Square Garden concerts on that 1969 North American tour showed a delighted John Genzale, later better known as New York Dolls guitarist Johnny Thunders, in one crowd shot.

Yet the music wasn't the central attraction. Instead, the leading role was played by the unsettling sense of lawlessness at Altamont, with the biggest act on the planet very publicly losing their grip on the reins. The Rolling Stones were reduced to helpless, frustrated onlookers, surprisingly pleading for calm as the brutal theatre around them became the show.

Mick Jagger: '[The Stones played] as well as the conditions allowed! As you say, you don't really listen to the quality of the band's performance when you're watching that movie.'

Commercial radio in Australia at the time consisted of the voodoo shimmer of the Beatles' 'Come Together' and the rollicking 'Get Back', the raspy swamp odes of Creedence Clearwater Revival, and the Kinks singing about Lola. This was all harshly countered by the nightmarish drone of 'Cold Turkey', the alleged ode to heroin withdrawal by John Lennon and Yoko Ono's Plastic Ono Band.

More broadly, the country was limping along after the fact with its own Woodstock, in the Pilgrimage for Pop festival at Ourimbah on the NSW Central Coast. Rob Younger camped out on site, as much an odd man out as Billy Thorpe and the Aztecs—which included guitarist Lobby Loyde—who were conducting a volume war among a sea of kaftans and sandals.

Rob Younger: 'There was a lot of prog bands around the place, but the one thing I can never recall seeing is rock bands at a lot of these things. Rock wasn't that big in Australia around that time. I think that's possibly why Billy Thorpe got so much traction. It didn't have to be any good, in particular. I actually liked his pop phase better than that later ponytail rock trip, but all that numbing *dah dah dah dah* [boogie] shit was what passed for rock and roll in Australia around that time.'

A later trip to a Victorian music festival with Warwick Gilbert put a nail in the coffin of any such future outings.

Warwick Gilbert: 'It got rained out and we didn't hear one note. We got washed down the hill with our tent! And got bogged in the car park!'

The way the weekend played out would have been a special kind of hell for Younger and anyone nearby. Suffering fools or situations, that, in his opinion, lacked merit was not his forte. He was endlessly capable of firmly providing supporting arguments while exposing the opposing views of others as just plain fucking wrong. Unloading on substandard bands at gigs was also almost a civic duty.

Warwick Gilbert: 'Rob would boo and express his displeasure in some way. I was an accessory to that and thought it hilarious!'

There was little need to heckle what was being created internationally. It was 1970 and England had the brute power of the Who, with *Live at Leeds* and soon the masterful *Who's Next*, the Kinks were elevating British rock to new heights, and the Stones were readying their *Sticky Fingers* LP, while Mott the Hoople, the Faces with Rod Stewart, Slade and T. Rex were marking up future punk templates. David Bowie's *The Man Who Sold the World* was a dark overlord sleeper and a further cultural ignition point for the coming years.

America had a veritable underworld in plain sight, with the Doors, led by 'Lizard King' Jim Morrison, now a leathered, cop-battling and baiting poetic Dionysus, calling up spirits of all descriptions. Plus, there was Steppenwolf, the MC5—with their second effort, the more radio-aimed *Back in the USA*—and Alice Cooper's next marvellously jolting release, *Easy Action*, which again had their sales team in tears.

Alice were part of the bill of the Cincinnati Summer Festival in June, but the Stooges stole the day, with a bare-chested Iggy Pop—formerly Iggy Stooge—in silver gloves and a dog collar.

Iggy Pop: 'I was sort of walking on top of this crowd in the middle of a baseball diamond and stoned out of my head! And on TV!"

A stunned older commentator clearly unaccustomed to such displays tried to explain the spectacle to the viewing audience with Iggy's savage yet balletic dance almost an instrument itself.

Iggy Pop: 'I really like John Coltrane and his brand of playing sax. I always thought, "Wouldn't it be cool if I could do, with my body and voice, the kind of thing a musician like that is doing?" He seemed to be there in the moment as well, so I wanted to keep that always in our show.'

The Stooges' second LP, 1970's *Fun House*, totally recoded rock and roll—just as Iggy's physical expression did to James Brown's moves—into hormonal chemical warfare, with songs like 'Down on the Street', 'Loose' and 'Dirt'. It also introduced a new dialect, with terms such as 'T.V. Eye' and, in the song '1970', the flow of words appeared to form something called 'Radio Birdman'. The Stooges were mutants from the best kind of monsters, but Iggy throwing what was thought to be peanut butter at the Cincinnati Summer Festival crowd and a number of feature articles weren't going to be sufficient to propel the outfit onto radio, and the record was deleted from sale as quickly as their first effort.

On the other hand, the Velvet Underground's *Loaded*, the last with Lou Reed, was free of the grinding fury of the past and instead carried such gossamer pop drops as 'Rock and Roll' and the three-chord wonder 'Sweet Jane'.

Lou Reed: 'It's four chords, actually. There's a little extra chord in there.'

But in Australia, multiple faceless groups felt the need to perform a tepid pop song called 'Yellow River', while

Melbourne's the Mixtures released and had a hit with a version of 'In the Summertime' by British act Mungo Jerry, as the English unit was still receiving plenty of coverage with their own rendition. And no one blinked.

Halo of Flies

The rolling boogie of Daddy Cool's 'Eagle Rock' was the unofficial Australian national anthem in 1971, when Rob Younger made a discovery in a tiny, unassuming record store in Sydney's Imperial Arcade that was light years away from a John Lee Hooker rhythm.

Rob Younger: 'There was a box of albums on the counter and they appeared to be imports. In it was the first Velvets' album with the pink banana which, as it turns out, was what was underneath the yellow skin. The peelable banana [edition] would be worth a fucking fortune now. Perhaps the coolest debut LP ever.'

However, the big international rock concert tour of the year, featuring Deep Purple, Free and Manfred Mann at Randwick Racecourse, was all about England, rather than the seamier side of New York City.

Warwick Gilbert: '[Deep Purple guitarist] Ritchie Blackmore's snake-charmer scale—I was trying to get my head around that. But it was a direction of music that kind of went belly up, with Led Zeppelin's largesse and all that. All those bands got bloated and successful and the music sort of fanned out into twenty-minute solos, and they lost sight of the tunes with clever pyrotechnics and all of that shit. Rick Wakeman's "Square Knights of the Round Table"! On ice! Wasn't it on ice?'

The underbelly of America had expanded further. The Doors' *L.A. Woman* was a mix of sparkle and unease, from the breezy 'Love Her Madly' to the quiet threat of 'Riders on the Storm'. Jim Morrison's slow, menacing mantra in the title cut took on a far deeper meaning after his mysterious passing in July 1971, exactly two years after the equally shrouded loss of Brian Jones of the Rolling Stones.

Alice Cooper's relocation to Detroit had seen everything finally fall into place with their third effort, *Love It to Death*, the initial copies of which appeared to show the singer's exposed dick on the front. From the voodoo of 'Black Juju', the tale of a nervous breakdown and sectioning in 'The Ballad of Dwight Fry', a surprising version of the Rolf Harris co-written 'Sun Arise', and the hit, 'I'm Eighteen', *Love It to Death* was their breakthrough and first masterpiece. With a stage act that over the coming years would see the singer draped with a boa constrictor, nightly meeting his maker via either gallows, electric chair or guillotine—Alice Cooper were on the path to become a global flagship for decadence and teen rebellion.

Alice Cooper: 'We were as in your face as the MC5 or the Blue Cheer. We would ram it down your throat. We had no philosophy, we had no agenda. Our job was to kill the audience any way that we could, to absolutely destroy them and make them talk about us the next day.'

The Coopers would appear on the same bill with the Stooges and the MC5. With his growing audience, Alice talked up Iggy and co in his interviews in magazines such as *Rolling Stone*, leaving a trail for the curious to follow.

Brad Franks (Birdman devotee, artist, tribal heritage Darug, Cattai Clan): 'We've got to find out who these people are! If they're good enough for Alice, they must be good enough for us!'

Alice's second effort in 1971 was the masterful *Killer*, with its child-like front cover font and photo of a boa constrictor. Songs like 'Desperado', written about the late Jim Morrison, 'Dead Babies' and the stunning 'Halo of Flies' made it Halloween every night. It sold strongly and elevated the Alice brand further and prompted a ticket sales frenzy at the box office.

The Stooges had headed in the opposite direction. They'd split in a haze of drugs and mounting industry apathy months earlier, while the MC5 fired off a third and final shot with their peak-of-powers statement, *High Time*.

Warwick Gilbert and Rob Younger also took differing paths, with Rob hanging with a crowd in Como in southern Sydney, before meeting Englishman Mick Lyne while the pair were working at the Redfern Mail Exchange over the Christmas period.

Sway

The song from the Stones' *Sticky Fingers* was oozing through the public address system at the airport in Detroit. It was October 1971 and at first Deniz Tek thought the sound had somehow escaped from his head. Along with *Who's Next*, he had almost worn out his copy of *Sticky Fingers* over the past six months, and always lingered over 'Sway'. Hearing it again as he was about to embark on a long journey to Sydney to study medicine—a trip funded by working at the Chevrolet assembly line in Ypsilanti, Michigan, as a floor sweeper the length of the mile-long pits—felt almost ceremonial, marking his passing from one world to the next.

Deniz Tek: 'I was eighteen, an engineering student at the University of Michigan, but I didn't really want to be an engineer. My dad and grandparents were engineers, and I was expected to be one also. My dad was a professor there. If I'd stayed, I might have been in one of his classes.

'I had no idea what I really wanted to do but I thought that medicine would give me a lot of options. It was a chance to be free, travel, work anywhere, and do some good for whatever community I was in. Also, I believed a medical career could be part-time, so I could play music as well.

'I knew Australia was cool. Life was out there and I wanted to live it my own way.'

Tek's passage was via London and he took himself to the

Marquee Club where many of his English heroes, including the Stones and the Who, had cut their teeth. There, he witnessed the proto-punk sect that was the Pink Fairies destroying the place, and their epic reworking of the Ventures' version of 'Walk Don't Run'. It etched deep in his mind.

After visiting family in Turkey, Deniz took a ship to Sydney. He arrived in the first week of February 1972 to commence studying medicine at the University of NSW, as the country was still reverberating to the thunder of Billy Thorpe and the Aztecs' appearance at the first Sunbury Festival in Melbourne.

The summer radio was alive with the Stones' 'Brown Sugar', the Who's 'Won't Get Fooled Again', T. Rex's 'Jeepster' and the Doors' 'Love Her Madly'. He took in as much as he could tolerate of Led Zeppelin when they appeared at the Sydney Showground.

Deniz Tek: 'I really liked the first couple of Zeppelin albums, and I was a big fan of the Yardbirds, but their performance [in Sydney] lacked emotional fire and I found myself looking to get out of there early and get on a bus ahead of the crowd.'

Dave Brubeck at Surf City

Gazing upon Led Zeppelin's rock-god pairing of Robert Plant and Jimmy Page was what other people were fixated on. Ron Keeley's attention never left drummer John Bonham kicking the shit out of his overly large bass drum, and in the process violently vibrating the strange symbol it carried.

Ron Keeley: 'Bonham, the heaviest right foot in the business. I picked that up from him.'

There were no thoroughfares to heaven of any description in Ron's early life. He came into the world at an orphanage in Subiaco, Perth, and was taken immediately for adoption only to be back in the hands of the Catholic Church and the first of his boarding school experiences when he was eight. Learning piano lent some colour to his world.

Ron Keeley: 'I finished piano at fifteen. I passed to Grade Seven. My exam piece was Rachmaninoff's "Prelude in C Sharp Minor", a real bitch.'

'I was supposed to be the pianist in my first band—it could have been the Drifters and later Peter and the Drifters. I remember being fascinated by the drummer, and always wanting a go on his kit.'

In 1963 Ron joined the Australian Navy. He was based at HMAS *Nirimba*, a training facility rather than shipboard placement a good hour or more from the reach of any sea breeze, near Blacktown in Sydney's western suburbs.

As a 'sprog' or apprentice, his day was split between two very different activities: fashioning steel and brass to an exacting degree and marching while handling a rifle in a precise ceremonial manner. Keeley quickly noticed that the band creating the soundtrack for the laps of the ground were given breaks not afforded to the other recruits. At the earliest opportunity, he put himself forward for that more relaxed duty. Ron found he could keep clean uncluttered time—albeit on a side drum—and as an added bonus had something to do with his hands rather than constantly beating out 'the devil's tattoo' on every available surface.

Ron Keeley: 'I've always been an anxious, nervous, twitchy type and used to get chucked out of class for tapping on the desk. I suspect drumming was an unconscious way of burning off nervous energy and it was easier than learning to play a guitar, although I did toy with bass guitar for a while.'

He would acquire a drum kit while in the service fuelled by the electrical current of the Beatles' 'She Loves You' which almost threw him across the room. That near-airborne experience was superseded by hearing the Stones' version of 'Little Red Rooster', with Charlie Watts' tell-tale heartbeat tap and the rise and fall of a ghostly slide guitar drifting from the late-night car radio.

He also loved jazz including the near-regal Duke Ellington and the hugely popular, if anything but hip-looking, Dave Brubeck.

Ron Keeley: 'I really liked the Brubeck Quartet. Brubeck's understated but perfectly apt piano, Paul Desmond's cool, cool sax, and especially Joe Morello's drumming. In fact, he was without a doubt my favourite drummer, and I even learned to play along to "Take Five" and "Unsquare Dance".'

The way in which the drums seemed to glide beneath that music, gently underpinning it but directing its flow and stride appealed enormously to Ron, and this art soon came to imitate life at HMAS *Nirimba*.

Ron Keeley: 'I was appointed to oversee the visitors' room. The job wasn't difficult, mostly seeing nothing got out of hand, but I did have a budget to buy LPs to play as background music. So I bought Chuck Berry, Little Richard and Elvis, but also Ellington, Basie, the Modern Jazz Quartet, Lionel Hampton and others. I'd have to say they were my most important jazz influences, particularly the big-band drummers.'

The guitar twang and rolling drum rhythms of the surf-music craze also resonated deeply. When he was able, Ron would return to Perth and head to Cottesloe Beach—a favoured location—and the Swan River and join the gatherings for the surfie stomp dances in the summer heat.

In Sydney, the place to be was Surf City, a cavernous 'Sound Lounge' in Kings Cross. Although it wasn't exactly as waterside as the events in Perth, the place was routinely packed by as many as 6000 people on weekends to 'rock-twist, stomp jive-limbo' to the biggest acts in the country, such as Billy Thorpe, or for some just to test themselves against the bouncers.

While in the city on one such occasion, Keeley decided to become a permanently marked man and get tattooed. In mid-sixties Australia, this was strictly confined to seamen and those worth giving a wide berth.

Ron Keeley: 'It's an eagle sitting on an anchor, with the initials "R.A.N." below. It was done at a tattoo parlour on Oxford Street, just about opposite the old Greek Orthodox Church. Afterwards, I had a couple of large scotches at the Beauchamp.'

Back at HMAS *Nirimba*, Ron joined some of the other apprentices in a jazz band. While their repertoire was tailored to weddings and the like, as well as pubs and RSLs, they let loose musically when they could.

At one of their gigs at Blacktown RSL, Ron was given some advice by one of the senior patrons in the audience, that keeping Swiss-watch precision time wasn't the main game. Instead, he should let the music breathe and move; that is, swing.

Later, the outfit evolved into a more guitar-based unit called the Mobiles, and Ron was delighted to be able to display his sun-bleached surf-rhythm roots.

Ron Keeley: 'The first thing I played was the Surfaris' "Wipe Out". The Shadows' "Apache" was another one we did.'

In 1967, Keeley finally moved beyond attending Surf City in Sydney and the stomps in Perth with a posting that saw him on the open sea. He was bound for San Francisco, where the Haight-Ashbury district was the crossroads of the hippie universe with the Summer of Love. Despite his regulation-style haircut amongst the shoulder-length locks and bright tie-dyed clothing, for the first time in his life Ron found a sense of freedom—and quiet rebellion—as well as making his double debut: pulling on a joint, and tasting what, back in Australia, was still the exotic delicacy of pizza. Even the local airwaves seemed to be telegraphing a new world. It all made a considerable, almost life-changing, impression.

Ron Keeley: 'I very nearly jumped ship, actually.'

After returning to Australia, a stopover in Melbourne allowed Ron to witness the dual forces of nature that were the Who and the Small Faces in the southern capital. For all the visual action of Pete Townshend and Roger Daltrey, Keeley couldn't help being mesmerised by the rhythm jinx of drummer

Keith Moon, who also had a background in surf music and jazz, in among the wild abandon of his flaying.

Ron Keeley: 'That [concert] was mind-blowing. I used to try to play along with Keith Moon [on Who records] . . . hopeless.'

Jazz was the driver of many of the great rock drummers of the day, from Ginger Baker to Mitch Mitchell, but it was the first album by the Chicago Transit Authority—soon to be simply Chicago—that laid out the cutting-edge possibilities of merging brass instruments with rock and roll, with drummer Danny Seraphine pushing and pulling proceedings.

Ron was hooked, for the same reason he loved the Stones' Charlie Watts and John Densmore of the Doors.

Ron Keeley: 'The Stones without Charlie? Unthinkable. The Doors without Densmore? A very different band. Both showed me how to play with a jazz feel in a rock and roll band.'

It was further vital tutelage for a then-unknown future.

In June 1970, Ron farewelled the navy. However, just as he was regaining his land legs, the following year his adoptive father died. It jarred the former seaman, despite him not having a blood connection.

Later the same year, through an association with the experimental co-op Ubu Films—founded by Albie Thoms, Aggy Read, David Perry and John Clark—Ron met Bob Dickson, an artistic, flair-filled individual with a new-aged fashion sense.

He would be instrumental in Keeley taking a room in November 1971 at what would be a pivotal address: 99 Boundary Street, Darlinghurst. It also housed young English guitarist Mick Lyne, and Frank Caley, who played bass.

Ron met Rob Younger for the first time when Younger came to Boundary Street to see Lyne.

Keeley had another drum set by this point and began playing

with fellow residents Mick and Frank, while Bob Dickson added piano. Younger soon became involved on rhythm guitar.

The Boundary Street outfit was to be called Star, driven by Dickson, who planned an auspicious debut performance at the ever-elegant State Theatre. An actual functioning band—not to mention that dream—didn't ever eventuate.

With the start of the new academic year in 1972, Ron returned to studies—this time philosophy, psychology and sociology—and moved to 14 Abbotsford Street, Kensington, a large address and more local to the University of New South Wales. Once he hauled his possessions to the new location, he then assisted Rob Younger's shift into the room at Boundary Street he had just vacated.

It wasn't long before Younger made the acquaintance of New Zealand–born Jules R.B. Normington, who had moved next door.

Jules R.B. Normington: 'I had some acid and I'd just bought *Who Will Save the World?* by the Groundhogs. Side one, amazing! Side two, amazing! I better play it again! I just played it six, seven, eight times in a row! I had the window open and had it cranked and every moment was a new surprise, even though I'd been through that moment just minutes ago. Rob came over and said, "Can you stop playing that fucking record!"'

Over at Keeley Manor at Kensington, there were several empty rooms, so Ron put up space-to-rent ads at the university. Deniz Tek's current student share house experience had been a disastrous clash of cultures. He needed a place.

Deniz Tek: 'The ad was like a play on words. It said something like "Deviant distraught demented person needed for room", so I went there. Ron Keeley comes to the door.'

Once Deniz was settled, Ron introduced him to Martin's Bar, while Tek returned the favour unveiling the sounds of Alice Cooper and the Stooges, which pounded on the same door within Keeley that the Stones and the Doors had done. Like his San Francisco adventure, that music felt like an escape, a freedom. More than his beloved jazz, it would be the means by which Ron would finally break out and say fuck you to the discipline and restrictions of much of his life.

There was still a spare room at Kensington, until another student, this one undertaking a Bachelor of Science with a Maths major, answered the ad—John Needham.

Deniz Tek: 'He looked like [Alice Cooper bassist] Dennis Dunaway and was super-skinny and had hair down past his butt.'

Needham grew up south of Wollongong and in January 1967 his family had moved to North Parramatta. It was an area very much like the wild west at the time, with skinheads and others regularly wreaking havoc. The city even had its own gaol, just a few hundred metres from the Needham home.

John introduced Deniz to Frenchs, a wine bar he had been patronising since the late sixties, where the pair spoke in the common dialect of the Stones.

Anyone Seen Gawlik?

Rob Younger should have burnt his ticket for Led Zeppelin before the gig and saved himself and anyone who came into his orbit over the next few weeks the pain. Blues rock wasn't to his taste; the elongated version of the genre even less so. Younger's realm instead was *Creem* magazine, which he was now buying regularly from a newsagent at Wynyard in the city.

Although the copies were several months old when they reached Sydney, they still featured a world light years ahead of Australia, with acts such as Alice Cooper, the New York Dolls, Kiss and Aerosmith, some of whom were yet to release a record. One image from the Cincinnati Summer Festival in 1970 particularly fired Rob's imagination.

Doug Lonsdale (Birdman devotee): 'There was a picture of Iggy Pop and I remember [Rob] saying, "This guy has gotta be fantastic! This *band* has gotta be fantastic!"'

Twenty-two-year-old Younger then found a second-hand Australian copy of the Stooges' *Fun House*—which had been given a withering review in *Go Set* Magazine—in the vinyl hunting ground that was Martin's Records in the city, which he regularly patronised. Like Ashwood's, it had such discarded items for two dollars or less. *Fun House* moved the axis on which his world turned by several substantial degrees.

Rob Younger: 'We had a couple of big speakers mounted up on the corners in the ceiling in the lounge room and I rolled up a big joint of hash—and that's the condition under which they made that record—and I sat there and it just completely floored me. I can only think of a couple of times previously where I was a little unsettled by a record and that was when I first heard "Tomorrow Never Knows" by the Beatles and some of the first Jimi Hendrix *Are You Experienced* record. But *Fun House* had a tangible threat about it I hadn't heard in music before.

'The critics always say that it was just after the hippies, or right at the tail end of that shit, and it just flattened all that stuff and just ploughed it under. I kind of agree with that. It sounded really fucking . . . otherworldly. It was a really pivotal moment for me.'

When Rob found a local copy of the first Stooges' album as well, he knew he had to act in some way, to respond, armed with this new knowledge. But how?

The self-titled debut by New York's Blue Oyster Cult had an impact as well. The band arrived fully formed, an immaculate rock conception, with its own inbuilt mythology heightened by an umlaut above the 'O' in 'Oyster' and a mysterious symbol front and centre on the cover, designed by artist Bill Gawlik—or simply 'Gawlik' as he was credited.

The logo was a conglomeration of astrology, alchemy, Greek mythology and the unknown.

The music was a mix of firepower, flash and subtlety, with guitarist Donald 'Buck Dharma' Roeser at the centre of dispensing each, with songs that were both poetic and sinister, about mythical characters and places and blurred real life. There were references to the Canadian Mounties, murderous drug deals, salamanders, biker gangs and Altamont, and the romantic oral application of a strange barbiturate. In part, these themes were drafted by the band's manager, co-producer and sorcerer-like figure Sandy Pearlman, with input from rock writer Richard Meltzer and others.

Rob Younger: 'I remember getting the train out to Oyster Bay and buying a *Creem* magazine, and there was an article by Richard Meltzer about the Oyster Cult. Maddeningly, I left it on the fucking train when I got out at Jannali. I'd love to still have that issue. I hadn't heard them [BOC] and I thought, "Gee, this band sounds fucking fascinating!" So I got a copy of the album at either an import shop, or had it imported, and just loved it.'

David Bowie, meanwhile, was conducting a one-man rock and roll renaissance, with the follow-up to the *Hunky Dory* LP, *The Rise and Fall of Ziggy Stardust and the Spiders from Mars.* Like Roxy Music, *Ziggy Stardust* depicted a bright, blazing new metropolis of style for a generation of kids dying to escape their dead-end circumstances and reinvent themselves. Bowie's day had also involved providing support for an ailing Mott the Hoople and handing them what would be their biggest hit, 'All the Young Dudes'. His growing influence and business connections were also instrumental in getting Iggy Pop off someone else's couch and ultimately, the Stooges—Pop and guitarist James Williamson, with Ron and Scott Asheton on bass and drums—reconvening in London. They appeared at the Kings Cross Cinema in July 1972 with opening act San Francisco's Flamin' Groovies, who had made a string of energised LPs, including *Flamingo* and *Teenage Head.* The Stooges' brief performance left mouths agape, including that of future Sex Pistol John Lydon.

'The total effect was more frightening than all the Alice Coopers and Clockwork Oranges put together, simply because these guys weren't joking,' declared Nick Kent in *New Musical Express* (*NME*).

While in London, the revamped Stooges went into the studio and recorded what would be the *Raw Power* album.

Iggy Pop: 'James Williamson played me the riff to what would become "Penetration". When I heard that I got very excited, and believed I could use that structure to make a very, very, ultra-modern rock and roll in a direction no one else had taken.'

An ailing MC5 had moved down another path, with an appearance also in London on a huge fifties rock and roll revival show at Wembley Stadium, with Jerry Lee Lewis, Chuck Berry, Bo Diddley and Little Richard, which paved the way for the UK punk scene. The Michigan outfit's decision to take to the stage in costume was a major miscalculation.

Wayne Kramer (the MC5): 'Had we gone on with our leather jackets and Levis they would have loved us but with sparkles and spangles and Fred Smith dressed in his Sonic Smith character outfit with the cape and the gold lamé, the 60,000 teddy boys rejected us out of hand! They were throwing beer cans and we made the mistake of throwing a can back!'

This grand English gathering of American renegades was completed by the New York Dolls opening for the Faces with Rod Stewart and the Pink Fairies before 7000 people at Empire Pool, Wembley, in October.

The Dolls were a joyous explosion of ragged sound and a sexual blur of style, with high heels, thigh-level red boots, elbow-length gloves, repurposed women's clothing and perfect manes of just-been-fucked hair. They'd created their own scene during a long-term Tuesday-night residency at the Oscar Wilde Room inside the Mercer Arts Center in New York City, where they were witnessed by the likes of Bowie, and even Marlene Dietrich. The Dolls and the Mercer soon became a magnet for the socially marginalised, as well as those in the local arts scene who saw both hope and scope and created their own gold-dusted, wildly extravagant look. From that glittering pool, other bands, fashion figures, filmmakers and photographers sprang.

The secret weapon in 1972, however, wasn't a band but a collective of artists via a double record titled *Nuggets: Original Artyfacts from the First Psychedelic Era, 1965–1968*, put together by rock critic, and future Patti Smith guitarist, Lenny Kaye. It showcased a diverse and by then forgotten world of American bands who'd had minor regional to major chart hits in the sixties. These included the Seeds, 13th Floor Elevators, the Standells, the Count Five, the Remains and the Chocolate Watchband, several of whom received airplay in Australia.

Many had made significant TV appearances, with the Remains on *The Ed Sullivan Show* and the Elevators on camera on *American Bandstand* with their primal 'smash hit' scream of 'You're Gonna Miss Me' reaching the national US charts in 1966. Others were incorporated into sitcoms such as the Seeds in *The Mothers-in-Law* while an episode of *The Munsters* featured the Standells.

Nuggets didn't sell by the shipping container but tore open a rusted door to a hip past, and became a foundation stone for an approaching future.

Rob Younger: 'I've still got the *Creem* review issue. It was a big record but I was the only one that really had it. The Standells, no one knew out here. If there was anyone who knew those bands, they never presented themselves, and if they formed a band they never mentioned them as influences. That's a whole scene that hardly anyone who's a crucial ten years younger than me knows fuck all about, unless they'd been educated by someone else and shown this sort of thing. What a marvellous record!'

That year finally saw the Velvet Underground's first release in Australia, but rather than their defining debut or even second effort, it was the contractual afterthought *Live at Max's Kansas City*, recorded almost two years earlier at the ultra-hip, arts culture blending New York City venue and worse, documented Lou Reed's final appearance with the outfit.

Meanwhile, a future inner city scene in Sydney was being mapped out by the pages of *Guitar Army—Street Writings/ Prison Writings*, the book by former MC5 manager and figure-head of the White Panthers, John Sinclair.

Light Bulbs and a Prosthetic Leg

Australian artists had been mythologising America in song for years—'Arkansas Grass' by Axiom, 'St Louis' by the Easybeats and John (Paul) Young's 'Pasadena'—with an emerging Melbourne unit going so far as to call themselves Mississippi. Meeting an actual American or even hearing a Stateside accent was a rarity, though, so when Deniz Tek materialised outside any garage where a local band was rehearsing seeking like musical minds, many were taken aback.

In the end, Tek's future came, indirectly, to him when Ron Keeley's former bandmates in Star—Mick Lyne, Bob Dickson and Rob Younger—came to the Kensington address one evening.

Younger made quite a first impression on Deniz, who still had a room at Keeley's 14 Abbotsford Street digs, and not just from a death drop of hair that was far longer than the considerable locks of another resident, John Needham.

Deniz Tek: 'Rob's got a velvet suit, huge crucifix, hair like [Yes keyboardist] Rick Wakeman! He looked like this shining rock god! He was quiet rather than shy.'

Tek's friend Chris Jones was there, playing guitar along to some records, including Alice Cooper's *Easy Action*—which, like the Coopers' *Pretties for You*, never saw Australian release—and *Love It to Death*. It was new territory for the usually up-to-the-minute Younger.

Rob Younger: 'Deniz introduced me to Alice Cooper. I don't remember being aware of their first two LPs at all. No one I knew did. I found them somewhat old-fashioned, especially compared to stuff I was currently obsessed by, but I thought it was alright.'

Within months, the world would know of Alice with *School's Out*, which came packaged as an elaborate foldout classroom desk, with the LP itself inside a pair of paper panties. The Coopers were applying a further coat of primer for punk rock.

A firming of Deniz and Rob's friendship would take a little longer, the pair not meeting again for a year or so, with Ron Keeley once more the convenor.

Another visitor to Kensington around this time was record obsessive, artist and general stylish figure Lee Taylor. He came to see John Needham and sell some records by Frank Zappa, the hip, largely imported currency of the day—and Captain Beefheart. Taylor's mention of the Stones—and specifically Keith Richards—within earshot of Deniz again created an immediate bond.

Lee Taylor: 'Deniz wasn't famous but he had this incredible charisma. He knew he was good. I actually found myself talking with an American accent after a few weeks hanging out with him! I bumped into a friend and he said, "Why are you talking like that?" Deniz had this manner that was just infectious.'

Taylor also made an impact.

Deniz Tek: 'Lee was a reliable "fashion consultant"—if Lee agreed it was cool, it was confirmed! Lee introduced me to the Blue Oyster Cult. I recall the first time I heard their album in his room in his parents' house. They looked bad ass, anti-hippie.

'Lee and I were also into comic books and cartoon art. He was very good and actually got a job drawing Phantom comics.'

It was clear to Taylor that Rob Younger had already made a considerable impression on Deniz.

Lee Taylor: 'When I first met Deniz he said, "There's this guy, he looks like a biker, he's got the longest hair." So Deniz had his eye on him.'

By late 1972, Tek had teamed up with Chris Jones and his brother Steve as singer to form the Screaming White Hot Razor Blades. Rick Grossman, a schoolmate of Chris's, and future Divinyl and Hoodoo Guru, was also part of the circle.

Rick Grossman: 'I have memories of Deniz teaching us how to play [the Stones'] "Gimme Shelter", Chris and I, in Chris's garage.'

The Blades were informed by Deniz's records and experiences, and tackled an eclectic selection of songs by the Velvet Underground, the Stooges and Alice Cooper, along with Elvis, Bob Seger, British blues godfather, John Mayall, and of course, the Stones.

Their first gig was a Christmas Ball at the then Craven A Pavilion at Sydney Showground for Paddington Lions Club.

Chris Jones: 'We were shithouse, really bad. But because Dad was the president of the club, we got the job.'

The announcement that the Stones—in full sullen satanic wither—would be returning to Australia in February 1973 on the back of the *Exile on Main Street* album threw Deniz and Lee Taylor into a spin. Tek had called Australia home for less than twelve months and now his favourite band was being served up before him, in what would be far closer proximity than he could have ever imagined.

Deniz Tek: 'For myself, the Stones were far more significant than the Detroit bands. To me, the Stones are the ultimate American band, although they're British.'

As that juggernaut loomed, in early 1973, the Screaming White Hot Razor Blades morphed into the cringingly named Cunning Stunt, with Deniz on vocals and guitar, Chris Jones on guitar, Tek's housemate Giles Van Der Werf on bass, and Gerry Jones, no relation, on drums.

Thanks to Giles's connections, Wollongong became their stomping ground, at venues such as the Charles Hotel in Fairy Meadow or Caesar's in the heart of the city.

Chris Jones: 'Caesar's was a weird place. The police wouldn't even turn up there. Every time there was a fight the guns would come out. It was a pretty heavy scene.'

The Stunt would become, according to one poster, the steel city's 'most popular group' and a residency at the Charles on Friday and Saturday nights allowed them to spread their wings in a number of respects.

Tapping into—among other things—the mental notes Deniz had taken seeing Alice Cooper's early theatre in Ann Arbor, when Alice donned a collar and was chained to a doghouse on the stage, the Stunts wore raincoats, set off explosions, ritually destroyed defenceless watermelons and performed other antics.

Deniz Tek: 'Like a light bulb on the end of a cord and spinning it around. Guys at the Charles Hotel were all tripping on acid, going, "Oh my God!" because there'd be this feedback coming off the stage and there'd be this thing whipping around, which I imagine would have left this amazing trail of colour on their [brain] cortexes.

'I liked props. I had a prosthetic leg that I would dance around with. Theatre of the Absurd!'

Chris Jones: 'We had a pig's head on top of a mike stand, just painted up with eyes like Alice Cooper and red lipstick, probably Mum's. It was a real pig's head.

'We used to hand-make all the posters. No silk-screening, just one by one. We went to the newsagent and bought the cardboard and texta colours and a bit of glitter. We'd glue them all around town with a mixture of flour and water. Once I only had self-raising flour and all the cardboard posters were swelling out from the telegraph poles as if they were 3D, which looked cool.'

The band themselves were very much visually part of the act, with Deniz donning the spiderweb eye make-up showcased by Alice Cooper, and Chris Jones at times entirely painted blue like some alien emperor.

Chris Jones: 'When we first started it was just jeans and T-shirt and Deniz always wore a bit of black eye make-up. Me being the baby of the band, his girlfriend used to come over and do a bit of make-up on me before the gigs, and it just progressed to the full face make-up.'

Deniz made the role of front man appear effortless.

Deniz Tek: 'When I wasn't holding the guitar, I moved around quite a bit. It would be boring to just stand there, especially without a great singing voice. Not being tied to a guitar cord, I used that opportunity to get down on the floor, and into the audience. I would have got that from Iggy.'

And Tek wasn't above finding and distributing some of the stone tablets from which he was drawing. Martin's Records, or Ashwood's in the city, had copies of the MC5's *Back in the USA* and *High Time* records, as well as the first two Stooges' albums, just sitting in the racks, torches waiting to be carried forth.

Deniz Tek: 'It would be like a dollar or seventy-five cents or something. I always picked up whatever copies they had. Obviously, someone didn't like them and got rid of them. I just gave them to people and said, "This is where what I do comes from."'

Exiles on Main Street

The Queen swanned past Deniz Tek and Lee Taylor at Brisbane Airport. Lillian Roxon was now the matriarch of international rock journalism, who knew all and held court at Max's Kansas City. Her presence back in Australia spoke volumes.

Deniz had been working nights at the Davis Gelatine company in Pagewood over the summer, 'rendering animal parts into collagen for gelatine and adhesives' to enable him to follow the Stones' Australian tour as best as he was financially able, and hiring a super-8 movie camera and a tape recorder to document the experience.

When the Jagger and Richards juggernaut hit Sydney for two performances at Randwick Racecourse in late February—tickets just $5.20—Tek swung into action.

Lee Taylor: 'Deniz said, "Where's the phone book? They'll be staying at the hotel with the biggest ad." The largest was the Hyatt at the Cross. So he rings up and has the good sense to ask, in an American accent of course, could he speak to Bill Wyman, please—not Mick or Keith. They said, "Just a minute," Bill answers, and he hangs up and we run straight up there.'

The pair arrived at the hotel on William Street and hung out in the bar, trying desperately to contain their excitement with some of their heroes and crew seated just metres away.

It was enough of an initial dose and they then set off early for that night's first Randwick gig. Tek dressed for the occasion in a white boiler suit from the gelatine factory, with a Stones logo patch attached to it so he appeared to be a member of the band's crew. Tek secured a dream spot right up the front, which allowed him to film and also enact a plan he and Taylor had hatched months earlier.

Lee Taylor: 'Deniz had bought me a bottle of Old Grand-Dad [whiskey] for my birthday. When we knew the Stones were coming, I said to him, "We're going to give this to Keith!"'

They managed to grab the attention of founding Stones' member and then road manager, Ian Stewart, while he was helping set up the equipment.

Lee Taylor: 'I held the bottle up and he probably thought it's for him. He was very sweet and I let him down gently and said, "Could you please give this to Keith?" He sat it on Charlie's drum riser, and later, after the first couple of numbers or so, Keith looks down, sees the bottle and drinks from it, and we were going, "Oh my God!" Like teenage girls!'

The next day Deniz decided to take things up a notch and see if Keith Richards would be interested in buying his vintage guitar. He found the name of Richards' guitar tech, called the hotel again and got straight through to Newman Jones, who told him to come by after the gig that night.

Deniz Tek: 'I stopped in at Dare Jennings to get the guitar—I had left it there while I was at the concert—and went to the Hyatt. There were all these fans and the lifts were being guarded by a karate school—these black belts—so I'm thinking, "I'm never going to get up there." I just sat around for an hour and then the lift opens and this girl comes out. She's about seven feet tall, wearing leopard skin, this African girl, and she says in this loud voice, "The guy with the guitar can come up now." She escorts me past the security and we went up.

Newman Jones checked out the guitar and said, "Come on, let's show it to Keith."

'There was a party in Keith's room and he asked for somebody to bring in an amplifier. They had a tape of the concert at Randwick and Keith plugs into the amplifier, with this guitar I had brought, and plays along with some of the songs. Mick came up to me and wanted to know who I was and talked to me for a little while. Then the place cleared out, because Mick was going to show films in his room. It just me, Keith, [Stones guitarist] Mick Taylor and [saxophone player on the tour] Bobby Keys, who was unconscious, passed out. This would have been about two in the morning and, until about six, Keith played guitar and talked. He was very kind and friendly.

'He said, "How much do you want for the guitar?" I said, "I don't need any money, just give me any one of your guitars. It can be the oldest, most hacked-up guitar, I don't care. Just give me a Keith Richards guitar and I'll make you an even trade." He said, "I'd be happy to, but they're all packed up. Everything is at the airport—we're leaving today." I said, "Don't worry about it. Just take the guitar and send me one." He said, "I won't remember. Let me just give you some cash and you go buy something." I said, "Okay, fine." So he picked up the phone—"This is Keith, I need some money"—and puts the phone down. This guy comes running in with [an accounting] book and the money. I was so high [with excitement]! I couldn't believe it!

'The Stones and the crew had T-shirts for the tour, not for sale. We'd seen Keith in one of the T-shirts and it said "Guitarist" on the back, and I thought, "That is so cool!" So I asked, "That tour T-shirt, could I have that?" Keith goes, "I already gave it to somebody else, sorry, but hang on." And he's got this little bag and he pulls stuff out and goes, "Here, have this." He gave me a Stones' T-shirt from the '66 tour of the States.'

When he emerged into the early-morning light, Deniz, too wired up from the Stones encounter to sleep, jumped in a taxi and had breakfast with a gobsmacked Lee Taylor. He gave him a signed drumstick from Charlie Watts then went to Harry Landis Music in Park Street in the city and bought a new guitar with the cash from 'Keef'.

Tek's shoot of the Stones' Randwick show on 26 February 1973 is on YouTube.

Tyranny and Mutation

The dopey routines of comedians Cheech & Chong blaring through the PA system at Randwick Racecourse in the lead-up to the Stones' appearance were the type of thing that drove Rob Younger mad. He led with his eyes and made his way towards the stage as if being buried deep in the crowd might somehow shield him from the dumb-fuck hilarity.

For the second gig the following night, he took his motorbike, and used his helmet as an icebreaker to again better his position, possibly brushing roughly past Warwick Gilbert, Ron Keeley and Deniz Tek in the process.

There wasn't too much difference between the shows.

Rob Younger: 'They played the same set and most of them wore the same clothes. It was great, though. Really great.'

While the Stones had arrived in high style on the Randwick stage in horse-drawn carriages, the Blue Oyster Cult were a gargoyle atop some grand gothic architecture, dispassionately eyeing all below.

Their second effort, *Tyranny and Mutation*, built strongly on all aspects of their first. The cover image of a temple of some description topped by the band's logo was again the work of artist Bill Gawlik, while the record itself was divided into two sides and modes: the Black and the Red.

They additionally appeared to have created a new alphabet while the felt-pen that blocked out text on the sleeve and label of imported copies to avoid copyright issues seemed to have been done in the interests of national security.

Even the cover of the single 'Hot Rails to Hell' had weight well beyond its sound, with an image of a heavily decorated military figure standing against the American flag, while on the back was a shot of band members Eric Bloom and Buck Dharma crossing their guitars mid-performance, as if they were jousting for some dark prize.

Rob Younger: 'The great thing was the quotes on the single. One from *Rock* magazine and one from *Rolling Stone*. *Rock* mag said simply, "A portable Altamont," and the other was "A brilliant exposition of what the Stones would be playing today if they hadn't turned into such bourgeois hedonist auteurs". I thought, "That's great!"

'*Tyranny and Mutation* is their best record, I reckon. I used to lie in my flat, with my head between the detachable speakers, and listen and be completely thrilled. They built a fantasy world.'

The *Raw Power* album from Iggy and the Stooges also seemed to have come from a place of unknown otherness—certainly no longer a Detroit address—right from its shot by Mick Rock of an iridescent Iggy at London's King Sound the previous year. The mix added a hallucinogenic dimension, virtually an extra instrument, while James Williamson's searing guitar breaks spectacularly fell in and out of earshot like daggers, and the drums almost dragged the rhythm back slightly, rather than propelling it.

Iggy Pop: 'I don't think anybody put out something that pointed the way to the future as much as that record.'

In America, it received FM radio airplay and a massive billboard on Sunset Strip in West Hollywood, while a full-page ad in *Time* magazine, titled 'A platter of raw Iggy to go', contained grabs of several salivating reviews, including Lenny Kaye from *Rolling Stone*.

In Australia, *Raw Power* was included in a large advertisement, along with other recent CBS releases such as Paul Simon's *There Goes Rhymin' Simon* and Leonard Cohen's *Live Songs*.

Rob Younger: 'I bought *Raw Power* on my 23rd birthday. No one wanted to know! They didn't! You could clear rooms with that record! I instantly thought that was the fucking greatest thing I'd ever heard, and this is even after being knocked out and a bit scared by *Fun House* when I first heard it. *Raw Power* just sounded like it was from another world yet again, another planet or something. It's got that intensity about it, that malign sort of intent. I found it fucking exciting! I drove people mad with that record.'

But again, sales were well below expectations.

Iggy Pop: 'It *[Raw Power]* didn't really come out, it kind of fell out! Nobody really wanted it. Management didn't want it, nobody knew what the fuck to do with it! It was in the reject [bargain] bins for 39 cents shortly after it was released.'

There was also plenty of initial optimism around the first New York Dolls' album, with a specially designed font written in lipstick on the record label.

Nick Kent gushed in the *NME* that the Dolls '. . . can proudly stand beside Iggy & the Stooges' stupendous *Raw Power* as the only album so far to fully define just exactly where 1970s' rock should be coming from'.

Rob Younger didn't have to be told to be sold.

Rob Younger: 'The first review I remember was in *Rolling Stone*. I think the headline was "New York Dolls—What's it to Ya?" I've still got it inside the first album, actually. I put reviews or obituaries inside records; otherwise you lose them.'

The LP charted, hitting as high as number 45 on the Top 100 Albums listing, shoulder to shoulder at various points with the Carpenters and ZZ Top. But it wasn't going to be enough.

Imported copies of the first album by Aerosmith were also turning hip heads, while Lou Reed's bleak masterpiece *Berlin* was everything the previous year's breakout effort, *Transformer*, only seemed to suggest visually, and proved a powerful cleaning agent.

Rob Younger: 'I emptied a roomful of Bowie fans with *Berlin*. Side two, especially, was a bridge too far.'

Billion Dollar Babies by Alice Cooper, on the other hand, was the pinnacle of their jaw-dropping stage spectacle and commercial success, the once-outsider weirdoes now gleefully able to shower their past detractors with real and novelty money as their bodies floated past. Alice himself ran a mock election campaign with the song 'Elected' and had the support of *Creem* magazine readers, who would vote Alice 'Punk of the Year' for 1973.

Even the Coopers' earlier *Pretties for You* and *Easy Action* recordings were finally deemed fit for public consumption in Australia with the *School Days—The Early Recordings* double set.

By this point there were import record shops in Sydney, led by the Goliath that was Anthem in the concourse under the town hall. It carried a sea of records unavailable in Oz. Anthem was modelled on Melbourne's hugely successful Archie 'n' Jugheads operation, which had been the country's first rock and roll import record store—opened by David N. Pepperell and Keith Glass in March 1971.

An offshoot of Anthem, Ripple Records in the Angel Arcade,

was run by Chris Pepperell—a relation of the A & J's store co-founder—who would later launch Red Eye Records, which would become the largest store in Australia.

It was all music to the ears and wallets of Warwick Gilbert and Rob Younger, who, in the second half of 1973, reconnected via the bridging structure of the Stooges.

Warwick Gilbert: 'Rob brought *Fun House* around to my place and played it. I wasn't real impressed, because I was still into the blues rock sort of thing. Rob certainly looked different to anybody else by then. He was a presence on the street. He'd get guys in pubs going, "Look, this guy's a sheila! Bloody poofter," and Rob would walk over to them and scream at them, "You get fucked!" He liked a bit of a stoush, Rob!'

Gilbert had hardly been lost in the wilderness the previous few years. After a stint in advertising he had returned to animation as a member of a high-level team that had been specially assembled at Hanna-Barbera's Sydney studios. A trip to the UK saw him take in a series of shows at the famed Rainbow Theatre, including Mountain ('The loudest band I've ever heard!') and, far less inspiringly, prog kings Yes ('I left during an incomprehensible Steve Howe guitar symposium'). Back home, Warwick witnessed Sydney performances by the likes of Black Sabbath and the Stones.

Warwick Gilbert: 'I stood in front of Mick Taylor. I didn't even notice Keith Richards.'

His rebonding with Rob Younger was strengthened with the *Nuggets* compilation, Gilbert delighted that someone else also recognised its magic. Not long after, he saw a copy of the Stooges' *Raw Power* in a record store.

Warwick Gilbert: 'I thought, "There's that band that Rob likes." *Raw Power* was a nihilistic sort of blues, and to me was kind of scary to listen to. But it was amazing. They had that Motown chord structure that the Stones kind of used, the suspended fourths and all that kind of stuff, like in "Honky Tonk Women".'

As this awakening was taking place, Iggy and co were about to take their lives in their hands at the Michigan Palace in Detroit on 5 and 6 October 1973.

Like a Pontiac Firebird

Deniz Tek was living at Baxter College at the University of NSW when he crossed paths in the dining room with an enigmatic fellow resident from Canberra, who, like Tek, didn't fit into the animal-house culture code by which some lived.

Deniz Tek: 'I noticed this guy eating all alone, so I went over to talk to him. Conversation turned to music and he told me he played piano and had a classical and modern jazz background. He was a fan of Fats Waller, and he was getting into the blues.'

Pip Hoyle was one year ahead of Tek in medical school. Since he was seven he'd been sitting at a piano, climbing in classical tuition to Grade Seven. He harboured a desire to be a serious musician and composer.

For most of his high-school years he had played jazz on weekends. Rock and roll didn't loom large on his radar until he and Deniz got together in the piano-practice spaces at the university.

Deniz Tek: 'We jammed and hit it off well. We didn't know any songs that each other knew, nor had much in common musically, but I recall him showing me how to play [jazz and blues classic] "St James Infirmary". I knew he could add unconventional elements to the music I wanted to make.'

Cunning Stunt meanwhile had made a recording for a surf movie before the band name went out with the tide in favour of TV Jones—Tek, Van Der Werf and Jones.

Tek soon had the retitled outfit rehearsing in the piano rooms with Pip.

Deniz Tek: 'He didn't want to play straight 4/4 time, and his non-mechanical, fluid style confounded Giles and the other guys.'

The rest of the TV Joneses also weren't over the moon about Hoyle being a Tek ally and as threateningly intelligent. Nonetheless, they played a number of gigs together, with Deniz fired up after taking the sacrament of Iggy and the Stooges' *Raw Power*.

Deniz Tek: 'The Stooges were back! For me, it was an affirmation of life. The Stooges pointed the way forward.'

Late in 1973, Deniz went home to see his family in Ann Arbor and there had three pivotal experiences. One was acquiring a guitar once owned and played by the MC5's Fred 'Sonic' Smith.

Deniz Tek: 'At this convenience store on South University Street called Campus Corners, they had a noticeboard full of handwritten notes. There was this ad, "MC5 guitar Epiphone Crestwood $140," or whatever it was. I thought, "That's interesting, an MC5 guitar?" So I called the number and it wasn't Fred Smith—it was a guy named Fred Stoll. The band had just sold off a bunch of their stuff. I'm not sure how he managed to find out, and he bought that guitar and resold it.'

The second significant encounter was catching a rerun of the New York Dolls' jaw-dropping television appearance on the *Midnight Special*, which featured live performances by a number of acts each week. The Dolls had a dressed-to-kill flamboyance but at the same time didn't seem at all contrived—even the small doll hanging from the back of black-maned guitarist

Johnny Thunders somehow seemed natural. A few kids in the audience danced and one girl sang every word, in what overall was a coded broadcast direct to the hearts and minds of a legion of misfitted kids, like an underbelly screening of the Beatles on *Ed Sullivan*.

Deniz Tek: 'The Dolls were a revelation! They took the Rolling Stones' oeuvre almost to the level of cartoonishness, but it was super-cool! They hit us with a welcome dose of retro Stones' essence. I was immediately hooked.'

The third lightning strike of Tek's home visit came with the discovery of Garland Jeffreys, whose 'Wild in the Streets' was making a mark on radio.

Deniz Tek: 'I thought, "That's what the Stones *should* be doing!" Kind of in the same ballpark as the New York Dolls. I heard it in the car, loved it, but couldn't find a copy and then had to go back to Sydney. The record was unknown and unavailable in Australia. So I took what I could recall from it, mainly the chorus and guitar riff, and wrote another song around it with my own verses, called "Insane Alive", and I credited Garland Jeffreys with songwriting.'

In early 1974, TV Jones shifted their focus from Wollongong and staged theatre to the Sydney scene, where they were somehow able to gain a foothold in several major venues such as the Whisky a Go Go in Kings Cross and—thanks to Chris Jones's mum knowing major industry figure Harry M. Miller—a slot at Chequers, where AC/DC had made their debut a few months earlier.

TVJ secured a week's worth of gigs at the famed nightclub, but midway through the first engagement opening for Sherbet, Deniz's voice collapsed and he was forced to resort to a still-in-character, but unsuccessful, plan B.

Chris Jones: 'We got fired because Deniz was crawling around on the floor. All they wanted in that place was twelve-bar blues rock. They didn't want bands playing Alice Cooper and biting people!'

All the while, Deniz had been working up an image in his sketch pad, which had roots in the auto-manufacturing industry of Detroit, along with the vehicle he himself had driven in 1969.

Deniz Tek: 'The Pontiac Firebird [emblem] was a [stylised] symbol of a bird and its wings rose up around it. My drawing was sort of loosely based on that visual concept. It was like a combination of the Firebird symbol and the symbol for radiation.

'I was drawing a lot of cartoon art, and used it here and there on planes, spaceships and so on, but it never occurred to me to use it for the band. For one thing, we didn't have any products to put a logo on. TV Jones never had a T-shirt, no LPs, or anything where a graphic design could be used. Of course, I was well aware of the Stones' tongue, but bands having logos was still a relatively new concept. It wasn't until I saw photos of the Blue Oyster Cult using their Saturn symbol on flags draped over banks of amplifiers that it occurred to me that I could do the same.'

Rats in the Cellar

The walls of the tunnels at Eddy Avenue at Central railway station had long been a ragged mural of the social and political times in Sydney. As Christmas 1973 approached, the row of posters for 'Aztec Rock'—Billy Thorpe's appearance at the nearby Capitol Theatre in June—were partially obscured by overlapping advertisements and torn as if vermin of some description had been gnawing at them.

The onslaught of the Aztecs via Strauss Warrior amplifiers was one end of the scene. The hippie phenomenon of Uncle Bob's Band—formed from the ashes of Sydney's Original Battersea Heroes and not unlike the inner-city's Grateful Dead—and the folk music clubs the other.

In addition, every suburban guitarist dreamt of somehow being Led Zeppelin's Jimmy Page or Deep Purple's Ritchie Blackmore, while singers saw themselves as Free's Paul Rodgers or Zeppelin's Robert Plant. Purple's 'Smoke on the Water' and Free's 'All Right Now' were played by almost every act every night everywhere.

Rob Younger had an altogether different vision.

Rob Younger: 'I really despised a lot of the groups around at that time, and to my mind they became the enemy. They were the bands getting all the gigs and making mostly really slack-sounding rock records. It's the reason I started the Rats.'

He made his move when the means of production presented itself.

Rob Younger: 'I got a little money, like $1000 or $1500, from the sale of a house down on the south coast from my grandmother. I said [to Mick Lyne and Warwick Gilbert], "Why don't we buy a PA and start a group?"'

Lyne played guitar, as did Gilbert, who had turned his attention to learning the songs from the first New York Dolls' record, which Younger had also directed him towards—plus the material on *Raw Power*.

Warwick Gilbert: '[The Stooges'] James Williamson's favourite guitarist is Jeff Beck. I could hear that in his playing and it was an extension of the British blues that I related to. So I started learning that as a better alternative to heavy metal—all those guitar wizards that were out of my reach.'

Younger was going to front the band, an experience light years out of his comfort zone.

Rob Younger: 'I just wanted to be the singer. I didn't really know what to do, except hold the microphone really tight and yell into it. I didn't have any moves or anything. I put two and two together by seeing pictures of Iggy and David Johansen [New York Dolls]. I was just connecting the dots. Everyone starts somewhere.

'There were two records the band was based around mainly: *Raw Power* and the first Dolls album. I was really fucking nuts, obsessed about the Stooges. That was a catalyst. The Dolls, because of their great take on rock and roll, of course—also because Johansen's vocals seemed eminently copy-able.'

Warwick Gilbert: 'The Rats was a really great idea. It was Rob's concept and he picked all the records, cherry picking the best rock and roll. He was definitely well ahead of his time.'

Younger approached Ron Keeley as drummer, while firmly setting the boundaries from the outset: no 'jazz shit'.

All they needed then was a bass player. Frank Caley, who Ron knew from Boundary Street, wasn't the right fit, so Carl 'St John' Rorke, an imposingly built ex-member of the Australian Army and regular at Martin's Bar, was persuaded to sign on.

Their initial rehearsal took place in the front room at 14 Sims Street, Darlinghurst, where Ron was living.

Mick Lyne: 'We made an awful lot of noise and two of the neighbours came in and asked us please to turn it down. The usual story.'

Rob Younger: '[The New York Dolls'] "Bad Girl" was the first song I ever tried. We attempted [the Stones'] "Rocks Off" at our first rehearsal and I just couldn't get to it at all. I couldn't sing it. Now [laughs] it doesn't sound that fucking hard at all! Back then it was mysterious.'

Warwick Gilbert: 'Ron was the only experienced musician in the Rats. He had jazz chops and got up in the music and started slapping it around. Mick Lyne played great rhythm guitar. I couldn't play rhythm to save my life, so I just played lead and tried to make James Williamson–type noises. Carl couldn't play bass at all. Rob didn't hold back in venting his frustration at us, which was no fun.'

A Tutu and a Knuckle Glove

The January 1974 cover headline of Ohio's free weekly, *The Scene*, summed up the position with perfect clarity: 'Iggy and the Stooges; one step further than most people can stand.' The bloodied writing had been on the wall after the commercial failure of *Raw Power*, with the band now reduced to playing a small bar called the Rock and Roll Farm in Michigan—which had a heavy biker presence in the form of local gang the Scorpions—in the first week of February.

Ron Asheton (Iggy and the Stooges): 'One of the guys who wanted to be in the motorcycle club had to punch Iggy out. So we're playing and someone's throwing eggs, so Iggy just goes out in the crowd, and this big biker guy, he just slugs Iggy with his studded glove and [Iggy] comes back and he said, "Stop playing, we're outta here!" So we went back to the dressing-room and all these bikers come in and started giving us shit, and somehow miraculously the road crew got us out of there. But they wouldn't pay us and we were union members and the union blacklisted their club. No union bands could play there, so they promised revenge!'

Iggy Pop: 'I got beaten about the face while wearing a tutu by a rather large biker with a knuckle glove. That was pretty scary! I spent the night in someone's suburban bedroom unbeknownst to the family. I fled! With nothing but my tutu and the goodwill of a fan.'

Pop and the band went on radio station WABX and Ig called on the bikers to step it up a notch on 9 February at Detroit's Michigan Palace, where the Stooges had done love–hate battle with the local crowd in early October. The gang also hit the airwaves, warning of revenge.

According to some reports, the Scorpions didn't show at the Palace, which violates every known biker law. Other accounts had them there in force, but either way the band didn't escape unscathed, with the local audience—who were known to throw bullets on stage as a show of extreme disdain—again fired up by the promise of Iggy's now-legendary life and limb performance.

Ron Asheton: 'It brought out the weirdos in the crowd. And people themselves would want to get a little more violent. Then you get the lit cigarettes and the pennies [being thrown].'

The gig was chaotic, darkly comical and just plain sad despite Iggy's bravado. Like the Stones at Altamont, the beast Mr Pop had been challenging for years now roared back one hundredfold. It was an undignified tail-between-their-legs end for the Stooges.

Lou Reed's trajectory, on the other hand, had been reset with the *Rock 'n' Roll Animal* album, his head shaved in a slightly disturbing manner, tethered by a heavy collar, and glowing orange as though he had ingested some sort of radio-active isotope. Recorded at two performances at the New York Academy of Music on 21 December 1973 with a band including gun guitarists Steve Hunter and Dick Wagner, *Animal* featured supercharged workings of the back catalogue of Lou and the Velvet Underground into a virtual greatest hits that grabbed the attention of a new generation, particularly in Australia where the pivotal early Velvets' LPs remained unreleased.

Rock 'n' Roll Animal was the first of two critical Velvets-related injections that year.

The appearance by the Faces with Rod Stewart at Randwick Racecourse in February 1974 was raw joy to Lou's dark majesty.

Rob Younger: 'I was right in front of Ronnie Wood, about six or seven yards back, so I had a good look at it. They were very, very good. I had all the records, anyway.'

It was against this collective backdrop, and with the New York Dolls voted best new group of 1973 by the readers of *Creem* and also the year's worst by that same demographic, that the Rats made their first public outing as part of an afternoon benefit gig on the grounds of Paddington Women's Hospital.

Rob Younger: 'We were mere metres from the wards, where sick people presumably were, or women who were about to have babies, and we were playing this really loud shit in the open air and never got any complaints from neighbours.'

Warwick Gilbert: 'Someone filmed that. There were people leaning out the windows.'

Rob Younger: 'We just played furiously through the songs. We didn't stop to take a breather or anything, and everything was all a bit one paced and desperate. I was just standing there, pretty much. A bit more like Joey Ramone, actually [long pause]. Before Joey Ramone, I might add.'

In addition to the Stooges and New York Dolls, the Rats tackled 'Cold Turkey' by the Plastic Ono Band, along with 'Rock and Roll' and 'I'm Waiting for the Man' by the Velvet Underground.

Rob Younger: 'We only played covers, perhaps eighteen or so. The stuff we were playing wasn't standards. Nobody knew what the fuck it was. No one would come up and say, "So, you know about that band [too]?" It just didn't happen.'

But there were small pockets of local awareness with an edition of the *Australian Women's Weekly* carrying a feature on the first Australian tour by Suzi Quatro, which mentioned her home city of Detroit being '. . . the birthplace of punk rock, the MC5 (Motor City 5, a once famous rock group)', while, elsewhere, writer Jeune Pritchard mentioned Quatro had opened for the New York Dolls.

In any event, what the Rats were undertaking placed them like Cunning Stunt and TV Jones in a sacred order scattered across the globe, including Rocket from the Tombs in Cleveland, London's Hollywood Brats, the Imperial Dogs in LA, the Modern Lovers in Boston, Doris Death in Sydney and Brisbane's Saints. Each was a satellite and laying the foundations of punk.

Jules R.B. Normington, another music and record obsessive and avid *Creem* reader, loved what the Rats were doing and had to be involved.

Jules R.B. Normington: 'I knew all the songs and they were ripping them out even more intensely than the original bands were. It was incredible! There was no place I'd rather be than at their gigs, so I'd go with them with the gear as a friend would.'

He soon learned how to set up the equipment and mix the sound, the latter a thankless task on one occasion.

Jules R.B. Normington: 'Rob goes, "The sound was fucking terrible!" I went outside and burst into tears. I was devastated!'

It was as if Younger needed those around him to rise, otherwise he felt exposed. He was his own harshest critic.

There were other combustion issues, with Rob and Ron Keeley being oil and water, personality- and character-wise—one with a travelled earthiness and, fittingly, a pipe; the other, a nocturnal urban intensity.

Rob Younger: 'It was always a bit volatile. I'm not saying he's a bad person or anything like that, but sometimes people just rub each other the wrong way.'

Ron Keeley: 'Rob and I never got on, never ever got on.'

Warwick Gilbert shuddered at each eruption.

Elsewhere, David Bowie was again offering an escape route for many with the *Aladdin Sane* album, which would in turn be furthered by the futuristic punkscapes of *Diamond Dogs*.

The New York Dolls presented their second effort, the all-too-prophetically titled *Too Much Too Soon*—Rob Younger was once more in raptures—but, like its predecessor, it was given Australian release but sold considerably fewer than their first effort and was again quickly deleted.

An imported copy of the first LP by a group of mysteriously painted newcomers from New York City called Kiss—who had already caught the attention of the NY Dolls and future Ramones' members—also snared Younger's interest.

Rob Younger: 'We [the Rats] did "Strutter", which wasn't the one I really wanted to do. I liked "Black Diamond". That first Kiss record had some good songs, better than anything they did later. I really hate fucking "Rock and Roll All Nite"!'

Warwick Gilbert: 'Rob was good at finding stuff first. We vetoed "Strutter" when everyone else picked it up.'

Rat rehearsals would sometimes take place at an old warehouse at Woolloomooloo, where grass was growing up between the concrete, and an early AC/DC also made a racket.

Warwick Gilbert: 'It was like some old stables, and it had a pony's courtyard, down the bottom of the Domain somewhere. It had cobblestones. AC/DC would carry their equipment out and then we'd bring our crap in.'

Jules R.B. Normington: 'One day we needed the keys to get in and so we drove to Angus's house to get them.'

Despite their sound being well away from the norm, and most likely through Ron Keeley's local connections, they managed to score a residency at the Oxford in Taylor Square, Darlinghurst, the site of one of Warwick and Rob's first Saturday-night teen initiations. A tiny ad for the Rats' gig at the pub mentioned the outfit's 'vermin rock' but they looked more decadent than rundown.

Rob Younger: 'Mick and I used to share clothes sometimes. It was a combination of New York Dolls style and . . . maybe just the Dolls. I remember having a really nice grey, silvery jacket, quite tight plus red crushed velvet pants, and I bought some boots from St Vinnies or something. They were women's boots and they came up just below the knee and high heels. Mick was as skinny as a rake. He was built just like Mick Jagger and a nice-looking guy too—long blond hair, the girls loved him. We used to go to Frenchs and Martin's [Bar] in these clothes. That was what we wore around Darlinghurst, with eye make-up and stuff like that.

'One night coming home from the Oxford, a guy pulled over and offered me a lift. I got in and he saw I was a bloke. You could see his horror. I said, "I know, mate, I'm just up the road about five hundred metres. If you drop me off, that'd be great!"'

After about eight gigs, two lots of four weekends in a row, time was called on the Rats' experience at the Oxford.

Warwick Gilbert: 'We were a pretty sullen bunch and no one else was doing that sort of stuff, so we were pretty much in a vacuum.'

Deadly Earnest

The custom-built hearse, white with black windows, seemed to glide by—fittingly, like a ghost—attracting reverence at first, until Warwick Gilbert was noticed behind the wheel and the rear packed with amplifiers, rather than the dearly departed. The pop-up seat next to where the body would traditionally be placed was usually occupied by Jules R.B. Normington.

Warwick Gilbert: 'It wasn't one of the great long ones [vehicles], but you could fit a coffin in it. It was used to take the body from the house to where they embalm it. I just saw it as practical. It was really nice.'

Gilbert's artistic brain was constantly ticking over and came up with something special for the front of Ron Keeley's bass drum.

Warwick Gilbert: 'It was this little child with a rat in its mouth. I ripped it off Salvador Dali. It was great! It was repulsive! I was a big Dali fan.'

Rob Younger: 'It was a really nice rendering. It didn't have a name or anything on it. Like, "Fuck! That's cool!"'

The Rats' other rehearsal space was at Studio 20, which resembled a concrete bomb shelter, located around the corner from the Oxford in Darlinghurst. With other bands also coming and going, the rodents were often face to face with all Rob Younger stood against.

Rob Younger: 'I thought what the Rats were doing was hipper, but we weren't even doing our own shit. At least, we weren't ploughing the same fucking furrow as those berks. We used to heckle other bands something fierce. Then you realise, oh, you're in a band and you shouldn't be doing this, because it makes it look like you're saying you're better than they are, but . . .'

On one occasion the conflict wasn't with the other clientele.

Ron Keeley: 'The owner objected to our volume and had a bit of a go at us, and I had a go back. He stormed off and came back five minutes later with a pistol. Just across the road was the Oxford Street cop shop, so I went running over and reported this guy waving a bloody pistol around. It turned out he was a licensed private detective.'

Rob Younger: 'This prick said I'd threatened him! We had to piss off, completely fucked over. But it was educational.'

Keeley had given away his studies, but was working at the Menzies Library at University of NSW as the audio-visual technician. Here, he bumped into Deniz Tek for the first time in a while. Tek showed Ron the logo he had been working on.

In return, Ron played Deniz a tape of the Rats at Studio 20, including a version of the New York Dolls' 'Personality Crisis'.

TV Jones, with Pip on keyboards, had done some recording themselves at Earth Media studios in North Sydney, including 'Eskimo Pies'—co-written by Chris Jones—and Tek and Jones's 'Skimp the Pimp', which Deniz wrote about a colleague at the assembly plant at Ypsilanti, along with 'Monday Morning Gunk', 'Man with Golden Helmet', 'Snake' and 'Insane Alive'.

When Ron mentioned his encounter with Deniz, Rob Younger initially vigorously refused to believe anyone else in the country knew of the Stooges and the New York Dolls. Then, after Rob realised Keeley was talking about the individual he'd met a few years earlier, Ron facilitated a reconnection between the pair, most likely over a schnitzel at Martin's Bar.

Tek and Younger were diametrically opposed but both had a distinct intensity in all they did. They were the perfect yin-and-yang combination.

Rob Younger: 'We got along really well. I thought, "Here's a smart guy, someone who knows something. He's studying, he's got ambition, but he finds time to do everything." Deniz is one of those people who makes time work for him. I'm the opposite. I've always been a drifter and I react to whatever's going on.'

Deniz Tek: 'I became friends with Rob and he and I would get together often for record-listening sessions, and smoke and drink beer and listen to mostly Rob's record collection. He had a fantastic pile of records.'

Lee Taylor: 'Rob was uber-cool but in a very different way to Deniz.'

Younger was soon turning Tek onto a previously unknown world of music.

Deniz Tek: 'There was a lot of British stuff I only learned about from Rob. I didn't know about the Pretty Things. I didn't know about the Shadows. That stuff never made it across the Atlantic. So Rob opened up a whole universe of British music I had not been aware of. Particularly, his knowledge of the late-sixties Michigan rock scene was exceptional.'

It wasn't long before the idea of TV Jones and the Rats playing in a double bill was hit upon. The outfits appeared together on two separate occasions at Corrimal Community Hall near Wollongong.

Warwick Gilbert: 'That's where I met Deniz. He liked my guitar playing and was really keen about what we were doing. But TV Jones were more glam rock, like a Status Quo. I think they did "Raw Power", but it sounded like an Oz rock boogie band to me. We were all feeling around in the dark back then.'

Not long after, TV Jones landed an opening spot for former Easybeat Stevie Wright at Taren Point in Sydney's south.

Deniz Tek: 'Rob had a huge crucifix that had an actual figurine of Jesus on it, and he loaned it to me to wear at the gig.'

Some of Tek's TV Jones bandmates already thought he had an overdose of his own divinity.

The Other Glimmer Twins

Ripple Records were selling the usual stock of Yes, Pink Floyd, King Crimson, Crosby, Stills, Nash & Young, Black Sabbath and Frank Zappa, when Deniz Tek came in wanting what he wanted, no more and no less.

Chris Pepperell: 'He said, "Do you have any Ted Nugent records?" I looked up the Schwann Catalog, which was the only import catalogue we had at the time, under "New", and he was, "No, no man! Nugent! N-u-g . . ."'

Mark Sisto knew the name well. New York–born but Detroit raised and shaped, Sisto, like Deniz Tek, began a lifelong fascination for the military as a child and had his first gig-going experience at a double bill of the Who and Pink Floyd at the Grande Ballroom in 1968.

By 1974, the Motor City Mark loved had collapsed and he wanted out.

Mark Sisto: 'It was like the city was sacked by an army of death spirits: the lowering of the drinking age, a plague of heroin and downers. The crisis of the oil embargo kicked the big three (General Motors, Ford and Chrysler) in the guts, a blow that knocked them down so hard they never recovered. I wanted to find beaches, and summer means fun.'

He arrived in Australia in June 1974 to the sound of the Sweet's 'Teenage Rampage' on the radio when his ship approached Port Phillip Bay in Melbourne. Making it to

Sydney, Sisto settled in Darlinghurst and embraced the new world at Frenchs and parties.

His signature brown bomber jacket—proudly made in Detroit, with a map of Michigan sewn on—somewhat aligned with the partial biker slang title of Aerosmith's second effort, *Get Your Wings*, with a crude logo to match, and the Blue Oyster Cult's third, *Secret Treaties*, with their dark mystical powers writ large, backed up by songs such as 'Me262'—with its sounds of soldiers marching, sirens and bombs—and 'Dominance and Submission'. This time there was no Bill Gawlik cover art—the artist having disappeared, if, as some believe, he ever existed in the first place—just a drawing of the band around a German World War II jet fighter, a Messerschmitt Me 262 with the BOC symbol on the tail.

Import record stores were expanding further in Sydney, with Jules R.B. Normington landing a job at Ripple Records with Chris Pepperell, the Record Plant opening in the Imperial Arcade, and Mark Taylor, a Velvet Underground fan who was also carrying a major torch for the Stooges, unveiling what would be the pivotal White Light site.

Mr White Light, White Heat himself, Lou Reed, embarked on his first Australian tour in August 1974. It was probably the country's debut experience of a truly decadent American rock and roll star and the scenes in the toilets of his Hordern Pavilion show paid homage. Even when nowhere near a stage, Reed didn't disappoint. At his televised Sydney media conference and from under cropped blond hair and behind sunglasses, Lou seemed like some fragile alien creature as he moved through a range of unsmiling emotions—from clear boredom and contempt to dark, sarcastic humour. 'No,' he simply replied to several questions, 'Sometimes' to others. And so it went.

The screening on the ABC's *GTK* program of Reed performing the Velvets' 'Rock and Roll' at the Hordern was just as riveting, but with a now-frantic, seemingly possessed Lou. Rob Younger was at each Sydney show.

Rob Younger: 'He had these really cool stage moves. Like he might have danced one-to-one in a club with somebody. There was something groovy about it. That was a great gig for me. It left quite an impression.'

But rather than riding something of the wave around Reed's visit, the Rats fell apart, after Warwick Gilbert could no longer take the often-blazing, occasionally projectile-heaving tension between Rob Younger and Ron Keeley, compounded by upheaval at work.

Warwick Gilbert: 'It was a really stressful period and I just rang Rob up and said, "I can't do it anymore. I'm leaving the band." He said, "Oh, right." Then I said, "I won't be coming to practice next Saturday," and he said, "Well, if you're not in the band, there's no point!"'

Deniz Tek continued battling on in TV Jones.

Deniz Tek: 'What had been a smash hit in Wollongong absolutely did not fly in Sydney. Venues were clearly not ready for it. Audiences might have adapted, given the chance.'

Worse, the development of polyps in Tek's throat forced him to stop singing. With the Rats disbanded, Rob Younger was open to reasonable offers and Deniz figured his friend could fill TV Jones's vocal vacancy, a move which amplified the more extreme musical approach some other members were already keen to move away from. Neither party took to the other and the move was short lived. Along with Pip Hoyle's more lasting injection and general disquiet in the Jones' camp, this was Tek's seemingly final strike. In late August 1974, he found himself cast out of TV Jones.

Deniz was living at 14 Sims Street in Darlinghurst, having taken over the lease from Ron Keeley, when he was told his services were no longer required.

A visiting Rob Younger struggled to contain his astonishment that anyone would dump the band's clear star. He also couldn't believe his luck.

Younger moved into the Sims Street address. He and Deniz would form a formidable, intimidating alliance—a joint divining rod for all things.

Chateau Sims Street

Stocked with piles of *Creem*, *Rock Scene* magazine and San Francisco's revolutionary *Zap Comix*, as well as a sea of records in a pooling of Rob's extensive collection and that of Deniz, Sims Street, despite the less than luxurious environment, was a resort of high cool.

The Blue Oyster Cult, accentuated by Younger's determined sermons, was a critical feed into their planning, with the pair going so far as to join the BOC fan club.

Rob Younger: 'I sent away for their lyrics so I have the words of the first three LPs on that old-fashioned computer paper with the perforated edges and faintly lined.'

1969: Velvet Underground Live was a vital missive that year and only the Velvets' second Australian release after *Live at Max's Kansas City* two years earlier. It would be a further significant educational tool, and not simply due to its subversive and distracting cover art.

Late one night, Deniz had a near-fatal lapse of concentration himself, as he made his way up the stairs, which had no railing or banister. He stepped on a loose board and fell backwards two metres. Fortunately, Younger was behind and was somehow able to catch him. It wouldn't be the last time Rob had Deniz's back.

Rob Younger: 'We were crossing South Dowling Street near Taylor Square. We'd been to Frenchs, or somewhere like that, and were just about to walk across the road, when he just stepped out in front of a car. It was five metres away and it was going to hit him and I just reached out and pulled him back out of the way. That definitely saved his life.'

Part of Rob and Deniz's drafting of their future involved seeing what they were up against on the local front. Witnessing the Coloured Balls led by Lobby Loyde open for American rock and roll legend Bo Diddley at the Hordern Pavilion was neither inspiring nor instructive.

Rob Younger: 'The Coloured Balls wasn't even all that punishingly loud or anything. It was just head down, long guitar solos, *dah-dah dah-dah, dah-dah.* It wasn't much different to me to Status Quo. Just boogie. The tiredest shit. It seemed old hat to me even back then.'

For Tek and Younger's new outfit, they recruited Ron Keeley on drums, despite his at times volcanic relationship with Rob in the Rats. Pip Hoyle was enlisted on keyboards and Carl Rorke, also from the Rats, on bass.

What was needed was a name. The winner ended up coming from their interpretation of a line in the Stooges' song '1970' from *Fun House.*

Deniz Tek: 'The original lyric is supposed to have been "radio buzzin'", according to Ron Asheton. We heard "birdman" and liked that well enough.'

Given that so few people in Australia possessed *Fun House,* much less had made note of the lyrics, Radio Birdman was perfect.

All the while, Rob Younger had been working on bettering his craft as a frontman. He had greatly admired Deniz in his leading role in TV Jones but was now taking on those duties himself in front of Tek.

Rob Younger: 'Deniz had good moves and I wanted to be like that. But basically, I was a shy person and a bit self-conscious. I had to push through some barriers to be a performer. Probably harking back to a few humiliations I suffered trying to do something in a school play, and doing it badly, and how shit I felt after failing at that sort of thing. An inner fear of that repeating itself, maybe. I wasn't too sure of myself at the best of times.

'Deniz did tell me about certain moves based on Iggy, and another by James Brown. The "thousand-yard stare" [a term originally coined for battle-fatigued soldiers] was Iggy's. Just gazing vacantly while completely motionless and staring way the fuck in the distance longer than you really should. Basically, appearing completely disconnected from everything happening around you.'

Younger had been smiting the world with a similar gaze since his teens. All he had to do now was perfect it. He was soon to shoulder quite a responsibility.

Deniz, with his background in Detroit, songwriting talent and guitar skills—coupled with a formidable aura and fierce self-belief—would be seen by many as the leader of the new outfit. But the flamethrowing spirit the Radios would embody was a direct reflection of the life ethos of the equally charismatic Younger.

To the singer, everything was personal, all the time. Reactive—torch first, ask questions later—with few above initial suspicion, his tolerance level set the bar for all that the Birdmen would represent. While he possessed a razor-sharp dry wit and could be utterly charming, Younger, although mostly softly spoken, would be the inside and outside voice of the band, and their impending fight against the world also his own.

In any event, Ron Keeley could see storm clouds approaching. He was a Tek man.

Ron Keeley: 'I wasn't happy with the idea Rob was running the band. Whether he actually was at that point is another question. I did say I wanted Deniz to be the man, but he didn't want to have the responsibility. Deniz was the songwriter, the brilliant lead [guitar] player, and it just didn't make sense for him not to [be in charge]. It was just obvious. I wanted him to assert himself more.'

Despite his proven credentials in TV Jones, Tek had no desire to lead Radio Birdman as singer either.

Deniz Tek: 'From the very beginning I never imagined or conceived of the possibility of Radio Birdman without Rob in front.'

Nonetheless, the scale of Tek's role and influence was blindingly obvious including the design of the band's logo, which had come to rest on a final look after years of the guitarist toying, reworking and evolving the image.

Deniz Tek: 'The central area [inside the circle] could sometimes contain a flaming skull, lightning bolts, a hand with an eye in the palm, a Horus symbol, etc., but none of those variants ever made it off the sketch pad.'

The stage was set. The Stooges, the MC5, the Doors, the Velvet Underground and the original Alice Cooper band were no more, with the New York Dolls fatally shaky on their heels.

In Australia, AC/DC were starting to find their feet with new singer Bon Scott, Sherbet were the conquerors of the screaming teen masses, and Skyhooks with their theatrical pop had just unleashed what would be their phenomenally successful *Living in the 70's* LP. At the same time, the annual Sunbury

Festival was now a dark behemoth, an alcohol-fuelled shadow of the Woodstock peace and love dream.

Pockets of hip kids interested in the Stooges and the New York Dolls, informed by US magazines such as *Creem*, *Rock Scene* and *Circus*, were dotted across Australia, but Radio Birdman would be much more than simply part of a scattered stirring. The Radios were going to make a fist less than eighteen months after the last of Australia's troops withdrew from the Vietnam War.

Those in thrall of the Stones, Led Zeppelin, Alice Cooper, Slade, Kiss and even Yes and King Crimson were about to take up positions before new gods. They'd leave others to party to the Commodores' disco era pre-empting *Machine Gun* album.

Get Your Wings

The eight-word headline in England's *NME*, accompanying an interview with Keith Richards, carried more bite than almost all of the Stones' apologetically titled *It's Only Rock 'n Roll* album: 'You're never alone . . . with a Smith and Wesson.'

It was late October 1974 and Carl Douglas's 'Kung Fu Fighting' was on the jukebox when Radio Birdman arrived at the Excelsior Hotel, an old-world Australian pub in Surry Hills.

The small back room would host their first gig proper—after they'd moved the pool tables out of the way, with the help of friends including Alley Brereton, Doug Lonsdale, John Needham and Jules R.B. Normington.

With the band logo positioned on Ron Keeley's bass drum, they launched into the set. Two elderly ladies danced, totally unconcerned by the strange spectacle of Rob Younger on his hands and knees on the carpeted floor, straddled by Deniz Tek, the pair partially illuminated by an equally bizarre beam.

Ron Keeley: 'Carl [Rorke] produced this disco light that he put behind the kick drum for an effect. That was Carl.'

Alley Brereton (Birdman devotee): 'It was really loud! You could feel there was the start of something.'

Rob Younger: 'I think we had five in the band and we outnumbered the audience. We didn't know how to go about getting a gig and I don't know how we got that one. They wouldn't have sold many drinks.'

After the pool tables were returned to their original positions, the Radios took home less than ten dollars. Nonetheless, a string of weekend return engagements were booked.

The sound of the Birdmen was much more than the sum of TV Jones and the Rats. However, despite the geographic spread of the new band's influences—from New York and Los Angeles to London—their energies would come to be known as the 'Detroit sound' due to their advocacy of the Stooges and MC5. To most Australians, the Motor City was a distant and mysterious place, making it ripe for plundering in the Antipodes, or at least smart shorthand appropriation. The fact that Deniz Tek was in possession of Fred 'Sonic' Smith's actual Epiphone guitar didn't hurt. Especially as Deniz had recently been exposed to further evidence as to its previous owner.

Jules R.B. Normington: 'I had an issue of *Creem* or the *NME*, with an article on the MC5 in it. There was a photograph of Fred sitting on the floor, and next to him was the guitar. I showed Deniz and he went berko! He was literally bouncing around the room.'

Detroit provided a forwarding address, a physical territory and a musical pulpit from which to preach, just as the raw magic of Muddy Waters, Howlin' Wolf and Bo Diddley had done for the Stones in their early days.

Deniz Tek: 'We admired the way they [the Stooges and the MC5] were able to play their music with tremendous energy and commitment and sometimes at great personal risk. They were kind of kindred spirits to us. I was probably trying to spread "the gospel" of the Michigan bands. [But] I'm pretty sure I wouldn't have made a secret of my affinity for the Stones, if asked.'

Few would. Welcome to Detroit, Darlinghurst, Australia.

In these early days, Birdman had a performance-art component of which Rob and Deniz wrestling on the dancefloor was only part. Late at night, they'd collect old radios and televisions discarded in the street, then, during their epic versions of songs like 'Cold Turkey', smash them on stage.

Rob Younger: 'There'd be fucking glass everywhere! Those TV cathode-ray tubes, they're a vacuum, they implode!'

Deniz Tek: 'It was less straight-up rock and roll, and more "artistic" and weird. We were impressed by things like Alice Cooper's stage presentation, and the Velvet Underground with the Exploding Plastic Inevitable, and these audiovisual happenings. So we thought, "Why be restricted to just the music, when we can throw stuff round and have a good time and shock people?" I suppose it made up for some lack of musical acumen as well. Pip was the only one who was a really good musician.'

The keyboard player was the unit's secret weapon and major point of musical difference. He was closer to a member of John Coltrane's classic quartet, more the jazz flights of McCoy Tyner than a key-pounding Jerry Lee Lewis.

Away from the stage, Frenchs and Martin's Bar were the band's favoured hangouts to kick back or strategise.

Deniz Tek: 'Martin's would play all four sides of the Stones' *Exile on Main Street*. It was sort of our clubhouse.'

Ian Hartley: 'It was like Max's Kansas City. [Actor] Jack Thompson would go there, advertising executives would go there, [actor] Kate Fitzpatrick would go there, Norman Gunston would go there. It was covered with billboards and posters, so it was barely visible. A member of Radio Birdman brought in Lou Reed's *Sally Can't Dance* album, which was played in its entirety.'

Enter Mark Sisto, via a woman he met at a party.

Mark Sisto: 'She inquired where I was from. Detroit. Oh! I know a guy from Detroit. You must meet him. Yes I must! So a few days later, around New Year's, she brought me over to the Sims Street house. My first impression of Deniz was one of familiarity. Like, "Oh him, I know this guy," but I didn't. The second thing I noticed was the strong focus he had just in the act of walking down the stairs to greet me. I thought, "That's interesting. He seems to give a lot of importance to his inner world, doing a mundane thing like walking down some stairs." It made me curious as to why he would make such an effort. I had this impression for a long time he had some secret knowledge, and I wanted to know what that was.

'He told me about his band and the style of it. I thought this was most fantastic! The preservation of the spirit of Detroit, like removing an endangered species from its native environment to some new and isolated place, to preclude its destruction.'

But that experience was no longer available at the Excelsior. After a month or so of hosting Birdman's weekend assaults, which by then were pulling a few people, the pub's management called time on the band's back-room activities. The police CIB headquarters had recently moved into the area and those who drank at the Excelsior had made their disapproval known. Certainly the Radios did not want a visit from the Force's heavyweight, in every respect, 21 Division.

Deniz Tek: 'The cops said, "Whatever that noise you had in there was, we don't want to hear it again!"'

It was the first time Radio Birdman had been shut down, but it wouldn't be the last. The Rats had been reasonably well accepted at some venues, as had TV Jones, but even at this early stage there was something about Birdman that set the teeth of some on edge.

Perhaps it was their visuals as much as the sound, which Jules R.B. Normington handled, as he had for the Rats. Sheets carrying their logo covered the amplifiers, the fabric utilising red and black, the Blue Oyster Cult's colours proclaimed on the *Tyranny and Mutation* album.

Deniz Tek: 'On some of the early amp flags, the logo was centred inside a black cross, like a big plus sign.'

These stretches of material, some of which were also used as stage backdrops, were initially the legacy of Tek and Younger's very brief foray into the world of film.

Deniz Tek: 'Rob and I got some casual work as extras in a movie, where we had to stand around in a restaurant bar. After hanging around all afternoon and then not getting paid, we stole a couple of red tablecloths from the place.'

Certainly, the local police were taking note of the band, and made a visit to the Sims Street address on one occasion.

Doug Lonsdale: 'Rob and Deniz had the front door open and these two blokes came to the door both in suits. They were detectives and one of them had a girl's watch in his hands and said to us, "Any of you blokes know about this watch? Your girlfriend lost a watch?" And they were looking around the room. So they [Birdman] had the authorities against them even back then. It was very different in the inner city in those days. You had to be really careful. The cops didn't like anybody.'

Having a song called 'Smith and Wesson Blues', the first tune Deniz had written for Radio Birdman, wouldn't have helped their defence. It, and other ideas, came together while Tek worked overnight at the massive computing centre at the university, grabbing some sleep when he could, and during winter using the massive machine for warmth—its hum some sort of lullaby. He would arrive back at Sims Street in the very early morning and then head, sleep-free, to uni for the day's lectures. It was a process again facilitated by the implementation of the 'Tek way'.

Deniz Tek: 'What I tend to do is strive to achieve the maximum possible result with the resources available. I don't accept less than full effort from myself. What I am able to do is to work exceptionally hard. I have a high degree of self-discipline and try to instil the same ethic in others around me by setting an example.'

'Smith and Wesson Blues' would soon join a number of songs carried over from TV Jones, such as 'Monday Morning Gunk', 'Insane Alive' and 'I-94', formerly known as 'Eskimo Pies'. That material was among the tunes aired—after some wrangling, and with the support of John Power, later of Jo Jo Zep and the Falcons—at a gig at Frenchs wine bar, early in 1975.

David Williams (Frenchs owner): 'At the time, we mainly featured blues and R & B bands, like Foreday Riders, with a few others like Richard Clapton of a weekend. So after being asked many times I agreed to book them [Radio Birdman] on a one-night trial.

'By the end of the second number, everything had been knocked over or worse. The band were great, but the dancing, or whatever, by patrons created a mess, along with a lot of broken glassware. There were quite a few—not regulars—who were real dickheads to staff and other patrons, so at the end of the night I suggested they [Radio Birdman] would be more suited elsewhere, and I wouldn't be booking them again.'

Birdman clocked it up as a win. They'd converted some and repelled others. It was all part of what would be an ongoing program of slowly, but savagely, thinning the herd of any potential gig options in what was almost a pre-determined act of self-defeat. The Radios were to be accepted without amendment or deviation.

Jules R.B. Normington: 'The majority of the bands that were around didn't have much integrity. Birdman was full-on integrity, uncompromising. "We will not alter anything we do for anyone whatsoever." They were never going to play by the fucking rules. They had their own rules.'

For the band's friends—a travelling unit of a dozen or so—Radio Birdman, anytime, anywhere, was utter bliss.

Lee Taylor: 'When you went to one of the gigs you knew everybody in the audience, because there were hardly any people there and they were all right down at the front, so everyone's doing dives, just stupid dancing, which is kind of easy to do after you've had a few drinks. Even I would do that.'

Jules R.B. Normington: 'You couldn't help being physically involved in it. So we were just throwing ourselves all over the place. You'd end up with grazes on your knees, your jeans would rip and it didn't matter, because you were being transported by this intense music that was just so fucking good!'

Radio Birdman's own means of transportation to deliver this exhilaration was an initially white Ford Transit van that Ron Keeley—who was handling band finances, as well as being something of a Mr Fix It—bought for $750. The Blue Oyster Cult logo was soon emblazoned on the driver's door.

Ron Keeley: 'I think I was the only one who had a bank account. It was at the CBC Bank opposite the Oxford Hotel in Darlinghurst. Carl and I bought the van. We went down to Parramatta Road and came back in what became the Bird Van. Sliding doors at the front, double doors opening at the back so we could get all the gear in. I paid for it initially. When we started making a little bit of money, some of it trickled into my account and paid the van off.'

Lee Taylor: 'Over the years it fell to pieces. At one stage they lost the driver's seat; then the seat alongside disappeared. Then they lost the sliding door.'

Birdman were about to face an audience that wanted to shove them from a moving vehicle.

Sydney's suburban hordes may have seen shock horror pictures of Alice Cooper in the *Daily Mirror*. However, they probably never expected to see such beings on a stage at their local pub, where they just wanted a background soundtrack to sinking a thousand beers and picking up a companion for the night.

The Kicking Out of Jams

With straight, strawberry-blond hair falling below the waistline of his gold lamé pants, and eyes shuttered by heavy make-up, Rob Younger, slim and bare chested, was a picture of supernatural corpse chic. And as part of the new season's range, he was also reintroducing gloves as formal attire in the public houses of Sydney. Not in clean, elegant white but elbow-length, bright green, pink or red, or black satin. These had been purchased from the theatrical store adjacent to the Sydney Town Hall in Druitt Street.

Younger's accomplice and silent partner was Govinda, a human skull sourced from India for medical study, which kept a vigil on a microphone stand at the front of the stage.

Birdman wanted to reach a larger audience—or at that point, any audience at all—and had to swallow some of the poison of the straight world in order to do so. With a foothold established in such territory, they could then go about subverting that position to their own ends, as Alice Cooper had done with such spectacular success.

Their first crack at the world outside the inner-city limits arrived in the form of Mike Hurst who had seen the Radios several times at the Excelsior Hotel at the urging of Deniz Tek's girlfriend, Colleen Skinner. In his day job, Hurst was a journalist at the *Daily Mirror*, occasionally writing about music.

He wrote a review of one of the Excelsior shows but the accompanying photos by Skinner, including a shot of Tek straddling Rob Younger, were deemed 'obscene'—allegedly by Murdoch himself—and somehow not fit for the traditionally risqué *Mirror* and the piece was dumped.

Mike Hurst (early Birdman manager): 'Deniz and/or Rob said the band needed a manager. No one put their hand up so eventually I said I could do it. I had no experience in organising anything at that time. I was only in my early twenties and had no great life experiences to call on. So I did what I thought I was supposed to do. I had zero contacts, but as a journo I was comfortable making cold calls and I truly believed Birdman were fantastic.'

Hurst nonetheless not only secured some gigs but engagements on the Millers pub chain, major players on the local hotel circuit with several cavernous beer barns across Sydney—including Coogee, Manly Vale, Brighton and the Sundowner at Punchbowl—which had ignited pub rock in the harbour city a few years earlier.

The problem was the Radios were not about to reshape themselves to fit into this foreign environment, playing the hits of the day, such as Joe Walsh's 'Rocky Mountain Way' or Ike and Tina Turner's 'Nutbush City Limits'. They certainly weren't about to sing 'Happy Birthday' to Mick or Susan, turn down their volume to a polite level, or have Rob Younger thank and congratulate those assembled for being 'such a great audience'.

Quite the opposite. The game plan was to hoist their flag—literally—then shit in the nest of the hosts, and bite the hand that attempted to clean up the mess. It was self-immolation as a business model.

The first gig was at Millers at Brighton in Sydney's south.

Across from the beach, it was one of the biggest pubs in the city and infamous for hosting lovely-legs competitions, regular brawls and dispensing oceans of beer. It was an alpha-male domain, with the bouncers, by sheer physical necessity, the top dogs.

Mike Hurst: 'It had a huge auditorium with lots of tables and chairs spread around. Within the first two songs the crowd was polarised—half flocked to the foot of the stage mesmerised and the other half fled the pub. It was bad for business when half the pissheads departed en masse.'

This was just the beginning. When Rob Younger crawled across the sparsely populated wooden dancefloor, he created a punter exclusion zone of ten metres in each direction. Then, Deniz Tek's girlfriend was roughly escorted outside by the bouncers seemingly for daring to dance in bare feet.

Tek didn't take this lying down and abused the venue's security. This fired up the rest of the band, their supporters and, of course, the venue's hired thugs. Birdman then roared suitably into the MC5's revolutionary anthem 'Kick Out the Jams', to which management responded by cutting the power. Undeterred, the Radios urged on their backers in the room with the strength of their voices and heat of their emotions alone. Somehow the electrical current was restored and, fittingly, they blasted into Iggy and the Stooges' 'Search and Destroy'.

The bouncers were furious. At the end of the night, Birdman were forced to make their escape, with those who were carrying amps being escorted by two others brandishing microphone stands as clubs, which ended up being the point of defensive difference in the carpark.

Again, it was deemed a victory. And they delighted in it.

Rob Younger: 'How many bands actually get the proprietor

pulling the plug out? It's one thing for people to talk about it, but it happened. And we liked it because we already knew Alice Cooper got their [recording] contract from clearing rooms [in LA in the late sixties]. I loved the idea of a band being obnoxious, or somehow such an affront that people would get up and fucking go, rather than sit there and suffer—or the proprietor would tell you to stop, because he hated it, or because the crowd was complaining. Whatever it was, it happened.'

Next stop was Manly Vale Millers on Sydney's northern beaches. Again, the Birdmen had some fans at the gig, none more enthusiastic than Mark Sisto, gulping down a music that had died in his homeland years before. He danced with vigour and abandon with an immediate understanding of Birdman's roots.

Jules R.B. Normington: 'There was this guy doing all this crazy dancing like James Brown, and he had his head in the speaker boxes and it was loud. This guy was committed.'

Sisto managed to get onto the stage and took his game up a notch, crawling about growling like Iggy Pop. He then commandeered a microphone to sing back-up vocals on 'Kick Out the Jams'. It was a stunning audition for a job that didn't yet exist.

After the gig, Sisto gained entry backstage and grandly verbalised his enthusiasm to Deniz. He wanted to form a band with his compatriot, with Sisto singing. The pair had previously bonded on a homeland level, but there was now a higher plane on which they were connecting.

Such was Sisto's impact that night, he was packed away in the truck with the band's equipment—but positioned tightly in the back so he was unable to move and damage himself much as a removalist would do with a valuable antique. It was as if his worth had already been recognised and professionally appraised.

Mark Sisto: 'I was very pleased with the whole thing, bringing out the spirit of Detroit and inflicting it on a virgin audience. What a great idea! Birdman was very intrusive. Either you took it in or braced yourself against it.'

Mark in turn would have a considerable impact on Radio Birdman, heightening their intensity, mythology and sense of manic fun.

Deniz Tek: 'Mark was very important to us, both as a muse, and as a sort of mad monk and spiritual guide, in his own way. He was at the nexus of crazy intersecting streams of culture that included the Michigan music, a *Creem* magazine sort of ethos, an angle into the paranormal, anarchy and freedom, all lived with a hedonistic and fearless Hunter S. Thompson kind of intensity. He recognised no limits of any kind.

'Mark really was fearless, and had no hesitation injecting himself into any dangerous situation to help pals, or in some cases just for the sheer experience. Always with a fabulous sense of humour and fun, too! Regardless of what it might have looked like from the outside, we never did really take ourselves too seriously, and I believe we had Mark to thank for that as well. Without him we might have been a "serious artistic rock band" or something equally awful.'

Additionally, Sisto would take dancing to and from new heights.

Jules R.B. Normington: 'Long before stage diving, we used to get up on stage, me and Sisto and a couple of others—Sisto was the first to do it; just throw himself into the crowd, and there wasn't much of a crowd—and then do his dead cockroach dance on his back on the floor. And no one would catch you, you'd fall on the floor.'

You're Going to Have to Pull the Plug!

The character-building performances under Mike Hurst continued at the Bondi Lifesaver.

Mike Hurst: 'The audio cut [in and] out, and the longer the gig ran, the more frequently the sound completely died. It was a sickly pantomime. The wiring was faulty. The venue manager stormed up to me and declared: "You will never play here again." He probably said plenty more, but I didn't hear him. We packed up, pissed off, and needless to say with no payment, again.'

Surprisingly, the band later returned to the Lifesaver, one of the very few venues that would have them back.

No doubt with leverage from Hurst, the *Daily Telegraph* ran a story on the Birdmen in March 1975, with the headline 'Teeth 'n' all guitar' and a photo of the band on the beach, with their human skull and Deniz holding an old radio. The article plugged a coming two-night, early-evening engagement at the Grange, later the Grange Disco, a small place in Pitt Street in inner Sydney. It had hosted the likes of Buffalo, the country's ultra-loud answer to Black Sabbath, but for the Birdmen it would be just another shit-fight on a different day.

Mike Hurst: '[This was the] straw which broke the camel's back for me. It was a well-established live music venue at the time. Lots of people were there after work in the CBD, so dressed in suit and tie. It was a pretty straight audience, but they enjoyed Birdman. However, one or two friends of the band were totally off their face and jumped up on stage, swearing obscenities at their audience, screaming at them to take off their ties, etc.

'I guess I wasn't into mayhem, at least the obscenities. The boys may remember it differently, but for me it was just a case of anything goes, and I don't think the performance was enhanced in any way by letting their mates abuse the paying audience.'

The venue's management were just as unimpressed and the second night of the engagement evaporated. Mike Hurst had also had enough.

Mike Hurst: 'I wished them well. They seemed unwilling or maybe unable to accept advice on direction. I was probably wrong, but I remained a huge fan. My abiding memory of my time with Birdman is we got sacked from each of the five gigs I booked for them.'

From the Radios' perspective, however, they'd emerged from the string of engagements triumphant and defiant, having not deviated from their path.

Rob Younger: 'We always liked the confrontation. That fuelled us. That "us against them" trip and the fact that we were making an impression, we were getting slung out of places. We really thought it was a good thing. There's no doubt about that. It's not a retrospective view to flatter ourselves. We had a perspective on it and we knew there was a value in it—in these people not appreciating us.'

Deniz Tek: 'We were like, "We're Radio Birdman. We play hard the whole set. That's what we do. You knew that when you booked us."'

Volume was another issue. Unlike every band in the country that had a PA system which filled a two- or three-tonne truck and was capable of pumping out several thousand watts regardless of the setting, the Radios' rig to further project what they were blasting out on stage was a tiny fraction of that size at only 160 watts. But, the intensity of their delivery and attitude were key, as if their character added several decibels to their performance.

Lee Taylor: 'I was backstage watching one gig and the publican or someone said, "You're going to have to pull the plug!" I said, "I couldn't live with myself if I did that!"'

The band's appearance and anti-fashion dress sense were seemingly another point of confrontation. Rather than the standard suburban dress of the day of very specific red-tagged Levi's jeans, Miller's western, flannelette or plain T-shirts, the Radios donned wild, disjointed-looking gear. Deniz Tek had an endless array of sunglasses, a top carrying an ad for Ann Arbor institution 'Krazy Jim's Blimpy Burger', plus snakeskin and striped garments. Rob Younger, on the other hand, pulled on lamé pants and heavily torn or multi-patched jeans, with the singer doing his own denim repair work.

Rob Younger: 'We went out of our way to not look like everyone else, by ripping our clothes and smearing them with food and food colouring, and burning things so they looked singed. We used to find stuff in St Vinnies and so forth. Shitty-looking things that might look pretty cool on stage.

'The proprietors didn't like our crowd either. We'd start playing and our lot would get up and start throwing themselves around. They also didn't like the look of the people we brought with us, and it wasn't very extreme. I could never really fathom it.'

Birdman's extracurricular stage activities were a further recipe for alienation. On a whim, or when equipment malfunctioned,

Deniz would take centre stage, its lip, or the dancefloor, to recite the incendiary Black Power spoken-word work of the Last Poets' 'Wake Up, Niggers' and 'The Revolution Will Not Be Televised' by Gil Scott-Heron, as well as Edgar Allan Poe, often pivoting around the free-form tribal drum patterns of Ron Keeley playing with his bare hands.

Deniz Tek: 'We used those numbers to stay engaged with the people. All you needed was the drums behind you to do it. We would put Jim Morrison's poems to beats. Read from Baudelaire or Rimbaud or Dylan. Anything and everything. No rules in those days.'

For a short period, Rob Younger—complete with a briefcase containing pictures of the band and a cassette of a live gig—had the task of advocating the Radios' merits to prospective publicans and booking agencies, the very people he knew didn't know shit and who he despised for it. Although Younger was good on his feet and could be engaging, it wasn't the best of individual-to-vocation matches and very few wanted to know about him and his colleagues.

Radio Birdman's manner—not just burning bridges but vaporising them—was never going to see the outfit slide easily into the established order of the local music industry. This forced them into an outlaw position they had been quietly courting all along.

Deniz Tek: 'Once we got used to being outcasts, we saw things differently. We always viewed ourselves as the good guys, fighting for artistic freedom. We never got disillusioned. We felt empowered and free and opened our minds to the idea of creating alternative contexts to work in.'

Fortunately, others were also seeking to transform the music media.

War Lord

Handing Rob Younger a Hall and Oates LP was not the way to begin a working relationship. The singer enjoyed writing and was obsessed with records, so he approached Anthony O'Grady, editor of Sydney's new national fortnightly magazine, *RAM* (*Rock Australia Magazine*), about doing some reviews. Rob wanted to express himself as freely as the staff at *Creem*, raving about what deserved praise and gleefully piling endless scorn on anything else. He did several pieces under a pseudonym, including an appraisal of a Johnny Winter album. But his work was edited as was customary and thorny edges removed, which didn't sit well. Younger then approached *Rolling Stone*, only to be given the task of reviewing the performance of Melbourne progressive rock outfit Ariel at the State Theatre.

The upside of these interactions, particularly with *RAM*, was that he got to mention Radio Birdman to O'Grady, which aroused the editor's interest.

The magazine had already carried a tiny ad, announcing simply that Birdman were 'available to selected venues and clientele . . .' It included the name and number of Jules R.B. Normington, who had graduated to manager, as well as now running the Ripple Records store. Jules was a true believer in all the Radios were doing, and he had an easy way with people. His appointment to the role was virtually confirmed after one particular gig, when he'd taken it upon himself to confront a venue owner and their group of heavies in order to secure the band's fee for the night.

But Normington's contacts in the music business were largely limited to record companies, rather than booking agents and pub owners. He sought counsel from Anthony O'Grady, who arranged for a veteran of the Australian industry, who managed Hush, Marcia Hines and Mark Holden, and later created the ARIA Awards, to give Jules a crash course.

Jules R.B. Normington: 'I rang Anthony and said, "I don't really know what a manager does, or about contracts or anything like that. Could you introduce me to a manager so I can ask what I'm supposed to do?" He rang me back and said, "Come over Saturday." So I went to Anthony's place and there's Peter Rix. He was so nice and told me all this stuff, but I didn't know what he was talking about. I remember him leaving and Anthony saying, "So, did you get all that?" I didn't really . . .'

Nonetheless, the Radios landed a gig at another established venue, the Vicar of Wakefield at Dural in Sydney's outer northwest. No one knew what the fuck was going on when Deniz made his way off the stage and onto his back on the dance floor. When AC/DC's Angus Young similarly ventured into the crowd, it was fun, almost comical, whereas there was something unsettling about Tek getting up close.

Rob Younger: 'We were booked into a few places that should have been "normal" gigs, but turned out to be disastrously at odds with what we were doing. A lot of those early shows revealed how out of step we were with what was expected of a rock band. Obedient to management, friendly to the audience, dressed in an appropriate manner, playing stuff people were familiar with, etc.'

There had been a shift in the Radios' ranks, with the departure of bassist Carl Rorke. Frank Caley was again considered as his replacement, but in the end Chris Jones from TV Jones filled in for the band's unlikely second appearance at Frenchs.

David Williams: 'Rob and Deniz remained patrons [at Frenchs] and with a new area downstairs functioning, I decided to give them another night, just to get them off my back!'

Warwick Gilbert was at a senior level at Hanna-Barbera and hadn't played in a band since he left the Rats; however, he'd kept his hand in with the guitar. He went along to Frenchs at the urging of Jules R.B. Normington.

Warwick Gilbert: 'He said, "Have you seen Rob's new band? Radio Birdman?" I didn't quite understand. What? Birdman Radio or something? He said, "They're playing at Frenchs."'

From the stage, Rob Younger was projecting in a confident, commanding manner, the band were firing and focused—the smashing up of other's people's stuff a thing of the past—and the place was packed. Gilbert was taken immediately.

Warwick Gilbert: 'When I first saw the red flags [depicting the Birdman logo] in Frenchs, I liked that ragged colour. I think that's what first attracted me. Rob was fully formed then. He was enjoying himself. I liked the tremendous personality of the band and it was funny. The third song they did—I think it was "Insane Alive"—and I thought, "Shit, that's a good song!" They played enormously loud! They were just really bloody arrogant. I had a bit of an epiphany.'

Deniz Tek: 'The place was beyond capacity. We had a great night—really slamming, musically, but the crowd went from pushing and shoving into open brawls. The stage got overrun. There was nothing I could do but try my best to protect the guitar from getting smashed.'

David Williams: 'The night ended up the same as the first, with a few minor scuffles amongst non-regular patrons and too many dickheads in one place—so that was their final gig. They continued to be patrons but I was glad not to have to deal with the crowd attracted to them.'

But for Warwick Gilbert, the night was the roar of opportunity.

Warwick Gilbert: 'It put a bug in my ear, really. I went up and spoke to Rob and he was really friendly. I thought, "Thank Christ for that!" He was happy—he'd found something he liked. We got along like we always got along. And he said, "Drop in [to Sims Street]."

'Deniz said, "I know you play guitar, but would you be interested in playing bass?" I said, "Yeah, sure, I'll give it a shot. I'll play bass. I'll play the kazoo!"'

Just as Lemmy Kilmister had applied his guitar skills to bass in Hawkwind, and later Motorhead, Gilbert set about crafting a position front and centre in Birdman's sonic architecture rather than simply underpinning the rhythm.

Warwick Gilbert: 'I hadn't played bass before. I based my style on [the Stooges'] "Down on the Street" and added a bit of [Beatles' close associate] Klaus Voormann for variation as a template. I played bass like a blues lead guitarist. It wasn't proper bass playing—more like a third guitar pitched lower to boost the guitar hooks and tie them in to the drums, which it did. I came up with it to fit Ron and the nature of the songs.'

And he went in at the deep end at rehearsal one at Sims Street.

Warwick Gilbert: 'The first song was [Iggy and the Stooges'] "Search and Destroy". It was like a bomb going off!'

Ron Keeley: 'Birdman always rehearsed as we played. That is, flat out!'

Two weeks later on 30 May 1975, Gilbert played his first gig with the Radios at a self-organised event at the Heffron Hall in Burton Street, Darlinghurst. A sign that read 'Steve McGarrett', the lead character in television's *Hawaii Five-0*, was stuck to Tek's amplifier.

Deniz Tek: 'We were running our own shows when we could afford to. We just set it up, put up our own posters, charged a dollar at the door.'

The Heffron was a 'dance', and tickets were available from Ripple Records, where Jules was an endlessly enthusiastic evangelist for the band ('Of course they're better than AC/DC!'). He also brought into the Birdman fold any newly arrived records of note, such as the gloriously dumb pre-punk effort Dictators' *Go Girl Crazy!*.

Gilbert's bass work tightened the band, his quiet enigmatic presence as much an anchor as his playing. However, that first outing was not what he had hoped for.

Warwick Gilbert: 'Deniz was an arsehole right from the start. He pulled a rock-star trip on me onstage in front of his pals, just to establish the pecking order. And that was after I'd bought a WASP amp stack and I'd sold my Gibson '59 335 to buy a bass, and I wasn't real happy about it. I was seriously considering whether I'd do another gig, but I thought, "Well, fuck him. I'll do it to spite him." And that's pretty much how it went from there.'

Gilbert sensed the opportunity not only to continue what the Rats had been doing, but take that model several sizeable steps further.

Warwick Gilbert: 'I saw that Deniz centred Rob and provided a focus. Deniz was someone who commanded Rob's respect.

'It was volatile and dysfunctional in the Rats, but Birdman was volatile but briefly functional. It was possible to kind of continue that music and I think Deniz gave it credibility.

'Australians didn't give a fuck about Australians back then—they were all towards America or England. There was that kind of cultural cringe happening, so Deniz was like an exotic creature. We were awed by Americans. I think Deniz walked into that and we all started talking like Americans and saying American stuff. It was either "cool" or it was "bogue", which is bogus. It was kind of fun, for a while.'

Although Tek's personal intensity was unnerving for some, he was a powerful orator and motivator. Following him in his charge over the barricades against enemies both real and imagined simply made sense. And while Deniz fired up the troops, Warwick quickly worked out who to look to in Birdman's musical hierarchy.

Warwick Gilbert: 'I saw Ron Keeley as the leader of the music. It grew up around him. Rob was the conductor of the band's electricity. He was the guy that interpreted the music.

'Ron *was* Radio Birdman to me—the sound of what he did. He was an amazing drummer. More of a jazz player and he has a swing [to his playing] and Rob has natural rhythm, you've seen him dance. So the two of them together, there's a definite quality and relationship in the way they move and play. But Ron was able to articulate it from the ground up. So I followed Ron and worked in with him to make it seamless like a machine and aiming it at Rob.'

Ron Keeley: 'I took a lot of cues from watching Rob's back—watching what he was about to do next and if I could kick that along.'

The ferocity of Birdman's sound mightn't have been Ron's first musical love. However, playing with Warwick gave the rhythm section a rolling fluidity that allowed him to apply his jazz background and get under the music and lift it upward.

Ron Keeley: 'It was always a joy playing with Warwick. I don't think anyone else could have kept up and still stayed so solid. After gigs his forearms would be cramped up, because he was playing so hard and so fast. Warwick had his 300-watt bass amp directly behind me, and I used to come off stage with sore kidneys from being punched from behind [by the sound] all night.'

Mark Sisto: 'The band was great, especially after Warwick joined—there was always great improvisation. You never knew what you were going to get next. You can call it a great example of Dionysian art, as opposed to the Apollonian school. Summoning spontaneous creative forces from who knows where, either from each other or from the audience.'

As for Sisto, he was finding his own platform.

Mark Sisto: 'I had found some ways to contribute, like carrying boxes, doing the intro—like Brother J.C. Crawford did for the MC5—drawing handbills, and all that stuff.'

The blankness of the canvas in front of Birdman was glaringly obvious in one radio chart in mid-1975. Sherbet's 'Summer Love' was riding high in the singles, while the albums included *An Evening with John Denver*, and not one but both of the wildly pompous concept records by former Yes keyboard wiz Rick Wakeman—*Journey to the Centre of the Earth* and *The Myths and Legends of King Arthur*.

The Red and the Black

The sinister-looking limo outside St Paul's Chapel in Vista, New York, pictured on the cover of the Blue Oyster Cult's *On Your Feet or on Your Knees*, carried the band's symbol on a flag attached to its hood—as if the vehicle was ferrying the head of some secret state.

Rob Younger looked like he had stepped from the car when Mark Taylor, owner of the White Light record store, first saw him in the street.

Mark Taylor: 'It was nighttime and he was in full black leathers, with super-long hair. I wondered if I should risk saying hello, expecting to be ignored or, if I was lucky, to receive a gruff response. In the event, Rob stopped and grinned, looked at me straight in the eyes—direct, friendly, polite, no airs or graces whatsoever. I asked questions about Radio Birdman, but he asked questions about me. I didn't expect that.'

The Oyster Cult had already been instructive on a number of fronts for Birdman, and the artwork of *Tyranny and Mutation* helped set the direction for Warwick Gilbert's creativity.

Warwick Gilbert: 'Rob had *Tyranny and Mutation* and they had the flag up, the upside-down question-mark thing, and the two guitarists were crossing guitars. That was kind of a rallying point for us. I thought, "Well, that's where we're going, so I can do the art." It was an arrow forward.'

The band had done their own posters and promotional art prior to Gilbert's arrival, but he saw a great opportunity to create a uniquely stylised brand with a distinct look.

Warwick Gilbert: 'I went on to try and develop the image of the band, a graphic image. All the elements were there before I joined. I wasn't thinking commercially, just pulling it together from an art point of view.'

His first poster attempt had a very brief shelf life.

Warwick Gilbert: 'I had an Me 262 [plane] coming out of the centre of the Birdman symbol, using black-and-white monochrome poster paint. I adapted the *Rolling Stone* magazine masthead typeface to Radio Birdman. There was only ever one poster and somebody snatched it off the PA stack during its only showing at a Heffron Hall gig.

'The experimental five piece with Pip was probably the most fun period of the band. But although it [that outfit] created a lot of stuff, the art didn't come together for some reason.'

Meanwhile, Lou Reed was back in the country. He'd hated Australia—or maybe just the mainstream media—so much the year before that he returned for a second bout in July 1975. Unwittingly, he would set the scene for something far more significant than the Radios' self-organised events.

Deniz again seized the moment. He approached his friend, Dare Jennings, who was running Phantom Textile Printing at Centennial Park, with Julie Mostyn.

Dare Jennings (Birdman devotee, founder of Mambo, Deus Ex Machina): 'It [his future empire] started in a gardening shed out the back. Screen-printing for some of the music stores, guitar logos and things like that. And Kenworth trucks! From little things . . .

'Deniz had this idea for a [Radio Birdman] logo. He used a

coffee cup to make the circle, and the straight edge of a record sleeve for the lines. He wanted some help. I had some Letraset for the typeface and then I made a positive to make the screen for the T-shirt. Deniz was saying, "Dare, we've got to go to the airport and give Lou Reed a T-shirt!" This shitty T-shirt with the logo on it. It was pretty embarrassing.'

At his media conference, Mr Reed was neither a blond, nor the strange being of his last visit. Instead, he was openly bristling, verbally launching himself at a journalist as soon as he entered the room. 'You're digging your own grave,' he soon warned another, whom he subjected to a flaying with each inquiry. 'Ask a nice reasonable question,' Lou said. He was in the zone. 'Are you happy being a schmuck?' he replied at one point.

The 'Let's give Lou a T-shirt' venture seemed doomed. Typically, though, Tek wasn't to be put off and made his move after the media conference wrapped up.

Dare Jennings: '[Deniz said] "Lou, we brought you a T-shirt." "That's so kind! This is your band? I was in a little band once. You've got to tell me about it, and if you're playing somewhere, I'd love to come along." It was this epic moment where Lou Reed went from this snarling angry person to . . . and full credit to Deniz. I would have bolted if it was up to me.'

The notion of the former leader of the Velvet Underground not only attending a Birdman gig—witnessing them playing the Velvets' 'Rock & Roll' or 'I'm Waiting for the Man'—but maybe, just fucking maybe, getting on stage with the Radios had nerve endings really crackling. But there was one problem.

Rob Younger: 'Fuck! We haven't got a gig! What are we going to do?'

Idea: the Oxford pub in Taylor Square, Darlinghurst, which Rob and Warwick had first visited as teenagers, and where they'd played with Ron in the Rats.

Deniz Tek: 'We said [to the publican, Theo], "We know Lou Reed and he wants to go out tomorrow night and he wants to see us play." The guy goes, "Well, if Lou Reed is gonna come, you can play." So I told Lou Reed's secretary we were playing at the Oxford and, of course, Lou doesn't show. But all of our friends had told their friends, so about 120 people turned up, and they drank a lot of beer and had a great time. It went so well, he gave us a regular Friday and Saturday night spot.'

Radio Birdman finally had a realm of their own on the first floor at the Oxford. It was in close proximity to Martin's Bar, Frenchs, Sims Street HQ, and just around the corner from Studio 20, where the band would irregularly rehearse.

More than that, the Oxford was in a rich catchment area for several colleges, and in the heart of a vibrant alternative culture.

Tara Anderson (Birdman devotee): 'It was a scene where people who were into art or theatre or music kind of intersected, so there was a creative energy around that part of the city. Taylor Square was a very important place and literally a crossroads. And it's where you changed buses!'

Alley Brereton: 'There were a lot of people who were maybe seventeen, eighteen that moved into Darlinghurst and got away from suburbia. Everyone was looking for change.'

The Radios' Oxford gigs could be as loud as they wished and boom out the windows across Taylor Square, with their own crowd wearing whatever and dancing however they wanted—and all shaped around the medical-school commitments of Deniz and Pip Hoyle.

Mark Sisto: 'Before that, it was like, okay, how long before the pub owners pull the power? They were trying to sell drinks and there's this *blaaaaoo*! Real loud noise in the background!'

A new kid in town was about to sign up to the cause.

The Guess Who

The fifteen-year-old guitar enthusiast had recently arrived from Canada when he received a three-act shot of Oz rock at Sydney's Hordern Pavilion with Band of Light—featuring master slide guitarist Norm Roue and Rose Tattoo co-founder Ian Rilen—along with an electrifying post-Easybeats' Stevie Wright. Billy Thorpe and the Aztecs were the main act. They had a reputation as the most deafening outfit in the country, and lived up to the billing.

Chris Masuak: 'It was the loudest, shrillest fucking thing I'd ever heard in my life! He [Thorpe] sang "Somewhere over the Rainbow", which I thought would peel the aluminium off the roof!'

Masuak didn't know it at the time, but he would later be part of a major offensive against Thorpe's almighty blues boogie wallop.

But as loud as Thorpe and co were, even the Aztecs wouldn't have been audible back where Chris was born in Kamloops, British Columbia, Canada—and even less so when his father was posted to remote Fort McMurray in Alberta on the Athabasca oil sands belt.

Chris Masuak: 'We lived in the frontier really, up on the edges of civilisation, and my dad was literally putting in the telecommunications systems from the ground up. There was no television, there was only radio, and only in the evening when the atmospheric conditions were favourable, so we had to entertain ourselves. We listened to music and my mum thought it would be a good idea for us to play an instrument. We had a piano at home and that's what we did. Came home from school, played piano, listened to music.

'My mum always wanted me to play flamenco guitar. I didn't have any guitar lessons, but I played bass lines to Beatles songs or something. It wasn't that I was particularly interested in bass guitar, but it was a fun thing to do.'

Records by the classical greats, along with opera, soared through the home, while Chris and his siblings' own sound portal, a small record player, provided a more youthful element.

The family returned to Kamloops when Chris's parents split and life began anew with his grandparents. Masuak immersed himself in piano interpretations of the harpsichord work of composers such as Bach and Scarlatti and intensive study via the Toronto Conservatorium of Music.

After his mother wed again, employment once more dictated a move and the family relocated to a small mountain village called Mica Creek—largely populated by workers involved in constructing a gigantic dam.

Chris Masuak: 'I used to visit my old man in Edmonton in Alberta every summer. He had a sister who had a home-made guitar and a little old Harmony amp in her basement and I used to go plunk on that. I found it really fascinating, and then maybe when I was about twelve or thirteen my dad gave me that guitar. That was more or less the end of my piano lessons, which I'd had since I was five years old.'

That guitar, although modified several times, would stay with Masuak for years to come and be used on some significant occasions.

The Stones had already made a permanent place for themselves in Chris's viewfinder, after he borrowed their *High Tide and Green Grass* record from a school buddy. The 1966 compilation album would feed his growing obsession with guitars.

His stepbrother helped build his sound archive.

Chris Masuak: 'He had a really interesting record collection, so I was listening to Steppenwolf, Vanilla Fudge, Iron Butterfly, Cream, but I never—and I've thought about this—really tried to play like those guys or play that stuff. Like Hendrix, for example. Someone gave me *Electric Ladyland* and I was blown out but I never actually tried to play like him.

'The first time I thought, "God, I like that guitar player," was John Fogerty, because everyone listened to Creedence in those days—it was universal. Parents liked it, kids liked it—they just cut across all the boundaries, those guys. Not only did I just love his guitar playing, but he played slow enough so I could work his parts out. So he's the first guy I listened to that I maybe tried to emulate a bit.'

Despite Masuak's geographic isolation, it was only a matter of time before he put some of these learnings into practice in his first band, Manta.

Chris Masuak: 'There were a bunch of guys in town who were musicians, and all of us got together somehow. The bass player was in school. I think he was a year ahead of me, so he was like fifteen or sixteen, and I think the other guitar player was eighteen. He was a lifeguard at the swimming pool. We had two drummers in town, so of course we had two drummers in the band.

'I was the—quote unquote—better guitar player, so I became the lead player and I was forced to learn at an accelerated rate! We played the stuff that was popular at the time:

Ricky Nelson's "Garden Party" and Three Dog Night songs and Creedence, of course, and a few country-and-western-type songs like Johnny Cash–type stuff. We got to be the band that played all the dances and bars, and I had to get special permission to play at bars. It was a fun time.

'[At home] I would hook up all the amps together, including our PA, and play through them. My parents were extraordinarily tolerant when I think back.'

Whenever Chris needed gear and could afford it, the Canadian Postal Service came to the rescue.

Chris Masuak: 'Sears & Roebuck, Hudson's Bay Company—they all had mail-order catalogues. It was the internet of the time.'

Equally, in the pre-YouTube age, seeing late-night American television shows like *Don Kirshner's Rock Concert* and the *Midnight Special* provided a portal to another world and Masuak's mind was blown by the Mahavishnu Orchestra, along with acts such as Johnny Winter.

The family briefly shifted almost 400 kilometres south to Nelson—where Chris quickly notched up his second band, Mossy Mountain Freeber—before their biggest geographic move of all: coming to Australia in October 1973, where they settled in the south of Sydney, in Maroubra.

Relocating from Canada to a beach and surfing culture in the lead-up to a typically blistering Australian summer was both a revelation and cultural shock. Chris would hit the waves before school, during lunch and after classes, but Year Ten at Maroubra Bay High was closer to blunt force trauma than tidal tranquility.

Chris Masuak: 'When I got to Australia it was very backward, the Australian accent was impenetrable, and the school system was archaic and brutal. I just wanted to get out of there.

'The teachers constantly wanted to hit me and I wouldn't let anyone touch me. I played football [rugby union]—once. They put me in the second row and I went, "Nah, never again." So the sports master punished me by making me do sports with the girls, which I really enjoyed, because I kinda liked girls.'

The upside was music.

Chris Masuak: 'I used to fossick through record stores all the time. I'd go into a shop and the thing that attracted me would be the cover which had the most guitars on it. So I bought *Humble Pie Live at the Fillmore* because it had a ton of guitar pictures, you know? *Electric Warrior* by T. Rex because it had a guitar player with a big amp on the front.'

Masuak met a Greek kid at school named Johnny Kannis and formed a band, along with another student, Steve Harris. The talents of Masuak on guitar and Harris on keyboards particularly were impossible to miss.

Chris Masuak: 'If there was a school production, we'd end up doing something in it. I always played guitar or bass and Kannis played guitar or bass. We had a pretty decent band there. We had a couple of good singers at school, so we did the musical *Bye Bye Birdie* and *Joseph and His Technicolor Dreamcoat* and it was listenable.'

The fret fireworks of Lou Reed's *Rock 'n' Roll Animal* record weren't lost on Masuak, and the group played a dazzling version of 'Sweet Jane' in the breaks at school concerts.

In time, the outfit morphed away from its school base under the name of the Jackals with singer Steve Jones.

Chris Masuak: 'We used to just rehearse in my living room and played a couple of [rugby league] football-club gigs. Most of the Aussie groups were doing the *chunka-chunka* thing and we were playing early Aerosmith and Ted Nugent songs.'

An appearance by the Jackals at a dance at Northmead High School in Sydney's west opened a door to the future. Deniz Tek and his former partner in TV Jones, Chris Jones, came along as moral support for Jones's brother, although Tek also involved himself in the Jackals' performance.

Johnny Kannis: 'These guys [Deniz and Chris Jones] were side of stage doing this crazy dance like Iggy Pop does. Who are they? And Deniz did this big dive off the front of the stage into the audience!'

Later in the night after the Jackals had finished, Deniz, impressed by Chris's guitar playing, invited him to see Radio Birdman. Soon, Masuak, and friends like Steve Harris and Johnny Kannis, were hanging out at Sims Street, where they also met Rob Younger, and Deniz introduced them to a range of new thrilling music. Who needed school when these classes were in?

Chris Masuak: 'Deniz and I got along very well and he had an expansive record collection I didn't know anything about, which I really enjoyed going through. We jammed to those records. I liked his style, I liked his sound. He was a very big influence on my playing. That's when I started to listen to the Stooges and the MC5 and pick up a bit more of an appreciation for other groups, like the Beach Boys and the Rolling Stones or whatever.

'We'd spend the day at school, and head into town and visit Younger or Tek—Tek was studying so he was in and out. We had free rein. They were very tolerant. So we basically went in and read all their *Creem* and *Rock Scene* magazines and listened to their music.'

The sight of a copy of *Raw Power* during one visit brought back a memory of the *Time* magazine advertisement for the record Chris had seen in the school library back in Canada.

Masuak soon became one of the guitarists in a short-lived outfit called Charlie, with former Rat and early Birdman bassist, Carl Rorke, along with Steve Jones on vocals and Richard Burgman on guitar.

Chris Masuak: 'It was basically a pretty terrible covers band—[Joe Walsh's] 'Rocky Mountain Way' type stuff, but it was something to do.'

What the outfit did provide for Masuak was an up-close viewing of Radio Birdman, when Charlie played a 'Super Rock Dance' at St Mary's Church Hall at Waverley in May 1975. TV Jones, who had continued in reconfigured form after Deniz Tek was dumped, were top of the bill, with Birdman somewhat gallingly in the second slot.

Like Warwick Gilbert, Chris was immediately drawn into the Radios' gravitational pull.

Chris Masuak: 'It was just so incredibly different. They dressed differently, they talked differently, they acted differently. They were like a little self-contained unit. They had their own style and thing going, which was compelling. I was very young and I'd never seen anything like it. The music itself was stunning. It was powerful. They didn't sound like the New York Dolls, which were an influence. They didn't sound like the Rolling Stones, which were an influence. They didn't sound like Alice Cooper. They didn't sound like the Beach Boys or Jan and Dean.'

Masuak then witnessed Warwick Gilbert's debut at the Heffron Hall, and in early June took in the Birdman experience again with Charlie, when the Lions Club of Paddington put on a charity event at the Sydney Showground's Wills Pavilion—with TV Jones again headlining.

Chris Masuak: 'I listened to and enjoyed a lot of different types of music, but nothing really "changed my life" until I saw Birdman.'

When Are We Playing?

The cops around Darlinghurst seemed to have missed the memo about the Beatles' revolution a decade earlier. Accordingly, anyone slightly out of the norm was regarded with aggressive suspicion. For some that meant a physical confrontation or a trip in the back of a deliberately swerving paddy wagon was only ever a misinterpreted look, mumbled response, unusual garment choice or tipsy stumble away. The standard fine for such crimes, though, was often no more than 50 cents, the same as the entry fee to see Radio Birdman at the Oxford.

The building of their fanbase began slowly, with numbers significantly less than the enthusiastic gathering hopeful of seeing Lou Reed. Instead, it was a scattered group of maybe twenty people, a mix of supporters and the odd curious passer-by.

Warwick Gilbert: 'A few surly audience members demanded we play "Stairway to Heaven", with Rob telling them to "*Get fucked*"! It was hilarious!'

However, those who got it really did so. Not only was the music of the Birdmen unique in Australia, but something in the physicality of their delivery connected with the mind, gut and nervous system of their devotees and demanded a full body workout of every muscle and ligament. Radio Birdman unlocked something instinctive.

Doug Lonsdale: 'I'd never danced in my life, but when they started playing at the Oxford one night I'd had a few beers and I just jumped up and started dancing! I remember getting punched in the face once and I just kept dancing.'

Future Sunnyboy Richard Burgman proudly spent his twenty-first birthday watching the Radios at the Oxford.

Richard Burgman: 'There was nowhere else I'd rather be! If you stood at the back and watched them, they were raucous, they were loud—too loud. It was almost like an aural assault and you could barely hear Rob. There was never a vocal PA that could keep up with those big guitar amps, and you could barely hear the drums for the same reason. But, on the bright side, if you got right down the front of the stage and danced? They were the best band in the land! They were fucking incredible! And that was the difference. If you stood at the back and listened, you'd think, "Shit, what is this?" But down the front, the grooves they'd get, the speed, the power, the precision—it was all there.'

Paul Gearside was working in animation at Hanna-Barbera with Warwick Gilbert, when a colleague asked Warwick if the band he was in would be interested in playing at a party.

Paul Gearside (Birdman devotee, artist): 'I didn't know he was in a band and Warwick said, "Do you want to come?" "Sure, I'll come." It was a straight Double Bay party with straight people and a bit of music playing in the background. Then the band arrived. They looked the way I wanted rock stars to look. You could feel their presence in the room. They started playing and people were shocked! They moved outside.

'I was shitting myself! I thought, "This is two cultures colliding! And I'm standing in the middle of it!" By the third song I was climbing the walls! This was the best thing I'd ever heard! In the middle of [Alice Cooper's] "Ballad of Dwight Fry", Deniz was riding Rob around the room! It was mayhem and there was furniture and things falling over and I was dancing! There were a couple of other people with the band and they were going a hundred miles an hour as well.

'I was totally obsessed from that point and looked at Warwick in a whole new way. I couldn't wait to see him again on Monday. He couldn't go anywhere without me. If he went to the toilet, I'd follow him. He'd say, "What are you doing?" "I'm just making sure you're okay."

'I just wanted to know everything Birdman were doing. When is the band playing again? When are *we* playing? We. I just wanted to attach myself to them. I didn't want to let any of them out of my sight, because I'd found something. I hadn't been waiting for anything, but when it arrived, I thought, "At last!" I knew it. It was like I had a meaning in life. It was like when you fall in love and can't get the person out of your mind.

'It was a movement already and there were other people who, like me, knew. Just knew. We were it. Nothing could touch us.'

Along with friends like Johnny Kannis and Steve Harris, Chris Masuak was now also witnessing the Radios at every opportunity, with nirvana just a bus trip from Maroubra to Taylor Square.

Chris Masuak: 'I remember at one gig Younger called to me from the stage to "Settle down". I was kinda excited.'

Steve Harris (Birdman devotee): 'I was a nutcase! I used to dance, dive, roll around on the floor! Radio Birdman were not like the other children! It was a very hypnotic sound.'

Kannis seemed to have a bright future ahead of him in rugby league, with his talents coming to the attention of South Sydney. However, now a very different life path was stretching out before him.

Johnny Kannis: 'The family wanted me to marry a good Greek girl and become a motor mechanic, and I didn't want that. I wanted to rebel. I found my own way through Radio Birdman. I became reborn.'

For the Radios' August 1975 return appearance at Heffron Hall, there was another transformation, in presentation, which also served to dampen the sound and soak up the booming echo.

Ron Keeley: 'We got these banners made, about sixteen foot long and about four or five feet wide, dyed red. I've got a feeling they came from the army surplus store on Oxford Street next door to Martin's Bar. We had three or four of these across the hall.'

Meanwhile, across town, another subculture was at its peak. Balmain Town Hall had capacity problems and was creaking under the weight of a large enthusiastic crowd. The occasion was an appearance by Captain Matchbox, featuring washboard, kazoo and ukulele, and the wildly popular Uncle Bob's Band. Despite having released no records, UBB were a major drawcard and at Balmain, with its sprung floor, people seemed almost to be airborne while dancing, lost in the euphoria.

Bob Yates (promoter, writer): 'Uncle Bob's Band would pack the joint with 800-plus dope-smoking, barefoot hippies! The place would fucking go off! During one gig, the floor bounced so much it shook the ornamental plaster ceiling castings and cornices from around the light fittings, and sent them crashing onto the grand old council chamber table and chairs below!'

That adoring audience wasn't one-eyed about their heroes. Writer Toby Creswell, later a major figure in Australian music journalism, was a UBB fan, but went to see Radio Birdman at the Oxford at the prompting of Jules R.B. Normington.

Toby Creswell: 'It [Birdman] was very loud and I wasn't attuned to that kind of aesthetic, really. But I started going back and you could feel the winds of change happening. A lot of that music from the early seventies and late sixties had kind of run its course. And with the oil crisis, the political and social scene became more hard edged and more urgent. It was time for something new and this was kind of new.

'Radio Birdman were doing great songs like [Jan and Dean's] "Surf City" and [Tommy James and the Shondells'] "Hanky Panky", which were kind of considered uncool, but were really cool. They just had this new idea of what rock should be about.'

Tara Anderson: 'They [Birdman] were a great pop band when we first saw them. They played covers that were better than the originals. They were fun.

'A lot of the art-school kids were there [at the Oxford]. They were people who had drifted through from the hippie scene, the alternative scene around the area, so that kind of crowd in the room had a really different dynamic. They were a crowd that had grown out of [the vibrant counterculture] that was already happening in Taylor Square.'

Penny Ward (Birdman devotee): 'I could hear this sound, this band playing upstairs, and I thought, "Gee, I'd like to go in there," but I wouldn't have had the damn nerve, because I'd be on my own.'

Brain Capers

Warwick Gilbert's colleagues at Hanna-Barbera found there was a level of animation at a Radio Birdman gig more graphic than anything created at the office. And with an interactive component. Gilbert had been continuing to try and play down his life outside work but word had spread.

Warwick Gilbert: 'I didn't have the power of speech until I was about 30! I'd just go to work, draw and listen to Black Sabbath or anything decent. One day, someone else came up to me and said, "I hear you're in a band!" So, a bunch of them came along to the Oxford.

'When we started [the Stooges'] "T.V. Eye", with Rob yelling, the people from work nearly shat themselves! I could see them from the stage and thought, "Shit, this isn't going to go well when I get back to work!" They were covering their ears!'

And should have closed their eyes. Govinda, the permanently grinning human skull that witnessed all from the Birdman stage, was about to be the centre of proceedings.

Warwick Gilbert: 'I think Deniz and Sisto cooked up this plot, where they bought some sheep's brains and had one of those skulls where the lid comes off and they stuffed it with the brains. Sisto brought it through the crowd and held it up like a cannibal, shouting out, "The living brain!" The crowd parted and he knelt down in front of Rob. Rob took the top off the skull, lifted out a handful of brains and showed it to the audience. They were horrified! Then he stuffed it in his mouth and kind of went into a fit and starting spitting it out everywhere. People were getting hit by brains and shit! Everyone pissed off down the stairs!'

Mark Sisto: 'I just liked putting people on edge . . . then letting them off. I figured you needed to disrupt them from looking at some things from an attitude of the known. You jam the circuits, you create dissonance, and things become fluid or unfixed.'

Warwick Gilbert: 'The next day we went and got our amps and there were brains everywhere and they really stank! The sun was coming through the windows in the afternoon and heated up these bits of brains!'

Govinda would later disappear in what some believed were mysterious circumstances.

For Warwick, the evening hadn't only been about skulls and the violent spitting forth of sheep's brains. At the beginning of the new working week, he found, much to his horror, he'd become a minor celebrity.

Warwick Gilbert: 'I went to work on Monday and people were staring at me and I didn't like it. And I started getting girls come up to me!'

Back in Darlinghurst, Chris Masuak was on the up escalator. After gigs he'd demonstrate his skill and fandom back at Sims Street, where he'd re-play on guitar what Deniz Tek had fired off on stage an hour or so earlier. When Pip Hoyle signalled he needed time out from Birdman, some of the other band members went to view the young hotshot Masuak in action with Charlie.

Richard Burgman: 'There was a gig in Waverley and the brains trust from Birdman turned up. Jules Normington was there and Deniz and whoever else. Jules, bless his heart, thought I was the one they were going to pick! But no, it was Masuak.'

Warwick Gilbert: 'I was really happy with Pip. I liked the experimental nature of the band. I didn't care about being popular. It was a bit jazzier and I had more to do in that. But we all went to see him [Chris] play and thought, "Jesus Christ! We'll get him in the band when Pip leaves."'

There were no other candidates, or wider net cast, and after two rehearsals at Sims Street, the seventeen-year-old Masuak was in. He made his debut around late September 1975 at the Oxford.

Chris Masuak: 'I found myself in the band more or less like osmosis. I was just there. I went to all the gigs, I knew all the songs.

'I knew from the very beginning I had a big pair of shoes to fill, because they had a distinctive sound and I had to do something to complement what Tek was doing. That's where we came up with the so-called "dual-guitar attack". I was a very big fan of the Rolling Stones and I really loved that rhythm kind of approach, so there was a deliberate attempt to play the inversions [of what] he was playing, but also give the rhythm parts some velocity.

'Tek's style was very light, it was fluid. It had a really beautiful sting to it and he had quite a distinct sound. I had to find something different. And not only that, but I had the years of piano lessons, so I found myself being the guy that came up with the harmonies. I had a very active and distinctive role and I threw myself into it.'

With the meshing of Chris's technical skills and Deniz's more instinctive playing, Radio Birdman really began to fly.

Chris Masuak: 'For a young guitar player, [Tek's] real appeal was in the otherworldly energy, velocity and intensity of his playing. The real thrill—and enduring inspiration—was watching, and actually hearing the highwire act of a player on the very precipice.

'Tek was a real force of nature back then. He was a great player and, sure, maybe at that time he was at the edges of his abilities and you can hear it, you can hear him pushing. That's part of what gives it so much excitement and velocity, and there was nothing more exciting than that. Him and his presence and his charisma, but mainly his fucking playing.'

Masuak soon became former Rolling Stone Mick Taylor to Deniz Tek's Keith Richards. It changed everything.

Deniz Tek: 'Chris was so talented that he could pick things up in an instant. It gave me a bit of breathing room, too. I wouldn't have to do all the guitar, all the time.

'Of course, with Chris we also lost something. We became more of a standardised "rock band" with the two-guitar line-up. It was certainly more powerful, but less "out there", less artistic perhaps. More like the MC5 model, whereas with Pip we were more of a weird mix of the Stooges, the Velvets, and the Doors.'

Warwick Gilbert: 'We were able to play stuff more competently and scare the competition. Chris locked into what Ron and I had going, and made better sense of it. It sharpened up my bass playing as well. It put a fire under Deniz, so the whole thing took off.'

Chris Masuak: 'When it came time to tackle BOC [Blue Oyster Cult] covers, the guys would send me away to learn the song and report back with the right chords and riffs. Those were learning curves, for sure!'

Masuak had found more than a major musical outlet, he had secured a home.

Chris Masuak: 'I was dumped in a big city in a country that was alien and I was a guy without a rudder—and to me they were a family. They were friendly and very tolerant and kind. They were encouraging. I felt like I fitted in comfortably and just wanted to play. They were older. Twenty-five was much older than seventeen and I deferred to them. I was in the coolest band in Australia.'

Not long after Chris's recruitment, the Radios appeared at a dance at a Year Twelve formal event at North Sydney Girls High—schools were easier and more accessible marks than pubs. Most of the kids, not to mention the horrified teachers, didn't know what hit them.

Birdman would pay another centre of learning a more impromptu visit.

Chris Masuak: 'We were playing the Oxford on the night of my high-school graduation party and dinner. After the gig, the guys thought it would be nice to play for my classmates, so they loaded up the "Birdvan" and headed off. My classmates had the opportunity [of having] Australia's coolest band play at their soiree. Instead, they were horrified at the appearance of a scary bunch of weirdos and told us to kindly fuck off. They wouldn't even let us have a drink after all that effort. It was nice of the guys, though.'

Around the same time Johnny Kannis returned from an end-of-season Fairstar cruise with his footy team. He found that his school buddy Chris was now a Birdman, so he had more space at gigs to dance.

While the Oxford was the Radios' mainstay gig on a Friday and Saturday night, they had another crack at breaking into the broader industry by linking with Showgroup Management and could be hired for a fee of between $100 and $200. The phone didn't exactly ring off the hook, although perhaps they might have landed an opening spot for Alice Cooper, if his first tour of Australia in November 1975 hadn't been aborted. Younger had injured himself anyway.

Rob Younger: 'We were playing touch footy in Surrey Street in Darlinghurst and I had the ball under my arm and fell over. I didn't want to spill the ball because I'm a professional. My arm ripped open and it really bled. I went along to St Vinnies [St Vincent's Hospital] and they stitched it up and bandaged it. We had to play at the Oxford that night and the wound re-opened. It dripped through and there was just a pool of blood on the stage. And Deniz was going, "Oh man, he's bleeding for you!"'

Meanwhile, Paul Gearside had designed an image for Ron Keeley's bass drum head with a bandaged effect and a large safety pin, with the name 'Radio Birdman' almost soaking bloodily through it. He'd done something even more colourful for his own bedroom.

Paul Gearside: 'I painted the floor of my room red, gloss red, fire-engine red, and I painted the Birdman logo just near the door on top of that, like six foot long. You couldn't go in there for days, because everything stuck to it.'

How the Fuck Did You Guys Win?

Paul Gearside's allegiance to Radio Birdman was total and absolute, so he was less than comfortable about becoming a side show on Birdman's big day at the final of the *RAM* magazine and Levi's Battle of the Bands in early December 1975.

Paul Gearside: 'I had this badge my girlfriend at the time gave me. It was a swallow or something and I wore it everywhere. I took my shirt off and I didn't want to lose the pin, so I pinned it to my flesh. I was pretty pissed—we were all pissed. I remember there was a trickle of blood and people were grabbing me, saying, "I want to get a photograph!" I said, "Fuck off!" Then our band came on and I was just so fucking proud to be there! It was just a day I'll never forget. Well, it's easy to forget because I think I blacked out by the end of the day!'

Such competitions were a common occurrence at the time. More than 80 hopeful entries flooded in from across NSW, including everything from Status Quo-like boogie to bands with jazz influences. The Radios, on the other hand, were invited to take part.

The problem was that the Birdman unit was a man down. School had wrapped up and Chris Masuak had taken the opportunity to return home to Canada to see his family. Thankfully, Pip Hoyle, while still on a break, agreed to help out on a temporary basis.

Deniz Tek: 'We thought the contest was a bit of a joke, really. Anything outside of Darlinghurst or the Oxford was essentially enemy territory for us. But we saw it as an opportunity to take our band in front of a new crowd, get some chaos happening, and maybe increase our notoriety while going down in flames.'

Piss-take or not, victory would hardly damage their gigging opportunities, given the prizes included bookings at established venues, $300 cash, and studio time to record a single—something they'd been hoping to do for most of the year.

Not that the territory was entirely hostile, with the three judges including *RAM* editor, and now major Radios advocate, Anthony O'Grady, and Mac Cocker from the revolutionary new radio station 2JJ, which had been broadcasting since January.

The heats took place at North Sydney Police Boys Club. They began on a Monday night and ran through the week. Each of the 35 acts was allocated a fifteen-minute slot and all used the same equipment.

Future Midnight Oil frontman Peter Garrett was part of the crowd on Wednesday when the Radios appeared and powered through their set, including a ferocious version of the Stooges' 'T.V. Eye'. A bare-chested Rob Younger, his elbow still bandaged from his hard landing during that street football match, was a howling antithesis of every other contender—although he still found time to make some technical adjustments.

Warwick Gilbert: 'Rob got the microphone and smashed the shit out of it on the floor! Bits flew everywhere! The guy who was in charge of the equipment got really pissed off!'

While this was being thrashed out, Birdman's master plan was framed in a small but perfectly timed article in *RAM*'s

Grassroots section. It stated that the outfit's game plan was twofold: to open for the Stooges at the Michigan Palace—where team Iggy had infamously played their final show—and appear with Skyhooks, wipe the floor with the colourful Melbourne act, and 'get paid for doing both'. Publicans and venues owners, it was stated, were difficult to deal with, but 'so are we. Our time will come . . .' The entire piece read as if it had been penned by Rob Younger.

In the accompanying photo, the subversive focal point was an almost impossibly slim Younger, in long black gloves and eyes heavy with dark make-up.

As for the Birdman dig at Skyhooks, the hugely popular band were an easy target, but in reality their songs were close to the social settings evoked by the New York Dolls. Additionally, the Hooks would later cover 'Wild in the Streets' by Deniz Tek's hero, Garland Jeffreys.

RAM's Grassroots article laid a breadcrumb trail down a shining new path for many, including future Hoodoo Guru Brad Shepherd.

Brad Shepherd: 'Radio Birdman seemed like they knew what they were doing, even just in the photo. They seemed confident and defiant. And they were talking about the music that was like an alternate reality. It was a whole other universe to me that I was completely unaware of, and that seemed so cool. My imagination was being lit up just reading about the names of the bands and the songs they covered. It was very exciting for me to read in print for the first time. Like, "We do the New York Dolls' 'Personality Crisis'." I don't know what that sounds like, but I bet it's great!'

Shepherd's Deep Purple, Led Zeppelin and Black Sabbath records had to move over.

Brad Shepherd: 'I went to the Brisbane independent record store Wizard Records, upstairs in the Elizabeth Arcade, and purchased Blue Oyster Cult's *Secret Treaties*.'

Birdman progressed to the final of the *RAM* contest, which was staged outdoors in daylight at St Leonards Park. Among others in the running were White Heat, who featured Chris Jones, formerly of TV Jones; Thundaband, whose singer had hair almost as long as that of Rob Younger; and Vella, with Mark Gable, later of Choirboys.

But all the lead-up talk was about the Radios and allegations they'd destroyed $3000 worth of gear in their heat. A seemingly wildly inflated figure for a microphone and stand that simply happened to be in the wrong place at the wrong time.

Warwick Gilbert: 'The sound guy read us the riot act before we went on that, if we did anything to the gear, he was going to shut the power off.'

Like the Velvet Underground and Frank Zappa's Mothers of Invention, the Birdmen had a unique secret weapon: their followers, individuals whose very being was directed by the Radios and the possibilities they presented. Their support had been highly visible for the outfit's appearance in the heats, but now with triumph a possibility for *their* band they went up a gear.

John Needham: 'That inner-circle thing was very, very prominent and very, very intense. People were really possessive of the relationships with the people in the band. That little clique was as intense as the band were sometimes. And I think, with some bands, that propels them forward, being surrounded by that sort of craving and love.

'Why wouldn't you want to own them? Between seeing the Easybeats and seeing Birdman almost ten years later, I can't think of one other highlight involving local bands—that magic attachment. Suddenly there's a band playing the music you like, and there's nothing else going, so you grab onto it and you follow it and you become part of it.'

Alley Brereton: 'We wanted them to win. So we figured we'd turn out in numbers and create a big disturbance. For all the other bands, nobody really did anything. Nobody danced and just politely clapped. We all danced like mad!'

Paul Gearside: 'The ground around the stage was dry and grassless. This palm branch just happened to be lying there. I knew I had to mark our battle ground, so I started swinging and smashing it into the cracked ground and clouds of dust rose up! It was like a scene from that movie, *Zulu*, with warriors' feet and spears pounding the ground to Ron's battle drums. It was like a fucking rain dance or something!'

Warwick Gilbert: 'There was shit flying everywhere! It was fucking funny and making a hell of a racket! We weren't your typical band!'

John Needham: 'It was shit band after shit band. I was just pessimistic that they wouldn't win because they were just too radical.'

Mark Gable (Vella): 'They were on after us. I'd never heard or seen anything like it! But what really blew me out, apart from Rob Younger, was Deniz Tek tuning his guitar—at full volume! It got even better backstage because one of them had another guy and was spinning him around with his legs out, crashing into the furniture and beer bottles and stuff was breaking and they were screaming their lungs out! This was at a band competition!'

Abby Beaumont (Birdman devotee, photographer): 'After they played, I was chatting with a group of people and I said,

"There's absolutely no doubt Radio Birdman is going to win this!" The next thing I know, Ron Keeley picked me up and whirled me around through the air. He was just basically saying thank you.'

Initially, the result was declared as a dead heat for first place between Birdman and Thundaband.

Jules R.B. Normington wasn't having that and took his considerable and animated disbelief direct to the ear of Anthony O'Grady.

Jules R.B. Normington: 'I was like, "It can't be a draw, Anthony!" There's daylight between them and everybody else! He said, "I know! I know! We're going to have a recount!"'

In the end, Radio Birdman won, with Thundaband in second place and White Heat third.

It was a victory that didn't sit well with some of the other contestants.

Warwick Gilbert: 'One of them was calling us cunts and everything! He said, "I don't know how you bastards won it!" And as we accepted the award, he wanted to kill us! They couldn't believe they lost! I think it was worth it winning just for that.'

The spoils of the victory were far less important than the symbolism.

Radio Birdman had played a wild, unknown, against-the-grain music, destroyed equipment, acted in a fierce manner, rather than comical or welcoming, were hated by one judge—and still won.

Deniz Tek: 'We were pleasantly surprised in a way, by the win, because we needed the money, and enjoyed a bit of schadenfreude to see the other guys upset about losing. We were a little disconcerted also, because, what does it mean?

Are we now going to be "acceptable", on some level? It threw us off a bit.'

Alley Brereton: 'It was almost like, "Fuck you! We're here!" I got the impression it was a bit of a turning point. But they were still outsiders.'

Paul Gearside: 'I thought, "Those fuckers out there still won't understand," and there was sort of a feeling of "Good, because they're ours! If you don't get it now, you'll never get it, and we do, and fuck the lot of you!"'

I Wonder if Anyone Else Knows about This?

It was announced in *RAM* that Birdman would record a single of ‘Do the Pop’ with their winnings. There was also a slight stylistic shift in the magazine’s full page covering the contest.

The promotional badging of the event had seemingly and quite cannily been expanded in the piece to be a ‘punk band thriller’, even though the Sex Pistols had only performed live for the first time in early November 1975 and global public exposure for UK punk was a year away.

It was as if the *RAM* competition was now being framed as a changing of the guard, the promotion of a new cool.

Deniz Tek: ‘I’ve often wondered whether Anthony O’Grady was seeing into the future wave of punk, and wanted to get his magazine on board somehow, and our train was conveniently headed in that direction. Maybe he wanted to reimagine *RAM* as something between an Australian *Creem* or *Rock Scene*?’

In any event, like the earlier Grassroots story, combined with the magazine’s increasing mentions of the band’s obscure heroes in their letters page, the competition article—with its prominent photos of Birdman—made for high-impact publicity.

Bob Short (Birdman devotee, artist): ‘I lived in Wollongong and there was about three or four of us who had managed to find things like the Velvet Underground’s *White Light/White Heat*. I found an old import copy for $2.95. I also had the Dolls’ first album from a second-hand shop in Wollongong and another kid had the Stooges' *Fun House*. This music was our link against the outside world.

'Reading about it [Birdman] and seeing those pictures of Rob with those long gloves on, you immediately went [hypnotised voice], "Iggy Pop, New York Dolls. Got to find out more . . ." I have to see this band! Someone is actually doing it! It's real! If you got the bug for that underground stuff, you had to find it. You had to.'

Future Died Pretty frontman Ron S. Peno was living in Gosford on the NSW Central Coast. He was also entranced by the *RAM* coverage. It made a trip south to the Oxford to see the Radios in action mandatory.

Ron S. Peno: 'We just saw the last couple of songs, but it was enough for me to go, "Oh my God! Look at the singer's hair!" And he was wearing gloves and mascara and "Oh my God! Look at the guitarist!" I was taken immediately! They were the best band ever! Deniz, coming from Ann Arbor, was like a demigod. He was there. He saw it all. We were like, "Wow, Deniz Tek!"'

Peno had very briefly been part of a Gosford outfit called Uncle Mils, which tackled material by his beloved David Bowie, as well as most of the Stones' *Get Yer Ya-Ya's Out!* LP. But when he saw the MC5's *Back in the USA* in a bargain bin in the local Palings, the earth moved. They looked cool and sweaty and intriguing, so Ron handed over the $2.50. An introduction to the Blue Oyster Cult's *Tyranny and Mutation* was an additional life-rerouting exercise, but it was another trip to Palings that totally upended his world.

Ron S. Peno: 'I saw the cover of the New York Dolls' album and "Oh my God! I want to dress like that!" I loved the cover and with the "New York Dolls" written in lipstick! I thought,

"This is so cool!" Living in country Gosford, I thought, "I wonder if anyone else knows about this?"'

Soon, Peno, while wearing make-up, platform shoes and glam fashion, was attempting to outrun local school kids who were teasing him about his most unCentral Coast–like attire.

Arch Radios fan Doug Lonsdale was also on the move, working for BHP at Newcastle and then training it to Sydney on weekends to see his heroes. He met Angie Pepper at the steel city's Cambridge Hotel, where Pepper was singing up a storm on Friday nights.

In high school, art and music were Angie's great passions and she formed a group with some friends. She graduated to occasionally appearing on such local stages as the Newcastle University Student Union building.

When she wasn't singing, Angie was sewing for friends—one of whom scored a pair of leather pants—and her own needs.

Angie Pepper: 'I always had trouble finding clothes that I liked, so from about the age of ten or eleven I would design and make them for myself. For my HSC Level 1 Art submission, I designed and made a coat. I sourced, dyed and spun the raw wool for it and fashioned it using a variety of weaving, crochet and macrame styles, incorporating a bunch of natural objects like gum nuts and seeds, etc.'

After her final exams, Angie went to art school. One night after classes, she was convinced by a friend to get on stage with local blues outfit the Electric Jug Band. They had a new singer. The night they were invited to open for Bo Diddley at Newcastle City Hall, they nearly lost her.

About halfway through their set, Pepper became aware of a presence at the side of the stage. It was the rock and roll originator smiling from ear to ear.

Afterwards, Bo approached Angie and indicated how much he enjoyed the band's performance and her voice, advising Pepper to take her talents to America.

In January 1976, after art school, Pepper moved to Sydney and at Frenchs bumped into Doug Lonsdale, who introduced her to Rob Younger that night. A few weeks later, she took in the Radio Birdman experience for the first time at the Bondi Lifesaver.

Angie Pepper: 'The first thing that struck me was the Jekyll-and-Hyde transformation of Rob. The Rob I knew was mild mannered, polite, soft spoken, personable, engaging and witty, with a very clever sense of humour. A gentle fellow. There was absolutely no hint of the guy on stage now confronting the audience.

'The music was exciting and brilliantly executed. They were exhilarating and unpredictable. Like being close to a wild animal.'

Despite her anything but intrusive manner, Angie would come to exert a powerful stylistic influence and more on the band and their scene, much as Anita Pallenberg had done with the Stones. Yet without the slightest hint of Pallenberg's alleged walks on the darker side.

They Frightened the Shit Out of the Record Companies!

It was obvious something was very wrong when Radio Birdman arrived at the University of New England in Armidale, NSW.

Lee Taylor: 'They were setting up tables, with plates and things. And the tables were right up against the speakers, and I thought, "We're going to have to tell them . . ."'

It was the first of two curious Bird engagements in the region organised by former TV Jones member Giles Van Der Werf, whose own band, Siren, was also appearing. Most of the Birdmen, including inner sanctum member, Lee Taylor, did the trip in high style.

Deniz Tek: 'We took a small plane up there, and felt briefly like real rock stars!'

Chris Masuak, Penny Ward and Johnny Kannis drove up in Kannis's faithful Mini.

The uni gig was a formal occasion for students. Their parents and the organisers were taken aback, firstly by the Radios' appearance and then by their robust musical delivery.

Warwick Gilbert: 'All the parents started threatening us, and the guys in suits were calling us thugs and louts. The kids liked it and the parents wanted to beat us up! But Deniz and Rob were goading the young people into action, and they [the kids] were all riled up punching their fists in the air.'

Deniz Tek: 'After the first song this guy was begging us to stop, and after the second song, he said, "Feel free to stay and be our guest, but don't play anymore!" The guy had tears in his eyes and he's down on his knees, this guy in a tuxedo.'

Warwick Gilbert: 'He said, "I'll pay you if you stop!"'

Deniz Tek: 'So we hammered them with one more song and immediately went to the catering. Giles's band got up and they had to play lame covers all night at a low volume. We were kicking back, our feet on the tables. We're drinking champagne out of the bottle—you know, being real pigs, but just thinking it was so great we didn't compromise. And we were calling out requests. "You guys know [the Allman Brothers' twenty-minute-plus epic] 'Whipping Post'?"'

Ron Keeley: 'Sisto gave a master class on how to get the most buffet food on a five-inch plate. Carefully constructed from the base up. It must have been a pile six inches high.'

The second gig of the trip north was at Armidale Town Hall which attracted some local Indigenous kids. Unconcerned about it being a profit deal, the Birdmen let them in for free.

On the way back to Sydney, the PA system that belonged to Rob Younger, and which the band used at the Oxford, strangely vanished from the truck they shared with Siren. Without it, no one would be able to hear Younger sing. It was a serious blow, yet gear could be replaced, and Jules R.B. Normington subsequently bought a suitably red-and-black rig. The key point of the northern trip was that the Radios had once more stared down the squares.

Rob Younger: 'The us-and-them thing is really interesting. To separate yourself from the rest of the crowd. It does actually help things quite a bit. It brings attitude to the playing and so forth, and the people that like you feel like they're part of something . . . exclusive. It's not like musical snobbery. It's just saying we don't give two fucks what people think. You declare your contempt for other things and you draw a line and you deliberately do it.

'Being heckled isn't that much of a stretch from being wildly applauded. A strong reaction is the main thing. I think I got quoted by [*RAM* writer] Andrew McMillan about "It's not the band but the audience that's on trial". He loved that and really ran with it. I think it's kind of true.'

In the wake of Birdman's band-comp win, Anthony O'Grady was intensifying his efforts to help the group gain a solid foothold in the local industry. As part of this push, he was keen for others of influence to see the Radios in their natural habitat.

Peter Rix (manager of Marcia Hines, Jon English, Hush): 'Radio Birdman were Anthony's favourite band on the planet. One Friday night he said, "Come on, we're going up to the Oxford Tavern." No one in a million years expected the manager of Hush to go and see Radio Birdman, but I was the nice, sweet bloke at the back of the room, going, "Shit, this is good! Really good!"'

Getting something on tape to pass around to record companies was key to O'Grady's endeavours, but that was problematic.

Deniz Tek: 'Anthony took us around various recording studios—2SM [a facility run by Les Gock from Hush], EMI. All acrimoniously tossed us out after a few hours—the engineers couldn't handle it. Of course, we were a total pain in the ass, because our "No compromise" policy extended into areas we knew very little or nothing about!'

The only solid recordings to result—which included a returned Chris Masuak doing double duty on guitar and piano—were from Copperfield, a very downmarket establishment near Day

Street in the city, and Earth Media in North Sydney, where TV Jones had been put on tape.

At Earth Media, 'I-94' and 'Snake' were captured, while the Copperfield recordings were more substantial, with 'Descent into the Maelstrom', 'Do the Pop', 'I-94', 'Monday Morning Gunk', 'Murder City Nights' and 'Smith and Wesson Blues' and Chris Masuak's 'Death by the Gun'.

O'Grady took the tapes to industry heavyweights such as Mushroom's Michael Gudinski. While the offers didn't exactly pour in, there wasn't a blanket wall of resistance either.

Peter Rix: 'They weren't ignored by the industry—they were ignored by the record business, because they frightened the shit out of the old guys who ran the record companies. This is before I started the ARIAs, because that saw a major change, and someone in their thirties was suddenly able to recommend an act be signed to a label.

'Anybody who was in the management side or the agency side knew about Radio Birdman. Everybody did. They didn't frighten anybody who was listening to what was going on in other parts of the world. It all made sense but . . . you need a record label.'

The wariness cut both ways. The Radios distrusted everyone outside their direct circle, and even some insiders occasionally wore their wrath. Their manner would suck the oxygen from any corporate boardroom in seconds. As for playing the industry game of appearing on the ABC's hugely popular pathway program *Countdown*, and miming for the cameras, forget it. A weekly work sheet of national gigs was a further impossibility, given Deniz's study commitments and the working hours of his future medical career—along with the band's intensely physical and draining style of play, particularly for Rob Younger.

Add their utter intractability regarding their music and performance and it was a difficult, if not impossible, negotiation process, especially in a landscape where jazz-fusion act Ayers Rock had just been named Musicians of the Year in *RAM*'s 1975 readers' poll.

Peter Rix: 'It was very difficult for them to find a common ground to get to where they needed to get to.'

RAM ran their first major Birdman feature—unsurprisingly, perhaps, penned by Anthony O'Grady—across a page and a half in February 1976, with the piece peppered with references to punk, in line with the 'Detroit' tone the Radios were preaching.

Yet the music they were advocating wasn't just Michigan-centric. Deniz, Rob, Warwick and Ron had all grown up with, and been entranced by, surf music. The Radios embraced the Trashmen's 'King of the Surf', Jan and Dean's 'Surf City', and the Rivieras' take on 'California Sun', as well as directing instrumental elements of the genre into their own material.

Ron Keeley: 'Surf music had been with me a long time, and Deniz's songs gave that style a lot of scope.'

Toby Creswell: 'I really liked [Birdman doing] "Surf City" because I always liked surf music, but I also thought, "Culturally, what is Sydney about? Sydney is kind of a surfing town. We're basically about the beach."'

Birdman's musical catchment area expanded further. Several tracks from the *Nuggets* compilation—much beloved and introduced to the band by Rob and Warwick—such as the Remains' 'Don't Look Back' and the 13th Floor Elevators' 'You're Gonna Miss Me', also became part of the Radios' armoury. *Nuggets* would be reissued on the Sire label later in 1976 and become an important recording all over again.

For Birdman, that material joined other, more surprising inclusions in their repertoire by country rockers Commander Cody, the bubblegum pop of Tommy James and the Shondells, and UK proto-punks, the Pink Fairies, who blew Deniz Tek's mind at the Marquee in London in 1971. The Radios' church might have been less than tolerant, but its base was a broad one.

Nonetheless, Detroit-related records would still be pulled out each time the band walked into a party.

Deniz Tek: 'In those days, the pubs shut early and people would go to someone's house and party on. People would immediately put the Stooges or the MC5 on the turntable. We would be going. "Uh, yes, of course we love those records, but . . . could you please put something else on?"'

Tek would write a song called 'Radical Departure' in response. Not that they were able to record, much less release it. Nothing had changed in the few months since the *RAM* contest and the shine of their victory was dulling fast.

No Battle at Trafalgar

The risk of physical personal harm was never an issue for Mark Sisto. The act of exploration was what mattered and opportunities were rarely missed, even at parties.

Johnny Kannis: 'He was at the top of the staircase and did a dive right into the middle of the lounge-room floor. He was lucky he survived, to be honest, but he got up smiling and put his hand out to me and said, "Sisto!" And I shook his hand and said, "Kannis!"'

Mark Sisto: 'I was testing the flexibility of the floor.'

They would team up to form the Glutonics—a pre-Blues-Brothers-like pairing of backing singers for Radio Birdman on select songs—as well as continue their roles as wild dancers.

Johnny Kannis: 'I copied Mark Sisto. I'm quite happy to say that he influenced my dancing, because he used to dance like James Brown. When he and I were on the dance floor, there was no room for anybody else.'

By now, Kannis's wardrobe had expanded to include, at times, a white tuxedo.

Johnny Kannis: 'Birdman were playing at a party. Deniz invited me up and I sang three or four songs. You couldn't get me off the stage after that. The Dictators had released *Go Girl Crazy!* and [Dictators singer] Dick Manitoba was a bit of an influence. I read somewhere, maybe in *Creem* magazine, that he wore a white suit, so I just went and hired one in the city.

It just happened to be the same place Mark Holden was hiring his suits. It was the same one apparently and I didn't take it back! It was showbiz from there!

'I was into Las Vegas cabaret and artists like Elvis Presley, Tom Jones, Engelbert Humperdinck—all the crooners like Frank Sinatra and Dean Martin—and I was a big fan of the Rat Pack. They were dressed up and it was exciting to me as a sixteen- or seventeen-year-old. I became a shameless attention seeker.'

Kannis's love of Birdman was such that he had the Radios' logo tattooed on his arm in Darlinghurst one night, as Mark Sisto looked on.

Johnny Kannis: 'I was biting down on Sisto's brown leather jacket.'

Sisto's broader role in the scene was more mystical than defined. It would see him walk the streets in a dressing-gown with curious accessories, as if participating in some unseen ceremony.

Mark Sisto: 'I had different bathrobes and I wore them out in the street with a staff! I had this walking stick. I looked like I'd arrived from another century. And people were like, "What the fuck is this?" In those days, inner-city Sydney was a wonderful playground. Those were good times.'

There was still no record deal for Birdman. Then it seemed they didn't need one—to get on the air, at least.

On 2 March 1976, Double J beamed the outfit live-to-air from Sydney's ABC studios, before a tribe of followers. The band tore through a white-hot set that opened with 'Burned My Eye' and ran through the MC5's 'Sister Anne'; 'Dominance and Submission' and 'ME 262' by the Blue Oyster Cult; and the Doors' 'L.A. Woman', along with their own frantic, 'Do the Pop', and the epic, 'Descent into the Maelstrom'."

Bob Short: 'I remember the replay, wagging school to sit there, with each speaker of the stereo on each side of my head, lying down staring at the ceiling, listening with the tape recorder on to record it.'

Richard Burgman: 'They weren't trying be like Lobby Loyde or Billy Thorpe—that heavy three-chord Australian rock stuff that we grew up with. That didn't inform Birdman, because Deniz was American and Chris was Canadian. Birdman were different, radically different.'

And the Radios began implementing further rules and policies, while installing additional perimeter fencing. When *RAM* printed a letter of complaint of sorts from Deniz, about being framed as punks in their coverage of the band, it probably signalled the beginning of the Birdman practice of at least requesting they get to check any *RAM* articles before they went to print, a position also extended to other publications.

They didn't trust anyone else to get it right, and often submitted their own stories written by band members or close associates. Arguably, it didn't help Birdman's career trajectory—those in the local music industry simply weren't accustomed to being told how things were going to be.

A full-page feature in the March 1976 issue of Australian *Rolling Stone* seemed to make it out unscathed, with the headline, 'Radio Birdman: Blitzkrieg Machine Seeks Vinyl Success'. The Radios' presence in Sydney could now be sensed, even if the outfit was not regularly sighted. They were legitimised in part by Double J's support and backed with the band's own promotional material that was created on someone's kitchen table or lounge-room floor by a team of friends and associates, a full home-spun workshop. Each flyer or poster was individually stylised, with different cartoons and handwritten messages that screamed of an event, rather than just another gig or dance. A succession of them would hug telegraph poles near Taylor Square.

Johnny Kannis: 'People could rely on that as the media outlet for Birdman.'

Deniz Tek: 'We would write on them with textas. Mark Sisto wrote "Hand of Law" on one, and drew a hand with an eye in the centre of the palm.'

George Munoz, another Maroubra Bay High student, became similarly creative after being introduced to the band and the Oxford.

George Munoz (Birdman devotee): 'With Steve Harris and I doing art together, we started making our own Radio Birdman T-shirts, as well as for Blue Oyster Cult and the MC5. You couldn't buy T-shirts at the time by those bands.'

The Radios were confronted by a fashion from decades earlier when they landed an opening spot at the Canberra Theatre for Sydney's energised rock-and-roll revivalists, Ol' 55. Before the release of their *Take It Greasy* album, which would reach number three on the national charts, Ol' 55 had an enormous fan base. It was still daylight outside when the Radios stalked onto the stage. They hadn't had the chance to check the equipment, because the headliner's crew were setting up a trapeze for sax player Wilbur Wilde to swing out over the crowd.

Deniz Tek: 'No sound check for us resulted in the destruction of the hearing of all these seated kids, wearing mostly fifties' fancy dress costumes, like the cast of *Happy Days*. It was Dada-esque. It was just noise, weirdly taking on its own life.

The kids just sat there. They didn't make one sound. No one clapped. No one moved. They were stunned, with blank expressions, like we had erased their minds.'

Other gigs presented themselves, such as self-organised events at Balmain Town Hall, but getting a recording deal remained elusive. As a virtual last resort, Anthony O'Grady approached Trafalgar Studios at Annandale. Charles Fisher was a respected industry figure, who most recently had produced Ol' 55's *Take It Greasy*. Alongside him was veteran engineer and producer John Sayers. He'd worked with the Masters Apprentices, Billy Thorpe, and Lobby Loyde and the Coloured Balls. A former rep for Festival Records, Michael McMartin, was an all-round marketing wiz, future Hoodoo Gurus' manager and the third link in the Trafalgar operation.

Charles Fisher (Trafalgar): 'Anthony came to me before I met the band and said, "Look, Radio Birdman won the Battle of the Bands. We promised them a prize of a recording session in a studio—would you be that studio?" I said, "Why don't you bring them over and see what happens."

'They were hard to get to know, hard to penetrate, and I loved their arrogance. They didn't care about anyone and they didn't care about anyone's opinion. They had a real wall around them, a real us-against-them attitude. I said, "I'd really love to record you," and they looked at me and said, "Why the fuck should we record with you?" They didn't seem too keen on recording with anybody, to be honest.'

Michael McMartin: 'Deniz had this knack of seeming to be menacing or suspicious. He just knew that he had the look, the aura and that stare. It was "You're not one of us", but fairly quickly he started to figure out that while I may not be one of them, I certainly wasn't the enemy. Rob was quite a different character. He was "It's all going to fall apart—they're all fucked, anyway!'"

As the shock waves from the release of the Ramones' single 'Blitzkrieg Bop'—as well as their self-titled debut album—were being felt around the world, a deal was struck for the Radios to record at Trafalgar but only when the studio was free.

Parramatta Prison Blues

In his teens, John Needham could see the walls of Parramatta Gaol from his bedroom window. If he walked past at night, he could hear yelling and screaming from within, as if the sandstone blocks themselves were crying out. Now the racket inside was courtesy of a performance by Radio Birdman with Needham watching on.

John Needham: 'I was quite familiar with the Johnny Cash [prison] records. I remember [Folsom Prison Blues] when they all got up and cheered. So when the band said, "The next song we'd like to do is called 'Murder City Nights'," they all went, "Yeah!"'

Rob Younger: 'Afterwards, we went to a room and the inmates were serving us cups of tea. I just remember being uncomfortable with the idea of these people who can't leave—and probably not for fucking years and years—serving me a cup of tea.'

The unlikely gigs continued at a North Sydney bar and restaurant called Newts. Birdman were booked for a wildly optimistic six-night engagement from late April to early May, extravagantly billed as the 'Radio Birdman special' and an 'audio visual experience'. It didn't start well.

Jules R.B. Normington: 'The manager of the place asked me if we could do some covers, like "January" by Pilot!'

The Radios wouldn't oblige and, before a crowd that was mostly too straight, played sufficiently loudly that the power was pulled several times. The stint died on night one.

Rick Grossman, future Divinyl and Hoodoo Guru, however, was sold. He soon became a regular at the Oxford and anywhere else the Birdmen appeared.

Rick Grossman: 'I would have given my left arm to play in that band. One night after the Oxford, a few of us had to go on a ferry ride to calm down. It was so intense. They were great, great nights. I used to carry their gear up and down the stairs. I loved them! They were a scary band!'

Warwick Gilbert: 'The Oxford with Chris was the best and most creative period for me. We would never play the same set twice. It was more performance art, a real-time improvisation. An energy loop with the audience would occur: like stepping onto a light beam and being whipped along through time and space. The music exploded out when that occurred. I remember it clearly now.

'I remember once Deniz kind of tried to control it. He turned round and gave us the death stare and wanted us to slow down, but we were in this fucking loop! We just kept playing and ran right over the top of him and he wasn't a happy traveller. Then Rob started saying what cunts we were, and the audience was kind of digging the drama of it. Rob then got into it and he started dancing—and the audience started reacting and then we belted it up a notch. Deniz thought, "Shit! I better hop on board." When he joined in, everyone was so fired up it lifted the roof off the place. That was the internal dynamic of the band.

'Each gig was approached as if it were our last, and we didn't practise much, because it was about the explosive chemistry and you didn't want to use that up. It'd either fall in a heap or lift the roof off.'

Chris Masuak: 'That was the thrilling part. That was when we were making people come alive. We were invigorating. We were a life force.'

Angie Pepper: 'At times, it seemed like the band would be fighting to keep up with the beast they'd created, and at any moment it could all fall apart—but then they'd somehow pull their way out of the impending chaos and surge through to take the music to an even higher level. They were masters at accomplishing that and it was so exciting to witness.'

Warwick Gilbert: 'I used to close my eyes when I played and just listen to the music, just listen to Ron and sort of feel the room. That was my guide, but when I'd open my eyes I'd see amazing things! One time, this blast of heat went past my head and there was fire just spreading out on the ceiling. This fire breather had jumped on stage and blown fire at the roof! I thought, "Gee, that's interesting," but I kept playing.

'Another time, I looked down and saw four guys bashing their heads on the front of the stage in time to the music. On one other occasion, this girl climbed up on the PA and she was fucking the sound! With a smile on her face, so she was taking the piss, really, but it was just funny, actually.

'Even when the band wasn't very good, people would think it was the second coming of Christ, because it was *supposed* to be good! It garnered a halo effect and grew from there.'

All this magic also pushed Gilbert to further his design ideas in relation to the band's logo.

Warwick Gilbert: 'That was the line-up that inspired my art. I asked Deniz if I could rework the symbol. He said, "Sure." It wasn't working as a design for me, so over about six months

I boiled it all down to its basic component parts to a pop art kind of symbol.'

The Birdman inner circle was also involved to varying degrees in a wide variety of the band's operations—from poster/flyer creation and song selection to financial assistance, fashion and other aesthetics.

Angie Pepper: 'I used my sewing machine and sewing skills to help them visually style themselves. I patched and repaired jeans for Rob, Deniz and Chris many times, and stitched Radio Birdman symbol patches on clothing. Deniz had a piece of black fabric with the red Birdman symbol on it. I sewed that to the back panel of his cut-off denim jacket, along with a strip of snakeskin across the shoulders. I wasn't the stylist, I was the seamstress, but I'll accept credit for being a good one.'

Bob Short: 'A lot of the style that appeared in the audience was straight out of Angie.'

Alley Brereton also arranged for a tiger to be designed and embroidered on the back of Rob Younger's denim jacket.

Deniz Tek: 'We had a mission, and that took us beyond simply milling around looking after ourselves. It was never formally organised; rather, it was a spontaneously evolving community. We felt like we had a higher purpose.'

Tall Cool One

At six foot three, Jim Dickson was a towering figure in a number of respects, accustomed to viewing the world from on high. That was until he first witnessed Radio Birdman at the Bondi Lifesaver, while in Sydney as a member of Railroad Gin. Then even he had to look up.

Jim Dickson: 'Holy fuck! A mate of mine, Russell Handley, who was playing in a band called the Popular Mechanics, and was also a Townsville boy, said [during the Birdman gig], "Jim, you look all shaken up! Let's go back and have a joint and then come back and watch the second set." It was like, "Oh yeah! This is something else!" I resigned from Railroad Gin straight away.

'Birdman were a revelation! Rather than thinking, "Wouldn't it be great to be in Boston to see the Real Kids, or in London and see the Clash or the Damned, to actually have someone in Australia you could go and see who were putting out that energy was an extraordinary thrill!

'It gave you a kind of energy itself that you wanted to take an evangelical stance. Like, "This is really worthwhile, and I want to be a part of promoting this."'

He would be anchoring the object of his worship in a few decades.

Born in Ceylon—later renamed Sri Lanka—where he stayed until aged eleven, Jim spent three years in the UK and then in his mid-teens moved to Queensland. He first fell for the Animals and had been on a quest ever since. Magazines such as *Creem*, *Rock Scene* and the *NME* were his lifelines as was his friend Greg Foster with his vast record collection.

Jim's first musical outing was playing bass in a quartet called Midas. Alongside his friend Charlie Georgees, they tackled Alice Cooper, David Bowie, Lou Reed and Grand Funk Railroad.

By the time Dickson saw Radio Birdman, his buddies from Townsville and James Cook University—Colleen Giles, Greg Foster and Georgees—had moved to Sydney in search of the Birdmen, after reading about them in *RAM*. They were living in a five-bedroom house at Hampden Road, Five Dock, with numerous other exiles from North Queensland. The house and the Sunshine State would have a considerable impact on the Sydney scene in coming years.

With the fire of seeing the Radios in his veins, Dickson went north again. Working at Brisbane store Rocking Horse Records, he delivered Birdman and other sermons from behind the counter.

Back in Sydney, the Radios were recording at Trafalgar—when the studio was available and Deniz didn't have commitments with his medical studies. In the process, the original notion of recording a single broadened into something more substantial, as did Trafalgar's business model for the band.

Charles Fisher: 'We decided amongst ourselves we would do this EP. We wouldn't approach any record companies. We'd try and release it ourselves. It was only about six months after I'd done Ol 55's *Take It Greasy*, so it was a pretty weird segue for me. In fact, [then] I went from Radio Birdman to Air Supply.'

'Smith and Wesson Blues', 'Snake', 'I-94' and 'Burned My Eye' were recorded. The Birdvan brought in sheets of corrugated roofing metal from a building site to put on the studio walls, and in other strategic positions, to harden their racket. It was a technique used by acts such as the 13th Floor Elevators to produce an ambience when the sound waves struck the material. The other metallic addition to the sessions were beer cans, which were smashed on the heads of band members to the rapid-fire beat of 'Burned My Eye'.

Running wildly at cross-purposes to all this were some remaining trappings of hippiedom, with crystals, and even a pyramid, positioned in the studio control room.

It was a very different mindset to Birdman playing a party at an old mansion in Woollahra, where Dare Jennings and Julie Mostyn were living. The structure was marked for demolition and the festivities that night probably helped eased the burden on the contractors.

Then it was again back to the home sweet home of the Oxford, where, having got word of the Radios, Clyde Bramley ventured down from Toowoomba.

Clyde Bramley (Birdman devotee, later of the Hoodoo Gurus): 'It was like seeing the Rolling Stones in the corner of your local pub.'

The House Burned Down After They Played!

Paul Gearside had a Saturday-morning ritual: the paper, his cigarettes, and a few beers at the Union Hotel on Glebe Point Road in inner Sydney. His coat of many colours attracted celebrity attention on one occasion.

Paul Gearside: 'I had a denim jacket and I'd embroidered Lou Reed's silhouette face from *Transformer* on one side, and on the front was Radio Birdman [in text], with red teardrops dripping blood. Across the back in sky-blue cotton was the New York Dolls in script. I was sitting there, and this voice said, "The New York Dolls! What a great band!" I turned around and this guy sitting behind me looked a bit like Harpo Marx. We got talking and had a few beers. It was only when I got home that I realised it was Brett Whiteley!'

The Radios' ongoing enactment of the sounds of these heroes still wasn't to the taste of the broader community, including the no-nonsense organiser of one gig at Randwick.

Lee Taylor: 'He says to Rob, why don't you play some decent rock and roll? And quick as a flash Rob says, you mean like Johnny O'Keefe? And the guy said, yeah! That was very Rob. So fast. It was kind of a dare because this guy was tough and Rob shut him up.'

Jules R.B. Normington had stepped back as the band's manager to focus on the Ripple Records operation. Mark Sisto took the chair, handling band business from Jules's shop.

Mark Sisto: 'Where I was living at the time didn't have a phone, so I had to go down to Jules's record store and try and make phone calls in there.'

Meanwhile, with the recording for what was planned to be a four-track EP completed, the Radios continued to work towards a full album.

Several formerly underground American acts were now hitting their stride commercially: Kiss with *Destroyer*—on the back of the breakthrough phenomenon that was the *Kiss Alive* album—Aerosmith's *Rocks* and, most strikingly, the Blue Oyster Cult's fourth studio effort, *Agents of Fortune*, with the huge radio hit '(Don't Fear) The Reaper'. Some weren't overly comfortable with the minor change of instrumentation credits for Eric Bloom on the cover.

Rob Younger: 'I got suspicious when BOC dropped the "stun" guitar . . .'

Birdman were close to fully realised themselves. They were now tapping the high-energy rock ceremony of the MC5—minus their politics and freewheeling jazz element—the Stooges for raw animal ferocity and fury, the symbolism and mystique of the Blue Oyster Cult, the surly Altamont-era teachings of the Stones and Alice Cooper's pre-*School's Out* records. They were so hot, one showing on Bondi Road had a fiery conclusion.

Julie Mostyn: 'They played at a party of a friend of ours, Peter Brandon, who's now sadly passed away. Afterwards, the house burned down! Peter has never been so proud of anything in his whole life! That was his big badge of honour!'

The plan was for everyone soon to have such an item.

'Teengenerate: entitles holder to destroy himself' read one of the Radio Birdman fan-club membership cards. It was part of a range of promotional items, including bumper stickers, designed by Paul Gearside, who founded the club in July 1976.

Paul Gearside: 'I thought we needed a badge and, because of the look of the band, we needed patches and a newsletter. And I couldn't be Paul Gearside, so I became "Cloven Skull". I knew I could do a good drawing to go with it. I remember Warwick and I getting pissed one afternoon and just reams of paper lying around later, with all these cloven skulls we'd drawn.'

On the face of it, the coolest, most off-the-grid outfit in the country having a fan club might have seemed naff. However, this operation would be about so much more than sending members information about the favourite colour of their heroes; instead, it would play a major role in helping direct operations.

Besides, a few years earlier, both Rob and Deniz had written to Iggy Pop's fan club.

Rob Younger: 'The badge was a big one, about three-and-a-half inches in diameter, and it said "Iggy Pop—Hardcore Star".'

Things were firming up on other fronts. 'Roy Larsen' from the 'National Affairs Desk' issued Birdman's first media release, which was 'declassified' on 21 August 1976. Spiked with war imagery and terms such as 'offensive', 'attack' and 'tours of duty', as well as a blurring of fact that was part-theatric and part-mystical, it read like the earliest Blue Oyster Cult promotional material, stating that the true story behind the unit's beginnings were 'unimaginable to the human mind'.

The listing of the band personnel was just as interesting, with Ron 'Ya Habibi' Keeley—'Ya Habibi', bestowed by Deniz Tek meaning 'beloved', and also an eatery at Bondi where Ron enjoyed the Lebanese rolls—who was aged 'one third', Warwick '999' Gilbert, Chris 'Boy King' Masuak, Deniz Tek 'alias Steve McGarrett', and Rob 'Random Grooves' Younger.

In keeping with the MC5 and their early link with the White Panthers, the release also spelt out in a semi-lighthearted manner an associate hierarchy: Minister for Defence and Information was 'Marque Steiphane Sisteaux' [Mark Sisto], with Minister of Resources Jules R.B. Normington, and Chief of Security Johnny Kannis.

It all played into the notion of solidarity, an all-for-one code and gang culture, which was led from the front by Deniz.

Warwick Gilbert: 'Deniz was a uniting force and espoused a brotherhood. Those were the words he used. We even had our own kind of language.'

Chris Masuak: 'It was camaraderie, it was friendship, it was loyalty, it was commitment to each other and to what we were doing. There was a definite feeling of "us". We were separate from the rest and were clearly perceived as such. We did feel unique, in the true sense of the word.'

And that feeling would radiate outwards to those around them.

The new name in the media release was 'manager and agent' George Kringas, a friend of Gearside and Gilbert. Kringas was an architect who would be involved in the restoration of Sydney's historic Queen Victoria Building, while his brother, Chris, had spearheaded the design of the High Court in Canberra. George had no track record whatsoever in the music industry, but was a smart operator.

Paul Gearside: 'He lived up the road from me and I'd see him in the street. George was a beatnik. He'd have his calico linen hippie pants on and his beads and his hair and beard.'

The pair got acquainted and Kringas asked Gearside over one night.

Paul Gearside: 'We were sitting on cushions on the floor and he played some music like John Coltrane and it totally uninterested me.'

They became tight, however, and Paul took George to the Oxford. As had been the case with so many others, Kringas was transformed.

Paul Gearside: 'He put Coltrane on the backburner. He loved the Oxford.'

George's journey to becoming a larger-than-life character, with his nickname of Bu Riviera embroidered on his pants and being the life of any party, had begun.

One such soirée was at a shared terrace house on Bronte Road, the scene of Ron Keeley's very crowded 30th birthday party.

Sarah Bishop (Birdman devotee): 'It was a Gothic horror theme. Mark Sisto turned up in robes, with a fish head on a broom handle.'

Just as attention grabbing was the coming update to the manual for the coming punk movement which had been in production for several years. Rarely has a recorded disaster been so instructive.

New Homo Sapiens 2.0

The September 1976 release of *Metallic K.O.*, on French label Skydog, framed the Stooges' violent decline and thudding final stage fall. Subtitled 'Open Up and Bleed', it was said at the time to be a recording of 'the last ever Iggy and the Stooges show' from 9 February 1974 at the Michigan Palace in Detroit. Later, it was believed to be an earlier date of 6 October 1973 at the Palace on one side, and the final stand in February on the other.

In any event, the record was a suitably chaotic exit point and for many their introduction to the Stooges and Iggy's nihilistic, death-or-glory antics, the poor sound quality only adding to the air of car-crash fatalism. It would allegedly become the biggest-selling album in the Stooge catalogue, despite being an after-the-fact release to make a few desperately needed dollars.

Ron Asheton (Iggy and the Stooges): 'I saw this whiskey bottle coming [out of the crowd]. A pint-sized bottle with about a third left hit the end of the piano and exploded in spray. That was like, "Whoa!"

'They [the crowd] were going for Iggy, but everyone else was in the line of fire. The guy that just missed him with the beer can, you hear that on the record. I saw it come out of the lights and it was a full can of beer, and it missed his head by, seriously, two inches. It would have really done some heavy damage. I just went, "Good arm, man!"'

Metallic K.O. would have a huge impact worldwide, including the coming Sydney punk scene. Another incendiary device was set off during a lunch at the home of Anthony O'Grady.

Deniz Tek: 'I was sitting near [Skyhook] Red Symons and I didn't recognise him. He was saying something and seemed like he was bragging. I said, "Excuse me, but are we supposed to know who you are?" He took that as an insult. Rob [Younger] thought it was hilarious.'

Younger wasn't quite so jovial following a Birdman appearance at Hurstville Civic Centre. Although the venue's bouncers were notoriously firm, during the gig security were actually concerned that Rob, lying on the stage howling, was in pain and required assistance. They would not be quite so caring at a future engagement.

Mushroom Records head honcho Michael Gudinski came to the show to check out the band.

Rob Younger: 'I think Anthony O'Grady would have encouraged him to come along. I remember Gudinski swinging into the room going, "Good set, boys!" This sort of thing. I thought, "Who's this? Oh, I know who that guy is." Then you think, "Why would he be interested in us? Why would he know what we were doing?" We really thought no one else had a fucking clue what we were on about, and for someone from a record company to come in and say we were good, or we were bad, would have meant fuck all.

'And they offer an opinion about you, and you hear them speak about other things they might like—not that we talked to Gudinski at all, as far as I remember. Then you find out what the person's like and you probably prefer they didn't like you, because they're dickheads. They've got taste up their arse. I would have summed this bloke up in five seconds flat.

That was the thinking at the time, anyway. We had that outsider thing and relished it.'

The sessions at Trafalgar continued. They took an upward turn when Deniz, at the urging of Charles Fisher, tapped into his love of the Stones, the Kinks and the Who, and teen anthems such as 'Satisfaction', 'The Kids Are Alright' and 'Baba O'Riley'.

Deniz Tek: 'I came up with "New Race". The central idea is mutation, or transformation, from the human race into a less flawed type of being—Homo Sapiens 2.0. It has nothing to do with the idea of "racial" identity groups as currently understood. The word "race" is in it only because "race" is a much better lyric than "Gonna be a new species", although the meaning would be the same.

'So I had this idea, but the song was supposed to be a "teen anthem", per Charles Fisher's request. I started with Pete Townshend's "teenage wasteland" concept and welded the idea onto that. Of course, teens are going to mess up any new transformation, and the coming "enlightenment" is going to have a decidedly teenaged skew—it would have to include a lot of sex, drugs, and rock and roll!

'"Punching out" is the aviation term for ejecting from a damaged airplane. The sense here is of jumping out of the cycle of karma—circular time—and into a more linear—or at least spiral—upward progression. Nobody got that. Any teen movement needs a chant or a slogan. Ours comes from a Robert Crumb comic book that had a drawing of a beatnik playing bongos and saying, "Yeah hup". I often went to comic books—Crumb or Justin Green, mainly—for lyric ideas. Although there was a serious concept at the core of it, like most of the tunes I wrote in that period, the song was meant to be fun, humorous and delivered with a wink. Levity superimposed on seriousness.

'The crowd had already been doing raised-fist salutes, but it was more of a "Right on, motherfuckers!" sort of thing. Once we started playing "New Race", the [chorus] line sort of got merged with that.'

Charles Fisher: 'I fucking loved it! I thought if we could get this out on a commercial release, this was going to be a hit.'

Penny Ward: 'One night they [the band] said to Jules and me, "Come down to the rehearsal room at Studio 20 behind the Oxford." They'd been fighting, you could feel it, and they said, "We've got a new song. Do you want to hear it?" And they played "New Race" and oh my god! That was just an amazing experience, because it was a brand-new song and no one had ever heard it—and in this tiny room it was just incredible!'

In early October, legendary gonzo writer, and author of *Fear and Loathing in Las Vegas*, Hunter S. Thompson, spoke at Sydney Town Hall. Deniz and Mark Sisto could have done what Tek and Dare Jennings did for Lou Reed, and presented Thompson with a T-shirt. Instead the Birdman went one step beyond simply being a member of the audience once more.

Deniz Tek: 'I asked a question: "What's the most disturbing thing you have ever seen?" He said it was seeing a guy get his head pushed through the plexiglass front of a jukebox, and when he pulled his head back out, it cut his ears off. Then he said, "No, actually, it was Richard Nixon's inaugural speech." I got him to autograph a dollar bill and I kept it in my copy of *Fear and Loathing*.'

The women in Radio Birdman's audience at the Oxford had no need for either of those emotions. They weren't just eager participants and supporters, they gave the room and scene colour, shade, warmth, dynamics and a strength. There were no bouncers and there was no need.

Julie Mostyn: 'It was just the perfect music to rebel to and fantastic music to dance to—women love dancing—not just sort of bouncing up and down a bit. Radio Birdman wasn't just a male phenomenon, by any means. It was a female one as well.'

Tara Anderson: 'We were always down the front and no one hassled us, and we danced the night away. Boys didn't push you out of the way to get in front of you. We always felt safe.'

Alley Brereton: 'At the Lifesaver, you always had all these arsehole men trying to pick you up or grab at you, but you never had that at the Oxford. The guys didn't do that. They were more thoughtful.'

Abby Beaumont: 'Women could go there on their own. It kind of changed a lot of things. There were a lot more girls than would usually be going to see a band, because they wanted to see the band not because their boyfriend did.'

Alley Brereton: 'I guess it was sexually expressive. There were a lot of women, which the other venues didn't have. They were more male orientated. The music was quite sexual, it was quite attractive, so I think that comes into it as well. It was still a sexually charged place without the aggression, without the macho-ness.'

Mark Sisto: 'It was wild, but it was safe. Safely wild.'

For a time, at least.

The Blitzkrieg

The American accent on Illawarra regional radio, south of Sydney, in the second week of November 1976, was striking in both tone and urgency. 'We interrupt this program to bring you the following important message from Steve McGarrett high in the David Stott Building. Hit it!' Deniz Tek's voice then continued over a roaring preview of the Radios' recorded version of the Stooges' 'T.V. Eye': 'Radio Birdman will launch a blitzkrieg attack on Steel City [Wollongong] this Friday night. Killer rock and roll jams starting at 8 pm at the Corrimal Community Hall. Tickets two dollars at the door. Lord have mercy!'

The 'David Stott Building' was a reference to WABX, the legendary Detroit radio station that had helped fire Tek's youth. The announcement gave the impression the outfit's position—while growing in popularity—was far loftier than it was.

With rare exceptions, Birdman had studiously torched everything behind them at virtually every turn. Even Chequers in inner Sydney, which hosted every conceivable act in the country, didn't want the Radios—or their crowd—coming down their marble staircase, thank you very much. And there was no fucking way they were going to hang out at the Manzil Room at Kings Cross until 4 am, surrounded by industry people and every band they despised. But something had to be done.

Warwick Gilbert: 'We had an impromptu brainstorming session with George Kringas and Paul Gearside after a particularly exciting Radio Birdman gig at the Oxford. We were just thinking of how to push it forward and came up with the idea of the "Blitzkrieg", a series of half-a-dozen gigs with the military kind of metaphor of bombing the city, because the music was really powerful.

'George and I then presented the concept to the band with the proviso that, if successful, he would continue on as manager. I shared a house with George, who had been helping me manage the day-to-day band stuff.'

The idea got the nod. Kringas would finance the venture, which would be organised with the assistance of Trafalgar and led by Gilbert's dynamic poster.

It was a 'Martial Law production' and displayed a diving German World War II Stuka bomber—an idea from the cover art for Jefferson Airplane's *After Bathing at Baxter's* record and their Fillmore West gig poster Warwick bought in his late teens—with a banner of 'Radio Birdman Blitzkrieg' and the now-revamped logo, which had replaced the Blue Oyster Cult symbol on the Birdvan door.

The tone and appearance of the artwork reflected the Oyster Cult's *Secret Treaties* and fed into Deniz's lifelong interest in military history, particularly aviation.

Warwick Gilbert: 'It was inspired by the music of Birdman and the audience reaction and that fervour we tapped into. I'd seen a Messerschmitt [German jet fighter plane] and had an image of that since I was a kid and thought it was terrifying.

'Deniz suggested the Germanic Airkraft lettering for the poster which in turn suggested to me the image of a Stuka in a steep dive.'

'The concept was tongue-in-cheek on my part, designed to attract attention and stand out against the bland stencil-lettered posters of the day. It was to upset the squares, basically. That was the whole point of it. The biggest "Fuck you" we could find.'

And the colours involved were critical: red and black, which were already reflected in the band's flags and banners.

Warwick Gilbert: 'Red, black and white are arresting colours. They're used a lot in propaganda art and they pack a wallop on the street. I was in advertising for a while and did layouts for fashion magazines, and I went on shoots with models and rock bands, which came in handy for the Birdman artwork.'

The poster earned, or perhaps confirmed, Gilbert's new tag—although it was at odds with the man himself—and fed further into the notion of the band as a gang.

Warwick Gilbert: 'Deniz liked to give people nicknames. It was kind of showbiz stuff and it was fun—we all got into it. He and Mark Sisto thought it up, I think, and presented it to me at the Oxford one night. "Hey, we've got this perfect name for you. The War Lord!" I thought, "Oh Jesus . . ."'

The poster projected and heightened the general sense of foreignness around Radio Birdman, an intangible unknown, while the Blitzkrieg expression precisely reflected what the tour dates would be: a strategic, unforgiving lightning war on the eardrum and body in five 'offensives'. They'd take place, largely around Sydney, on Friday and Saturday nights—thus not interfering with Deniz's medical studies—kicking off on 30 October at Hurstville Civic Centre. Birdman would then move on to Balmain Town Hall, Hurstville Civic again, Corrimal Community Hall, and wind up at the Bondi Lifesaver, on 13 November.

Warwick Gilbert: 'The Blitzkrieg concept established the band's graphic image right there. That moment was the height of our career, I think. But if there wasn't a killer band at the centre of it, none of it would have worked.'

Promoter Bob Yates had run many highly successful gigs around Sydney, including huge nights at the Paddington and Balmain town halls, for everyone from Captain Matchbox and Uncle Bob's Band, to Skyhooks, the Sports and even Tiny Tim—as well as university folk shows. He crossed paths with Warwick while Gilbert was putting together the Blitzkrieg art at the Tin Sheds, the Sydney University Art Workshop, where posters-as-political-activism pioneer Chips Mackinolty had operated.

Bob Yates: 'I was there cutting a stencil for a silkscreen for the next Captain Matchbox gig and there was a guy working on the bench next to me very carefully setting up photographic screens. He asked for a hand to hold the screen or something, and I saw he was placing a plane onto what we now know as the Blitzkrieg poster. I'm not too sure he even told me he was the bass player!'

Meanwhile, Charlie Georgees had banded together with Rick Grossman and Mark Kingsmill—they were looking for a singer in the mould of Iggy Pop. The ad in *RAM* placed by Georgees was Ron S. Peno's moment writ large.

Ron S. Peno: 'It said, "Guitarist wants to form/join hard rock band into Dictators, Blue Oyster Cult, MC5," and I just went, "Oh, for fuck's sake!" "Needs lead singer" or something. Oh my God! That's my ad! I've been waiting so long for you!'

Ron soon moved into Jim Dickson's old room at Five Dock manor.

General Patton

In an era when gig posters carried only the base textual information in one colour, the mass display of German Stukas around inner-city Sydney declaring Radio Birdman's Blitzkrieg campaign was like an Andy Warhol art installation in wartime.

Ian Hartley: 'Everybody at school thought the Stuka was the best-looking aeroplane in the world. Spitfires were just plain, but Stukas looked like this demonic thing because the wings were almost Wagnerian.'

The first date of the Blitz was a return to Hurstville Civic Centre, although before only several dozen people. Bob Yates was entrusted with the tour's second.

Bob Yates: 'George Kringas asked if I'd promote the Balmain Town Hall gig. He was wearing tight leather pants and leather jacket and just looked like a try-hard! I told him I didn't think Balmain would work and didn't want to promote it. He then offered to pay me to do it. I did all the things I would do for the Sports or Captain Matchbox, Uncle Bob's Band, etc., but it bombed. Maybe 150 or so.

'They were without a doubt the loudest band to have appeared there—at that stage, anyway—and brought the cops from the station next door. There were three or four of them just standing at the doorway, gaping in astonishment at Rob Younger et al., and eventually left us alone. It was just me and my rather timid folk-singer friend Dan Johnson—one half of the Ward and Johnson folkie duo I managed—running the door. He was so disgusted with me for dealing with a band like that, he yelled in my ear, "These guys can't play for shit!" And he left me to it, after twenty minutes of them onstage.

'George was pissed off at me when it failed and didn't want to pay me, because he said he hadn't seen any posters up for it. I gave him all the poster locations and he must have driven round and checked, because he rang and apologised and sent me a cheque.'

The second appearance at Hurstville as part of the tour was a near riot—and not in a good way.

Warwick Gilbert: 'We used to graffiti dressing-rooms where we played, and put our name and the symbol up there. The bouncers locked us in and stood over us and tried to get us to scrub it off. Black-belt karate used by nincompoops. Because their girlfriends liked us, they were jealous and wanted to make an example of us, but George was really good. He got us out of that.'

Mark Sisto: 'It was just chaos. A free for all. You didn't know who to hit. There were a couple of big footy-player type bouncers and so it was a challenge to get out of there with the equipment and without being smacked!'

Down at Corrimal, near Wollongong, the lack of attendance was a disaster and the band mood pre-show was poor, until Deniz Tek marshalled the troops.

Warwick Gilbert: 'There was only about three people there. Kannis was in the dressing-room dejected, sitting in the corner and we were all a bit glum. Deniz was pacing backwards and forwards—which he did quite often if he had something on his mind—and at an ever-increasing rate. Suddenly, he blasted

Kannis with this General Patton kind of speech and said, "There's people out there!"

'It was such an energising, heroic address. It was astonishing and we all snapped out of it. By the time we got out on stage, we were ready to eat the curtain or something! And instinctively, we just took our hands off the instruments and let this feedback, this wailing siren of feedback, fill the hall, and we crunched into the first song and blew the shit out of the place. By the time we finished our set, the place was full of people punching the air. It was an extraordinary gig. Deniz with his American chutzpah. Us Australians would have given up and gone home!'

In contrast, the final date at the Bondi Lifesaver was huge—almost inexplicably so—before more than a thousand people. In response, the band clocked up almost three hours, playing every song they knew and several they didn't. They were elated by the response and the trays of drinks that were customarily brought to the stage never tasted sweeter. It gave them more than hope. This was vindication.

Warwick Gilbert: 'Five encores with a packed house. Sweat dripping down the walls and people standing on tables!'

Mike Hurst: 'They blew the roof off the venue. People jumped up on the longest bar in town and danced. I had a grin ear to ear.'

Hurst did a piece in the *Mirror* under the heading of 'Birdman—Underground Explosion'. 'Not a new FM station,' he wrote, 'Radio Birdman . . . have developed a sizeable following with their raucous brand of brutal rock. They are the focal point for the kind of energy interchange which existed . . . with the advent of groups like the Rolling Stones and the Doors.'

Despite the generally small crowds and bouncers with itchy trigger fingers, on stage the Radios soared each night during the Blitzkrieg run.

Warwick Gilbert: 'It was the perfect balance in that five piece. All kind of working together like the pistons in an engine. Like the Rolling Stones, it works one way and you don't fuck with it. I thought it was extraordinary. Most bands sounded like stodge compared to us. There was no fat on it. And I like the fact it was kind of aerodynamic. That was how I thought of it and how I approached the bass—to make the music aerodynamic.

'What happened was the guitars were actually turned up on the edge of feedback and they created all this extra ghost noise in the live sound. Stepping onstage, you simply knew it was the best band on the planet, and so did the audience. It was real, not imagined, not fake, which was what I loved about it. Raw power.'

Ron Keeley: 'There was a phrase we had in the early days, called "riding the razor's edge", which was basically about playing as hard and fast and pushing it as much as we could. If it all just fell apart into a great mess, then that was part of the deal.'

Deniz Tek: 'We were very deeply committed and when it didn't go off for us, it felt devastating. We would beat ourselves up. Zero complacency.'

Rob Younger: 'The Blitzkrieg period was when we couldn't pull anyone. We had a poster that looked far grander than what the band were doing. It made it look like something might have been happening.'

But something was. Lee Taylor had got used to walking through the streets of Sydney with Younger and having the singer acknowledged by passers-by. But when Deniz was approached at the Oxford one night. something seemed to have changed.

Lee Taylor: 'It wasn't a girl looking for an excuse to talk. It was a young guy and he asked Deniz for an autograph. Deniz took it all in his stride, but I was thinking, "Shit, this is something. They're my mates! They can't be famous!" It was the beginning.'

Personality Crisis

War wasn't just an aesthetic for Radio Birdman—it was art imitating life, in a grouping that was a fateful collision of very different individuals. It was a highly combustible alliance but one that generated a rapturous response from fans.

Animosity would often seep into plain sight, and theatrical physical altercations on stage were anything but a mirror of the play-acting of Alice Cooper. The conflict between Rob Younger and Ron Keeley was only one of the ongoing skirmishes that were completely indivisible from the music.

Jules R.B. Normington: 'I think it was during rehearsals at Studio 20 and they [Younger and Keeley] just went berko and I'm standing there trying to find the courage to speak up. I wanted to tell them off. Like, "For fuck's sake, guys! You're acting like children! What you're creating here is massively brilliant! Don't you fucking get it? Stop this stupid shit! Rob, leave Ron alone, and, Ron, just play the drums." That's what I *wanted* to say and I remember all this going through my head. But I thought [if I said anything] they'd tear shreds off me and I'd be out of the friendship group.'

Penny Ward: 'They created that music because of the conflict. It's hell for the band but it was good for the music.'

Brad Franks: 'You never knew whether they'd end up beating each other up on stage. There was many a night that ended in them fighting. They were so intense about the music.'

Warwick Gilbert: 'There is a price you pay to create something like that. I think the volatility of it was its essence. I mean, without even playing a note there were sparks amongst people [within Birdman] who rubbed each other up the wrong way. Everyone did—for whatever reason—in our own unique way! The different strong personalities created a certain electricity.'

Ron Keeley: 'It was us against the world, most definitely—but also it was us against each other from time to time. The personalities . . . could really screw it up.'

John Needham: 'Birdman had the unique ability to take all the inner hostility and conflict they had towards each other, and just get on a stage and broadcast it; sort of deflect it out into the audience. It had a transforming effect if you were in the crowd.'

There were other impacts. The Blitzkrieg campaign would have a magnetism well beyond its original scope and duration, particularly for some young males who—like Deniz Tek and Mark Sisto—had a fascination for military history, worshipped Sven Hassel's books about German soldiers during World War II, and owned Airfix replica kits of fighter planes, bombers, tanks and the like.

Richard Burgman: 'When they used "blitzkrieg" on the posters, it was like, "We are a war machine! We are at war with the world, man! We don't give a fuck!"'

Ron Keeley: 'It was like setting out to battle and we're going to kill 'em. That was very much the attitude. Send them home knowing they'd been in a maelstrom.'

But while the imagery held enormous allure for some, for others another element began to emerge.

Tara Anderson: 'It [Birdman] appealed to a different type of male. "New Race" is a perfect example. That was a fun dancing song, then it became like a war cry or something. It was quite peculiar how that changed.'

Way Above the Pay Grade of Mere Mortals

'Thank you! Thank you very kindly! It is a great pleasure to me to bring to you at this particular time, nationally and internationally known as the hardest-working man in show business, Rob Younger and the fabulous Radio Birdman!'

It was Tuesday, 23 November 1976, just over a week after the Blitzkrieg tour had concluded, and Mark Sisto was enthusiastically introducing the band to the audience of 2JJ, as if he was heralding the arrival of James Brown at the Apollo. It was Birdman's second live-to-air for the station that year and they blasted through a marathon sixteen-song session.

Pip Hoyle, or 'Doctor Gonzo' as Deniz tagged him—a character from Hunter S. Thompson's *Fear and Loathing in Las Vegas*—was back for the night, his keyboards dancing and cascading across the onslaught. Chris Masuak probably wondered what the fuck was going on.

Just days later, the Sex Pistols released their near-symphonic riot of a single, 'Anarchy in the UK'—followed by an infamous, expletive-laden interview with Bill Grundy on Thames Television. As England screamed, Rob Younger began the process of discerningly snapping up seven-inch items from the rising punk scene.

Rob Younger: 'As far as impressions go, I'd say "Anarchy in the UK", on first hearing, remains the most lasting.'

New York's Ramones had also made an impression.

Deniz Tek: 'The Ramones showed how we could be more simple, and increase the power level even further. I don't know if there would have been a "New Race" or "More Fun", if the Ramones hadn't come along.'

Radio Birdman hovered above the growing punk scenes of London and New York like an out-of-body experience. Not only had they been there first, drawing on the now-hip Stooges and New York Dolls, they were a precision power machine—as opposed to the spiky, snotty DIY musicianship of most of the new young punks.

Tim Pittman (later founder and director of concert promotion and artist management Feel Presents): 'Punk led you to believe anyone could grab a guitar, but listening to Birdman was to hear something way above the pay grade of us mere mortals.'

Chris Masuak: 'I wasn't interested in punk rock. The Ramones sounded fresh and the Sex Pistols clearly stood out from the pack. But they weren't inspiring from a guitar player's perspective. Birdman set their bar much higher.'

Yet for many, punk would come to legitimise the Radios, or at least place them in recognised space.

The outfit had already stripped down, almost as if in anticipation, uncoupling from the on-stage teaming of Johnny Kannis and Mark Sisto in the Glutonics as their backing singers. It had been an arrangement that the purist in Rob Younger was never going to endlessly tolerate.

Rob Younger: 'I saw this video of us and Sisto and Kannis, and it looked like a fucking mess. It looked comical. I said, "I don't want these guys anymore." I didn't want it to become sloppy and be a bunch of people just wandering around the stage looking clownish.'

Others saw pure bliss, like Shelley Kay, who had come to Sydney from Toowoomba.

Shelley Kay (Birdman devotee): 'I just felt like this [Radio Birdman] was a secret. It was ours. Other people didn't get it or didn't know it because they lived in a stereotypical world. I felt like it defined my difference in how I saw society and the world because that music was fierce and challenging and threatening and wasn't the norm and I gravitated to that so much. It was just the peak experience to me! It was very unconventional, counterculture, anti-fashion and it just was the best!'

Jim Flowers (Birdman devotee): 'I felt as though I was devoting my life to following Birdman. I really thought they were significant enough to give up everything that I had previously thought important, such as formal education and family.'

Frank Cotterell (Birdman devotee, Waterfront Records): 'Radio Birdman gave me a reason to know what I was doing every spare moment when they were playing. They were actually a lifestyle. They stood against mediocrity. I'm getting excited just talking about it now.'

Julie Mostyn: 'It would be a week of excitement leading up to a gig. It wasn't just the night itself. I was working for the Australian Opera and also had this other side of my life with wild rock and roll. It was a good balance actually. So by the time the night arrived for the gig, I'd be racing up the stairs, running at top speed! I remember Johnny Kannis saying once, he was standing at the top of the stairs, "That's the way everyone should come to one of these gigs!" The music matched the way we felt. We all would wear the T-shirts or the badges or whatever. It gave us that community.'

Paul Gearside: 'The nervousness that we felt, not even being in the band, before they came on! They're coming! They're coming! And they'd pick up their instruments and one of them might say hi into the microphone and we thought, wow! they're talking to us!'

Catherine Kingsmill (Birdman devotee, artist): 'It was a collective euphoria. You didn't care about school even though you were doing your HSC, it was just like, fuck that, all you could wait for was Friday night and Saturday night.'

Dare Jennings: 'We'd all drunk the Kool-Aid about Detroit and punk and we were believers. There was a revolution and we were part of it! We felt righteous! We were changing the world at that point and what we were doing was meaningful.'

Other conscripts were now coming from an unexpected quarter. Uncle Bob's Band, the inner-Sydney hippie phenomenon, had shifted operations to Melbourne. Some of their followers in the harbour city turned their attention elsewhere.

Toby Creswell: 'All of their fans started going to see Radio Birdman—the art-school crowd, I suppose. Everybody I knew did. They cut their hair and got tighter trousers. Uncle Bob's Band had this weird idea of mixing jazz with rock, and that was a different idea to Billy Thorpe [and his massively amplified boogie]. Birdman was the next idea that came along.'

That was until there was a forced break in the broadcast of the rebellion.

Deniz returned to Ann Arbor in December, as he had in previous years, but this time his absence was for several months and had a far greater impact.

Deniz Tek: 'It is true in retrospect Radio Birdman had momentum, and me taking an extended leave of absence was probably detrimental from a promotional or business sense. But I didn't think that way—the idea of a strategy for the band's commercial development, other than purely musical, never came into my head.

'That trip was for purely selfish reasons. First and foremost was seeing my parents and brothers. I also wanted to see friends. The other reason was to get plugged in to the local culture, primarily the music. I felt like I needed a recharge of my batteries, so to speak.'

Back in the USA

The Roadhouse in Ann Arbor was ground zero, and the last men standing with regards to the 'Detroit sound' were making an appearance: the Sonic's Rendezvous Band—MC5 guitarist the ice-cool Fred 'Sonic' Smith and Stooges drummer Scott 'Rock Action' Asheton, with Scott Morgan from the Rationals on guitar and Gary Rasmussen, bass. They were virtually just a local bar band. There were no country-crossing tours, nor spots on major festivals with the big acts of the day before tens of thousands.

One audience member, a former local and now resident of Sydney, Australia, was blown away by the SRB experience.

Deniz Tek: 'Seeing Sonic's Rendezvous Band was a revelation to me! It was *so* real and *so* great! The Stooges were finished, the MC5 were done—all that good stuff that was happening in Ann Arbor was over with. Then I went to see Sonic's Rendezvous and thought, "This is it! It's come back! That stream has bubbled up from underneath and is on the surface again, right here in this club. Right now, this is where it is." I was so happy. It renewed my faith in things.'

Tek hardly melted into the background. He was quickly noticed by another former Stooge, guitarist Ron Asheton.

Ron Asheton: 'I was sitting there, going, "Jesus, look at these two guys dancing!" They were almost busting their heads on the ceiling. It was Deniz Tek and his brother. They came up to me after the show and introduced themselves. Deniz called me up a few days later and explained all the stuff he was doing.'

Tek had taken a few preview copies of Birdman's soon-to-be-released *Burn My Eye* EP with him for family and friends. He played a copy to Ron and Scott Asheton and Fred Smith.

Ron Asheton: '"I-94" and "Burned My Eye"—we played the hell out of that!'

Asheton and Tek hit it off immediately—not just musically, but with a shared interest in military history—and started hanging out and jamming. Deniz revealed a song he was working on called 'Hit Them Again', which he and Ron played in a local bar with the MC5's Dennis Thompson on drums.

Tek was no doubt quietly pinching himself and made a rough cassette of the performance. Ron Asheton also had the tingles. He was without a band and here was this young hot-shot, arriving with great promise. It had to be a sign. Ron made repeated overtures about working together in a more serious manner, but Deniz wasn't staying.

The home fires back in Australia were kept burning with the Slow Death Obsession Test that was distributed by Paul Gearside via the fan club, and named in part after the song by the Flamin' Groovies.

Paul Gearside: 'We were into the Groovies, and [their song] "Slow Death" sounded fun and intense. It was just a chance for the fans to rave about their heroes. There were no wrong answers. Everyone was a winner!'

Radios devotees sent in typed or handwritten responses—one partly in French—to express their joy and devotion.

Up in Brisbane, another band had suddenly found themselves getting some love, and landing on the world map. Back in August 1976, unknown to anyone outside the Queensland capital and tired of industry rejection, the Saints independently released their first single, '(I'm) Stranded', and pressed 500 copies on their own Fatal label.

Following a review in UK weekly *Sounds* that declared '(I'm) Stranded' to be the 'single of this and every week', a fuse had been lit. It saw EMI UK demand the label's Australia wing sign them forthwith. The record company then relocated the band from Brisbane to Sydney in January 1977 and released their blistering debut album.

Although not on the same level internationally, Radio Birdman were making an impression in *RAM*'s readers' poll, while Melbourne's *Juke* magazine carried an article headed 'Radio Badman—Raw Rock Power'. Intended typo or not, it hit the mark.

Those closely associated with Birdman were enjoying the reflected glory.

Paul Gearside: 'People would come up to me and say, "Are you the Cloven Skull?" I'd say, "No, that's someone else, but I know him. Or her." "But you know Radio Birdman?" they'd ask. "Come and we'll buy you a beer and you can tell us all about them." They wanted in, and I was an in. That's how strong the band was. People wanted to be part of it and you couldn't blame them.'

Deniz arrived back in Sydney in February 1977. The volcanic fault line which ran through the Birdhouse, chiefly between Rob Younger and Ron Keeley, a clash kept to a functional simmer by Tek's presence, had wrenched open while he was away. It added to the general disquiet about his lengthy absence.

Deniz Tek: 'I found out later that some of them were unhappy about it, although they never voiced anything to me at the time. That was always one of the biggest internal band problems—refusal to actually communicate. So you only find out there is an issue when it's too late to do anything about it.'

Tek had got what he needed and more from his experiences in Ann Arbor. He was refreshed and fired up after both he and his band had all but been anointed by their heroes. Not to mention that he had a song with Ron Asheton in his back pocket.

Deniz Tek: 'When I came back full of energy and inspiration, my goal was to share it with them and make our band stronger. I didn't want us to *be* Sonic's Rendezvous Band, but I wanted to use some of their spirit and bring as much of that purity and truth as I could to my own band. Apparently, the guys didn't value it as much. I didn't feel completely welcomed. The negativity which I experienced came as a surprise.'

Tek was not genetically equipped to pull back and apologise. Nor was he about to go into negotiations. Birdman were a gang and a brotherhood, but as far as Deniz was concerned, although it was never openly stated, they were *his* gang. The Tek way kicked in.

Deniz Tek: 'When the others didn't contribute to the musical direction of the band, I thought I could just do it all myself. They could help me, or get out of the way, but I didn't expect anything from them, except to play as well and as hard as possible. I never considered what they might have wanted from me. I was "doing my own thing". I now have a better understanding of the value of team effort, but I was certain of the direction I wanted to go and that was my priority above everything else.

'Those guys brought a lot of talent and power to the equation. I was well aware of that, but I didn't think they had the vision thing down, and an alternative was never offered, anyway. My relationship with Rob—and to a certain extent Pip—was different. We were much more on the same wavelength.

'I wasn't a total dictator, though. I actually did encourage the others to write, and I did work with whatever they submitted. I was always open to try ideas the guys had, even in the recording studio, although if an idea didn't work for me and Rob, it would likely end up as an outtake.'

Some saw more than just a sharpening of the band's future direction.

Warwick Gilbert: 'It all changed. It wasn't any fun anymore. He [Deniz] didn't need us any longer. And let us know he was a friend of Ron Asheton and we could fuck off, basically. He didn't say that, but it was palpable.

'He didn't communicate directly with us any further, and he cut Ron and I out of the creative and financial decision-making process and installed George Kringas as go-between. Thereafter, Deniz made the decisions without consulting us. We were basically treated as session musicians. There was no camaraderie after that. It created a lot of terrible tension in the band and basically split the band into two groups.'

Ron Keeley: 'He did come back a different person. He was more distant and his songs had changed. The tonality was different.'

Masuak felt his views, even when sought, were now deemed of little consequence or use and so withdrew from band meetings.

Chris Masuak: 'There was this astonishing behaviour suddenly towards band members, as if they were suddenly some kind of enemy. It got very confrontational and became us against them—the triad of Tek, Younger and Kringas. That ruptured the friendship and the loyalty.'

150 Sonics' LPs

White Light Records, suitably positioned underneath the centre of Sydney in the Tank Stream Arcade, had recalibrated. Owner Mark Taylor, who would become one of the world's foremost collectors of sixties' garage punk, was already across the Ramones and the New York Dolls, having ordered 25 copies of the Ramones' first album, purely based on the look of the cover in *Billboard* magazine; the same with the Dolls' debut.

Mark Taylor: 'We came up with the concept of combining sixties' garage and Ramones-style punk rock. It was our reaction to the flood of disco and rock, such as the Eagles, that was everywhere at the time. We didn't know of any other store anywhere in the world that only sold punk rock, because, besides White Light, there wasn't one.'

The store had closed in January 1977 to redecorate, dump the old-world stock of Steely Dan, Rodriguez, Santana and bootlegs.

White Light reopened in late February, ushering in a new age and brandishing the first album from the UK's contribution to the punk movement.

Mark Taylor: 'The Damned's LP was released the same week we reopened. We had it in the window, directly airfreighted from the UK.'

The new store was an early seventies' *Creem* magazine come to life, with the racks filled with imported, near impossible to find records by the Stooges, the MC5, the Seeds, the Pink

Fairies, the Flamin' Groovies, the Velvet Underground and the New York Dolls. And not just an act's second or third album but multiples of their entire catalog. Seeing six copies of the Stooges' first LP was quite a moment. There were also cool overseas magazines, a sea of singles from the Sex Pistols to Dave Edmunds—rock and roll nerdvana, basically. For those deep in the suburbs, White Light was a charging station, a place to get supplies to take back into the wilderness.

Radio Birdman insider Lee Taylor—no relation—was hired for his expertise in sixties' garage punk, and rock and roll generally, and somehow managed to import 150 copies of the Sonics' out-of-print *Explosives* album.

Mark Taylor: '*Explosives*, together with the Stooges and MC5, is what really excited Sydney punters in 1976 and 1977. We bent over backwards to get the right stuff from all over the world. We knew we could sell hundreds of the Stooges' LPs, if only we could get them. They were only available in France, so we tracked down a supplier. Same with the Saints 45, "I'm Stranded". We bought 100 copies direct from [Saints guitarist] Ed Kuepper in Brisbane.'

The shop would also set fashion trends long before Kmart and Target stepped into that market.

Mark Taylor: 'White Light Records sold by far the first-ever Ramones T-shirts available anywhere in the world. They were printed for us by Dare Jennings to our adaptation of the first LP cover, a few months after the first Ramones LP came out. I wore one in New York and people were coming up to me in Central Park, asking where they could get one. Even John Holmstrom from *Punk Magazine* wanted to buy one when he visited the store in early 1977. I reckon White Light invented the Ramones T-shirt. Hell, I know we did!'

Hovering over it all were Radio Birdman, the virtual house band—although the shop was too tiny to ever permit a performance. It was an outlet for all the Radios loved and helped popularise, and with arch fans behind the counter including an actual Birdman in Rob Younger who worked there for a period. White Light would also act as a social network and secret musical appreciation society.

But while one door had opened, another seemed set to close for the band with the sale of the Oxford, their spiritual base. It seemed that, again, they'd be at the mercy of horrified venue owners and gleefully overzealous bouncers.

Thankfully, a petition circulated by the Radios' fan club and quickly filled with supporting signatures plus the diplomacy skills of George Kringas saw victory snatched from the jaws of defeat.

Deniz Tek: 'Our manager was astute enough to go to the new owner and say, "Look, we've got this scene happening and we want to keep doing it. We'll run the music. All you have to do is pick up the profits from selling the alcohol." The guy, goes, "Fine, great arrangement."'

The deal was for six months, after which the upstairs space would become a restaurant. In the interim, Birdman would run the room without interference and receive the door take.

Meanwhile, the band apparently rejected a test or sample pressing of their much-anticipated first release. Then a second. Then a third. This agonising level of sonic scrutiny ultimately saw the dumping of as many as five examples of the vinyl in order to get the volume just right. Or so the story went.

Bob Short: 'The legends are the things that fuelled the fandom.'

Burn My Eye

It was one hell of a recruitment-campaign image. The photo by Abby Beaumont of Rob Younger at the band contest as some primitive shaman appeared in *RAM* in mid-February 1977. It was the call to arms of a mail-order ad for Radio Birdman's long-awaited four-track, seven-inch EP *Burn My Eye*, which could be obtained from their fan-club address in North Sydney for $1.50, plus 30 cents postage.

It was an extraordinary moment. Not only had a Radios record finally seen daylight, but, unlike the New York Dolls, the Stooges and their other heroes, it wasn't on or linked to a major record label. It was all done in house at Trafalgar.

Michael McMartin: 'When the recording of the EP was done, Rob came in and we did the cover, manufactured everything ourselves.'

Charles Fisher: 'Michael was the studio manager and our business brain. I think Rob used to call him Michael McMarketing. Most of the success of the marketing was due to Michael McMartin.'

Boxes of the EP had arrived at Trafalgar in January. The Birdman logo was then imprinted in red on the label of each copy at the studio reception desk.

Angie Pepper: 'I remember sitting with Rob as he stamped the symbol on the labels. He was in a great mood and the gags came thick and fast. That was a lot of fun. I think Warwick was there too. I used to love hanging out with Rob and Warwick together. They would fire off each other and the comedy was absolutely brilliant. They'd have me laughing so hard, I couldn't walk. They could've killed it as a stand-up comedy duo.'

After the advertisement was aired, the band, their circle, the fan club and Team Trafalgar fielded the flood of orders from across the country. The Birdmen drew individual messages, grabs from song lyrics, cartoon-like graphics and calls to 'Fight the war against the jive'—the adopted catchphrase from 'Rock 'n' Roll Soldiers' by the New Order, an outfit featuring ex-Stooge Ron Asheton and former MC5 drummer Dennis Thompson—on the brown-paper packages that were then dispatched from Trafalgar.

Michael McMartin: '[Studio and Birdman publicist] Felicity Surtees was working with me in the office and the band were coming in and packaging, then going to the post office and sending them out. If you did a cost-effective analysis of postage and everything else, you'd go, "What are we doing?" But there weren't any overheads for anybody. There was this partnership.'

Contrary to what the ad in *RAM* stated, *Burn My Eye* was available from select stores, primarily those operated by friends and associates. These included Sydney's Revolver—formerly Ripple—which was managed by Jules R.B. Normington, Mark Taylor's White Light, and Anthem.

The artwork and cover layout were by Warwick Gilbert, as W. Lord [aka War Lord] and the live pic on the front taken at the Bondi Lifesaver. Continuing the tone of the Blitzkrieg tour poster, the EP was numbered Me 109, a reference to the World War II German fighter plane.

The surprise was the cosmetic adjustment to Deniz Tek's appearance, made while he was overseas.

Deniz Tek: 'To my great amusement, they airbrushed sunglasses on me!'

Sonically, the EP, produced by John Sayers and Charles Fisher, lacked the expected punch, but the four tracks were still a huge thrill. There was the freight-train rhythmic momentum of 'Smith and Wesson Blues'; 'Snake', with Chris Masuak on piano; the surf-guitar styled 'I-94' from the TV Jones days, concluding with a long passage of howling guitar feedback; and 'Burned My Eye', which clocked in at under two minutes.

Deniz Tek: 'Burn My Eye' was a Mark [Sisto]-ism—he used to say it as an exclamation of surprise, wonderment, admiration. I never heard anyone else say that. Mark was always drawing the Egyptian Horus [the all-seeing eye], and referencing it in quasi-mystical explanations for things. The eye in the hand was also a well-known Turkish icon. Of course, for me as a teen, there was also the Eye of Agamotto from Dr Strange comics.'

The song titles and Tek's lyrics alone demonstrated just how far Radio Birdman were operating from every other act on the Australian scene. 'I-94' referred to the highway that carves the United States east to west, winding through Ann Arbor and Detroit, while there were also references to Willow Run—the Detroit car assembly and former aircraft-manufacturing plant during World War II—Stroh and Rolling Rock beer, name checks of Garland Jeffreys. References to Jim Morrison, raw power, the O-mind slang from the Stooges' 'Down on the Street' and more were scattered across the other tunes. 'Snake' was about a relationship Deniz had with a woman who lived with a number of the reptiles. She would later feature in several other songs.

The guitars of Masuak and Tek had an interwoven serpentine quality themselves, with the rhythm section of Gilbert and Keeley one indivisible being.

Chris Masuak: 'There's a ton of country in those piano tracks. And more than a little Stones in the guitar parts. There are significantly more influences than people might imagine. That's what gave the band such colour.'

Each of the four songs also had traces of the Blue Oyster Cult's lyrical technique of introducing characters and places, while blurring time and fact.

Deniz Tek: 'Nothing was ever spelled out literally [in the BOC]—it was all metaphor and suggestive imagery. I found this to be an excellent tactic for a lyricist. Each listener can internally write his own story around the framework, viewed through the lens of his or her own life experience and personality. In this way, the power and magic of the storytelling can be amplified exponentially. I tried to write that way and even borrowed some of their memes from time to time.'

Clyde Bramley: 'We went back to Toowoomba and got the EP by mail order and used to just flog it to death. As country boys, we were impressed that you could do that sort of semi-independent thing of putting out things yourself, and then people heard of you and you got a following. So we moved to Sydney as soon as we possibly could, basically!'

Bob Short: 'I'd ordered the single and they needed some posters put up in Wollongong, so George Kringas rang me. I wagged off school and came up [to Sydney from Wollongong to pick up the posters] on the Friday afternoon and saw them rehearse, which was a little bit exciting! It was at Rob and Angie's house at Darlinghurst, in basically the garage out the back. They were playing all these records, like Kraftwerk and James Brown, to get in the mood before they rehearsed, and then [MC5's] "Sister Anne" and *High Time*. Rob had to put a sock over the mike to stop getting electric shocks off the PA because of shit electrics. They were like machines.

'Angie was like the den mother, the quiet voice, a presence. When I went to that rehearsal I got the immediate impression . . . they're in her house and everyone chills the fuck out! They didn't argue with each other, they didn't bitch and moan—which I'd seen them do on other occasions. They were on their best behaviour.'

The Fun House

The notion of rebranding the Oxford as the Oxford Fun House—or simply the Fun House—in homage to the second Stooges' album, had been tossed about for several months before firming into a reality around late February 1977.

'Strictly rock and roll,' the posters would soon read each Friday and Saturday night, 'from 7.30 pm to 10 pm.'

The admission fee jumped from fifty cents to one dollar, but the beer was still Toohey's Draught and KB, unless you had chipped in for a bottle of Jack Daniel's or Pernod. Mandrax remained a recreational choice although dancing was as always the major pursuit.

Several upgrades came as part of the Radios' new order for the venue.

Rob Younger: 'We changed the sign, using the lettering based on the *Fun House* album. It doesn't sound very original an idea now, but back then no one knew the record even existed. If you called a place the Fun House these days, everyone would go, "Oh dear . . ."'

The other big move was the installation of a jukebox that came to life when a band was not performing or between sets. It was mostly stocked with singles from Rob Younger's collection, as well as those belonging to Angie Pepper. There was everything from surf music and Motown to the Ramones' 'Blitzkrieg Bop' and the Sex Pistols' 'Anarchy in the UK'.

Lee Taylor: 'There wasn't a dud there. And it was stuff that was highly collectible. Not stuff to just be thrown on a jukebox!'

Rob Younger: 'They were simply cool 45s, befitting what we thought was a cool venue. We had to set the scene. You leave this stuff to berks and it's a disaster . . .'

A further change was a decree that ran contrary to the existing standards of some patrons.

Ron S. Peno: 'The Fun House had a "No flares, no platforms, no glitter" policy. A month before that, I'd been wearing all of the above, and all of a sudden I had to get rid of the platforms, the glitter and the cuffed Oxford bags [pants]. I had to take all my pants in and wear winklepickers and striped T-shirts and stuff.'

The policy was neither policed nor universally adhered to, but everything and everyone at the Fun House just clicked. It was meant to be.

Bob Short: 'By the time the Fun House happened, there was enough people. Like, if there's one weirdo in every school in the whole world and they've come to one place, you've got a critical mass.'

While Radio Birdman had a virtual indefinite residency at the venue, they didn't wish to play every week, nor were they always able to. So the net was cast for other likeminded acts, who had to get the nod from Rob Younger.

Deniz Tek: 'If Rob thought a band was too commercial or didn't dress right or wasn't cool enough, he wouldn't hire them.'

Mark Taylor of White Light Records had been playing guitar, and teamed with Five Dock crew members and fellow major Birdman fans Ron S. Peno and Charlie Georgees. Already an up-and-coming fret wiz, Georgees wanted to call the band the Hellcats—a name first hit upon by Rick Grossman—rather than the proposed Frozen Stiffs. Taylor wasn't interested in going under that moniker, so Ron and Charlie departed. The problem was Mark Taylor's outfit—who changed their name to the Psycho Surgeons—had their first gig at the Fun House looming. Deniz talked Taylor into going ahead with the performance anyway, and Peno returned to assist on vocals, with a particularly energised Tek along with Mark Sisto also taking the microphone.

Ron S. Peno came specially packaged for the occasion, and not just in the white trousers Stooge Ron Asheton had worn inside the cover of the *Fun House* LP, and which he'd recently given to Deniz Tek.

Ron S. Peno: 'I thought I'd wrap my upper torso in masking tape and then put on a leather jacket. It was sort of my debut. Letting everyone know I was this wild singer! I was the special guest and the song was called "Crush on You". Deniz introduced me on stage. And I was called Ron do Ron or something silly. After the Crystals song, I think.'

For Mark Sisto, the event was even more a seat-of-his-pants exercise. He had sung back-up as part of the Glutonics with Johnny Kannis, and acted as master of ceremonies at Birdman gigs, but this . . .

Mark Sisto: 'I had just read *Fear and Loathing in Las Vegas* and the whole thing was inspired by that madcap craziness. I had a set of words and Mark Taylor had a tune. We thought we would try to fit them together. Uhhh . . . nope. No time. Deniz egged me on, "Just do it! It'll be great!" So I high-dived into the pool in front of a packed house without having had time to look if there was any water.

'I said, "This is a little song I wrote while I was in DeNang. It's called Highball Dementia". DeNang wasn't a battle. It was a rear area where the Air Force was based, a place one might wait for a flight out. Anyway, Mark Taylor starts up this chopping droning on the guitar. I waited for about two lines and dived in: "For the last six hours I've been driving around in this Rikki Tik Taxi past the safe tree line. I hurled, unfurled, hard drank. Dementia. Both tired and wired dementia on fire. Dementia." Basically, the tale was about this rather traumatised service member who was desperately trying to unwind and relax before boarding a flight. He was self-medicating but it just made things worse: vomiting, fights with the gate guards, etc. He hit a few bars and had a "few more Highballs to mellow me down". He ends up missing his flight out and gets lost somewhere outside the perimeter. I had to make it to the end [of the song] or else the first impression I would make might be me dying on stage. It went over exceedingly well.'

While Sisto would not front another band for almost two years, the Psycho Surgeons became regulars at the Fun House. They recruited Radios fan club president, Paul Gearside, as singer, based purely on his wild dancing style. It perfectly suited their repertoire of Iggy and the Stooges, the Sonics and the Damned, as well as some originals.

The Hellcats, out of Five Dock Central, with Ron S. Peno—who would be dubbed Ronnie Pop or Ronnie Stooge by some—Charlie Georgees, bassist Garry Peterson, drummer Mark Kingsmill, also gained stage rights. They would become an act beloved by the Fun House crowd and a dream double header with Radio Birdman, with their virtual jukebox of rock and roll old and new, from the Ramones' 'Suzy Is a Headbanger' to Elvis's 'His Latest Flame'.

Ron S. Peno: 'We once got Johnny Kannis and Deniz Tek on stage—as "John and Den", mirroring Jan and Dean—to do the Beach Boys' "Fun Fun Fun".'

But even with Radio Birdman not always present, they were still firmly pulling the strings. They set up a strict black and white code, a new cool with tight perimeters regarding listening tastes and style. Venturing outside that compound brought on stinging eye-rolling disdain that no one wished to be subjected to.

Shelley Kay: 'You had to be very careful about how you expressed who you liked. If you said you admired the wrong band, you were really, really criticised. You were always trying to like the right people and stay abreast of who was cool.'

Jeff Sullivan (Birdman devotee): 'It really was a cult. If you were a fan of Birdman, you pretty well weren't allowed to like almost anything else, unless it was maybe the Dolls or Iggy Pop. You didn't like anything that came from outside.'

Julie Mostyn: 'They set themselves up as arbiters of what was acceptable and what wasn't. At that stage I was in a blues band called the Jive Bombers, and then the Kamikaze Kids, and if a Birdman came to one of the gigs, you'd feel honoured and sprinkled with a little gold dust. That was really special. They were sort of touched with that bit of authority. We all looked up to them because they were the beginning, the nexus of a movement that happened afterwards with a lot of people being inspired.'

As part of this, the Radios were a tutorial sending many down a secret tunnel on voyages of discovery of a new musical world occupied by not just by the Stooges but soul and surf music, sixties' girl groups and acts such as the Remains, the Sonics, the Flamin' Groovies, the Dictators and more. Many, enacting a scorched-earth policy, aided and abetted by punk's ground-zero ethos, dumped their old records and started afresh from the cheap second-hand racks at Martin's Records or Ashwoods where vinyl owned by Rob Younger and Warwick Gilbert—often marked with the Radios' red stamp from the *Burn My Eye* EP and their names inscribed—would turn up, traded in for better versions. It was like finding the Dead Sea scrolls, the actual original 'artyfacts' of Radios' influence.

And often, despite the outfit's growing stature, Younger himself could be found quietly browsing and, on occasion, acting in a customer-service capacity.

Brad Franks: 'I can remember being in Ashwoods and flicking through the records. Next thing I knew, Rob Younger was next to me going through a pile. I found some Doors album I didn't have and I lifted it up, and heard Rob's voice say, "Buy that!" "Oh! Okay!"'

The singer was also often on patrol at night.

Clyde Bramley: 'I used to drive cabs went I first came to Sydney and going through Taylor Square I'd see Rob crossing the road near the Fun House in leather, tight pants, all that kind of stuff and go, fuck! I've got to spend another twelve hours driving around in this fucking cab and there's Rob looking like a rock star!'

Meanwhile, fan-club membership was rising in line with Birdman's increasing profile, the impact of *Burn My Eye*, the support of 2JJ, and the growing patronage of the Fun House. But membership wasn't for everyone.

Bob Short: 'I never joined the fan club. I didn't even know there was a fucking fan club! I started hearing about it afterwards, but I thought, "Why would I be in the fan club? I'm here!"'

George Munoz: 'I wrote to the fan club and weeks and weeks went past and I didn't get anything. So I wrote again that my stuff hadn't arrived and at the end [of the letter] messed with the Birdman name and called it "Radio Birdshit". Ron Keeley replied with a lot of obscenities, [saying that] if I mess with the Birdman name again I'll be kicked out of the fan club! But I got my stuff.'

Mangrove Boogie Kings

The first Birdman gig back at their old stomping ground after Deniz returned from America was in late February. It was publicised by a single poster created by Angie Pepper, that carried no mention of the Radios and just a tiny logo and the insider-knowledge only pull line of 'Hand of Law Returns'.

Bruce Tindale (Birdman devotee, photographer): 'You [often] had to be connected to someone in the band, or one of the close followers, to find out when they were playing.'

Damien Minton (Birdman devotee, journalist, art dealer): 'I would go in [to Revolver Records] and ask Jules, "Where's Birdman playing?" Also [manager] George Kringas would make the mistake of putting his phone number on the bottom of the posters, so we'd ring him and ask, "Where are they playing?"'

One particular engagement was approached as a settling of old scores—with Ol' 55, as part of Orientation Week at Sydney University. The fifties' act were again top of the bill.

George Munoz: 'I was talking to the guy next to me and I was really putting Ol' 55 down, calling them all kinds of names. "They're crap!" And when Radio Birdman finished, this guy said, "I better get on stage. I'm in Ol' 55."

'I was wearing a Birdman T-shirt and standing right by the side of the stage. This roadie came over, totally pissed off, because they [Birdman] left all the amps at full volume, feeding back, and overturned everything. He said, "Are you guys fucking roadies?" "No, man, we're just fans." It was like he was prepared to hit somebody.'

Deniz Tek: 'We just destroyed Ol' 55 that night. They didn't even want to go on.'

Jim Manzie (Ol' 55): 'There was a woman up the back who had this cutting board and a serrated knife, slicing these tomatoes in half, so the Radio Birdman fans could throw them at us. I could see her from on stage! I thought, "This has been very smartly planned. Their fans are really organised and disciplined." Frankie [Ol' 55 singer Frankie J. Holden] did this big shimmy, like his Elvis Presley move, and this half tomato hit him right on the temple and exploded all over his gold lamé suit!'

The Radios were beginning to present themselves as a collective more sharply too. They'd been using rough banners for some time, but felt they needed something more substantial to hang at the back of the stage. Angie Pepper turned her hand to the task.

Angie Pepper: 'The fabric the sheet was made of wouldn't accept the dye to the full extent we wanted, and despite my best efforts it turned out more dark pink than red. Still, it was stencilled with the symbol and used for a little while, until Rob and Deniz fell upon a way to replace it.'

The Mangrove Boogie Kings had no need for such accessories. Hailing from the Hawkesbury area, north of Sydney, they were a roots rock-and-roll unit playing Chuck Berry, Muddy Waters and the like. In a sense, basically a local version of the UK's Doctor Feelgood, 'hard and fast and loose and not very polished'. They were already something of an inner-city institution when Birdman's roar of sound fell on them from above one night.

Warren Nunn (Mangrove Boogie Kings): 'After we'd play at Frenchs, we used to walk up Oxford Street. We passed the Oxford Hotel and from upstairs we heard this noise, and we looked each other and said, "Listen to that shit!" We were a blues band, a 4/4 sort of rock-and-roll band, and we were cool and everyone else was crap!'

They continued on their way but others stuck around. The Hells Angels and other bikers around Sydney seemed to like what they had heard about the Fun House, the band at the centre of it and the number of young women in the crowd. They liked it a lot.

A Planet Where All Was Good and Exciting

Doug Lonsdale would let out a primal scream on his arrival at the Fun House, a virtual sign the night's festivities could officially get underway.

The venue seamlessly consolidated the role of the Oxford before it as a personal pigeonhole for those who had yet to find a space for themselves elsewhere.

Johnny Kannis: 'An amp blew up one night so we had to refund people their dollar but no one would take it. A lot of people really relied on that place.'

Jim Flowers, Singapore born with a Caucasian father and Chinese mother, found his tribe at the venue.

Jim Flowers: 'I had begun to find it hard to fit in at school. The cool guys somehow turned to very nasty racism. The people at the Fun House on the other hand were so friendly and welcoming. I thought it was home. I still don't know why. I just felt I belonged.'

Alley Brereton: 'We all made our teenage friends really at the Fun House. Most of us are still buddies.'

Penny Ward: 'Birdman were menacing and that was appealing but not in a horrible way though because they were all really nice people and friendly, nice looking, intelligent and well spoken. That was the scene. Everyone was smart and clever and funny.'

Jules R.B. Normington: 'The people there were all the best people and all your best friends so it was like your lounge room and then the music started and it was as if you'd put your fave records on. It was like stepping onto some planet where all was good and exciting. Such gratitude for being in this place. Radio Birdman and the Fun House were the base everything sprang from.'

Bob Short: 'There was a lot of shy and insecure people there and it gave an air there was a toughness around it there really wasn't.'

Jim Flowers: 'I started wearing the small Birdman lapel badge at school. The guys who had been giving me a hard time actually got a bit freaked out by it. They became wary and didn't know what to make of me.'

Anny Douglass came to Sydney from Toowoomba and quickly felt comfortable.

Anny Douglass (Birdman devotee): 'I felt like a bit of a newbie at first [at the Fun House]. But, it never felt closed off to me. It wasn't a pick-up bar or nightclub. If you were there for the music, you were respected. I think average people were a bit afraid of going there, it had an aura about it.'

'Walking up those stairs, it felt like entering a secret meeting place or society.

'I felt I was doing something quite different to everyday joes.'

Catherine Kingsmill: 'There was always a sense of elitism, not that we felt we were superior, just completely different.'

Paul Gearside: 'I used to go up to the Fun House occasionally on a Saturday afternoon and just sit on the old lounge and the sun coming through those windows that overlooked Oxford Street would light up the dust in the air and the jukebox. To be able to be there by yourself and know that tonight is a gig and

I'll be collecting the dollar at the top of the stairs and that to see Radio Birdman you've got to get past me . . . I felt it was my job and it wasn't by any stretch of the imagination!'

There was now a steady stream of people headed for that first floor on Friday and Saturday nights and many would lie awake for hours afterwards, unable to sleep from the adrenalin still powering through their veins. Or have injured necks, arms, knees or backs after overexertion from dancing.

Bob Short: 'You just danced until they stopped and then you'd have a sit-down! Or a lie-down! It was too exciting! Dancing at a Radio Birdman concert was really different as well. Everyone would find space in the room. It wouldn't be like everyone packed up against the front. People didn't invade space either. And you didn't mess with the girls.'

Shelley Kay: 'I remember catching the bus home and you'd be completely spent. It was such a great workout. Just drenched. Hair matted, long hair clinging, just crazy sweat. I had to get the brush out at home to get all the knots out. It was like an exercise fix because the dancing was so intense. It was fierce. It was just . . . the best! I used to feel every note!'

Tara Anderson: 'The area in front of the band was for dancing and everyone respected each other. People who wanted to drink beer stood up the back near the bar. These days there is a constant movement of people going back and forth to the bar and pushing through the crowd with beer. Radio Birdman were riveting. Nobody left the front. It was all eyes on the band and dancing.'

For John Needham, one journey to the Fun House became a life memory itself.

John Needham: 'I was walking up Oxford Street and it was summer and the windows at the Oxford used to all be open.

The band were playing and the sound just barrelled out of the windows and echoed down the physical dynamic of Oxford Street. They were playing "Walk Don't Run" and I thought I was late for the gig so I started running. They always segued into [the MC5's] "Sister Anne" and I entered the room right at the minute they finished "Walk Don't Run" and started on "Sister Anne" and it was like a revelation! This is one of the world's greatest bands and I'm here and there's maybe fifty other people. Disobeying the song "Walk Don't Run" to get to the gig was ironic.'

During those summer months, the heat naturally became an issue in the air-conditioning-free Fun House.

Ron Keeley: 'I remember one night coming off the tiny stage first and the dressing-room was at the back of the room behind the bar and the crowd just kind of parted in front of me trying to get away from this mad-eyed horribly sweaty monster. I could wring a T-shirt into a schooner.'

Angie Pepper: 'Some of us would climb out onto that awning during Birdman's set break to escape the heat inside. I clearly recall one night in particular when it was just me and Penny Ward sitting together out there. We were saturated from dancing to Radio Birdman's first set. It was a hot night and a light breeze had picked up just enough to cool us down to a perfect temperature. I clearly recall thinking, "I want to always be able to remember this feeling". It felt like the night, the city, the whole shebang belonged to us. It was a really, really fun time in our lives. The memory of that night is as sharp as if it just happened and I can still remember how it felt, nearly half a century later.'

Above: Dressed to kill. Chris Jones (left) and Deniz Tek (in Alice Cooper spider make-up), from Cunning Stunt, Charles Hotel, Wollongong, 1973. Photo by Colleen Skinner, courtesy Angie Pepper Archive.

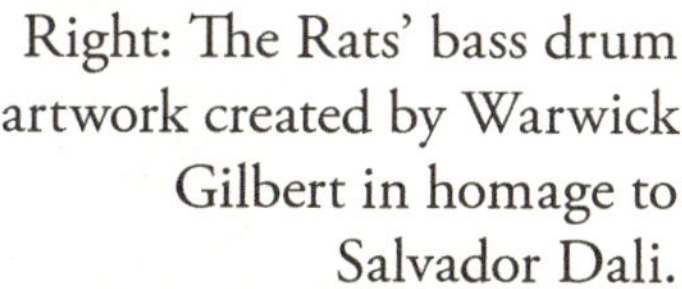
Right: The Rats' bass drum artwork created by Warwick Gilbert in homage to Salvador Dali.

Vermin rock. Rob Younger (left) and Warwick Gilbert, from The Rats, 1974. Photo by Ria Lyne.

Not remotely like everybody else. Radio Birdman in early 1975. (From left) Deniz Tek, Rob Younger, Ron Keeley, Pip Hoyle and Carl Rorke (partially obscured). Photo by Colleen Skinner, courtesy Angie Pepper Archive.

The first meeting of minds. Govinda, the skull (left), Mark Sisto (centre) and Deniz Tek, Manly Vale Hotel, early 1975. Photo by Colleen Skinner, courtesy Angie Pepper Archive.

Bandaged but unbowed. Rob Younger, with Deniz Tek, on stage at the *RAM* band competition, St Leonards Park, December 1975. Photo by Abby Beaumont.

Letting loose. Birdman fans dislocate their limbs, *RAM* band competition.
Photo by Abby Beaumont.

The Birdvan. (From left) Chris Masuak, Mark Sisto and Rob Younger.
Photo by Alley Brereton.

Blitzkrieg tour poster created by Warwick Gilbert, 1976.

The running of the mascara. (From left) Deniz Tek, Rob Younger, Chris Masuak (partially obscured) and Johnny Kannis, Balmain Town Hall, November 1976. Photo by Wiktor Zubenko.

Taking a stand. Rob Younger (with photographer Wiktor Zubenko in shot), at Balmain Town Hall, November 1976. Photo by Jim Swerydow.

The Iceman: Deniz Tek, 1976. Photo by Alley Brereton.

Bird(man) watching. Charlie Georgees (centre) and Ron. S. Peno (right) from the Hellcats, Balmain Town Hall, November 1976. Photo by Wiktor Zubenko.

The day Radio Birdman play at your party at Woollahra. (From left) Julie Mostyn, Penny Ward and Angie Pepper. Photo by Jules R.B. Normington.

The Glimmer Twins: Deniz Tek and Rob Younger (in front), 1976.
Photo by Abby Beaumont.

The red and the black at the Oxford Hotel, 1976. Photo by Glenn Rafferty.

Laying down the lightning. (From left) Rob Younger, Chris Masuak, Deniz Tek and Ron Keeley. Photo by Patrick Bingham-Hall.

Shaking some action, Rob Younger and friends, mid-1977. Photo by Patrick Bingham-Hall.

Lost in the maelstrom, Manly Vale Hotel, mid-1977. Photo by Patrick Bingham-Hall.

Rock 'n' Roll Soldier. Deniz Tek, mid-1977. Photo by Patrick Bingham-Hall.

Birdmen in full flight, Manly Vale Hotel, mid-1977. Photo by Patrick Bingham-Hall.

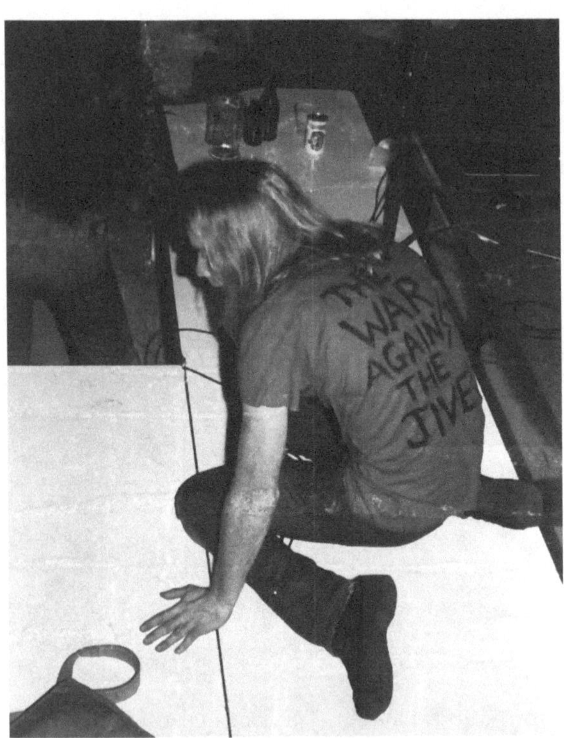

On your feet or on your knees. Rob Younger, Canberra, August 1977.
Photo by Bruce Tindale.

The Masked Marvel faces off against the 'War Lord'. Rob Younger (left) and Warwick Gilbert, Paddington Town Hall, November 1977.
Photo by Patrick Bingham-Hall.

Keeping the flame alive. The Hitmen, 1981. (From left) Brad Shepherd, Johnny Kannis, Mark Kingsmill, Chris Masuak and Warwick Gilbert.
Photo by Steve Lorkin.

Sonic Reducers. Rob Younger (left) and Charlie Georgees, from the Other Side, 1979.
Photo by George Munoz.

A memento from the Marine Corps Officers Ball. Courtesy Angie Pepper Archive.

The other Great White Shark: Mark Sisto (centre) with Deniz Tek, from the Visitors, 1978. Photo by Stephen Best.

Under the heat of the New Race lights. Deniz Tek (left) and Ron Asheton, 1981. Photo by Steve Lorkin.

What had been unthinkable for almost two decades. Radio Birdman reunion, 1996. Photo by Angie Pepper.

After doing the Pop with the Pop. Iggy (left) and Deniz Tek, at the Ron Asheton Memorial concert, Ann Arbor, Michigan, 2011. Photo by Anne Tek.

To the last. Radio Birdman: (clockwise from left) Rob Younger, Nik Rieth, Jim Dickson, Pip Hoyle, Dave Kettley and Deniz Tek. Photo by Anne Tek.

The Mercer Arts Center, Sydney

The convergence at the Fun House, plus the White Light record store, Trafalgar, and the ongoing support of 2JJ and *RAM*, placed Radio Birdman squarely in the middle of an expanding universe.

Rob Younger: 'I know I felt like we were the centre of a scene that was kind of new, and something was happening around the place that a lot of people seemed to be attracted to. There was some really fine people involved in all of that. It was a good time.'

And a highly creative one. Like such cultural epicentres as the New York Dolls' scene at the Mercer Arts Center and Max's Kansas City, music- and art-minded souls had come together at the Oxford, and now the Fun House.

On top of the emergence of bands like the Hellcats and Psycho Surgeons, the scene attracted and encouraged film, fashion and design students, artists, writers and photographers. Many had access to professional facilities—which for the camera heads included dark rooms and kilometres of film—from Sydney College of the Arts—where Chris Masuak was a student—Alexander Mackie College and the National Art School in East Sydney Technical College.

Some such as Dare Jennings, Paul Gearside, Warwick Gilbert and Toby Creswell were already well on their way.

Brad Franks: 'You can't manufacture that sort of stuff. Sydney was that moment in time. There was free education happening at a tertiary level, and you had lots and lots of cheap, dilapidated housing in the city, which is a great recipe for things to self-create. There were a lot of artists. You had three art schools, so you had this confluence of stuff happening. And, of course, everyone was sick of the kind of music that had been around for a while by then—that's the other key factor.'

Gregg Masuak, younger brother of Chris, would go on to become a multi-award-winning writer-director and producer, also creating music videos for the likes of Spice Girls, Kylie and Celine Dion. He enjoyed the fruits both of the inner Sydney arts scene and of Birdman.

Gregg Masuak: 'I spent all day studying like a fool and then dancing my bare feet off. They [Birdman] celebrated individuality, they celebrated creativity. I was freshly committed to the craft of film and a life of film. They were aligned with the dedication and spirit and that fierce energy that committed artists dive into. So it was kind of feeding my soul at a time I needed it. Radio Birdman inspired myself and others to dedicate, create, and put their all into their passions.'

Alley Brereton: 'With Radio Birdman doing everything themselves—like running the place, booking the bands, making the posters—that encouraged artists who [felt] restricted [or shut out] to do their own thing. People would come up and say, "We've got some great photos of the band," which Birdman could then use for posters, or "We can silk-screen T-shirts".'

Toby Creswell: 'Because they were so strong live, it really galvanised everyone. People went on to start record labels or fanzines or bands, because someone had done it, so it was an inspiration to others. The additional aspect was that do-it-yourself thing, which had never been happening in Australia much. That was really important. Make your own records, make your own posters—and be in opposition to whatever else was going around. The "squares", as Rob [Younger] might say. "Like, what are you doing for the revolution, pal?"'

Bob Short: 'I always thought the most important part was that gathering of the audience and that location. The whole new focus of punk rock was beginning to really rise up in the media. So you get a roomful of these kids who had basically grown up with the idea that they are the future and are going to take over the world. And there's this band that basically says something like that . . .'

Tara Anderson: 'There were really smart people in that room, who were alert and picking up that something new was going on. People who were culturally attuned. It magnetised an interesting crowd. The band themselves were great, obviously, but I couldn't overlook also the influence of who they attracted.'

Some even took the opportunity to reinvent themselves.

Bob Short: 'I had a nickname, "Bob", which came from [Sydney disc jockey] Bob Rogers, because of his glasses. I just went, "Okay, now I'm going to be Bob Short." I was going to be a new person.'

Jackson Browne & the Boys Who Lived Next Door

The large, aggressively pissed punter was happily taking on all comers in the crowd of more than 45,000 people at the Sydney Showground. It was March 1977, during Alice Cooper's first Australian tour. As a solo act, he'd risen far beyond clearing the Cheetah Room in LA in the late sixties, reaching mainstream consciousness with *Welcome to My Nightmare*.

Rob Younger wasn't among the heaving masses at the event.

Rob Younger: 'I was never interested in that level of theatricality. I just thought, "Gee, that must be tiring to have to put that on every night. Why the fuck would you bother?"'

Radio Birdman had just taken their first trip to Melbourne. It had been planned to tie the venture in with the release of their debut album, which had finally been completed after a series of intermittent sessions at Trafalgar. Thus, the tour was named after the record, and the LP, along with their coming single, was plugged on the poster. But neither were available when they travelled south.

Hitting Melbourne was a bold move for a band that hadn't clocked up many road miles outside inner Sydney.

The originally scheduled dates were 3 March, Matthew Flinders Hotel, Chadstone; 4, the Be Bop & Loo Bar at the Beverly Crest Hotel, St Kilda; 5, Martinis in Carlton; 8, Be Bop & Loo; 10, the Eureka Hotel in Geelong; 11 the Pier Hotel, Frankston; and 12, the Manhattan in Ringwood.

The gigs—a mix of city, outer suburban and provincial venues—were arranged at least in part with the assistance of the all-powerful Harbour Premier agency. Unfortunately, they coincided with a hugely successful visit to the city by Jackson Browne and Maria Muldaur.

Warwick Gilbert: 'The bookers were more interested in Jackson Browne.'

Nonetheless, the breathless pages of coverage in *RAM*, word of mouth and the *Burn My Eye* EP, which was available in select record stores in Melbourne such as Missing Link, helped pave the way.

The southern capital was a very different animal to the 'Detroit scene' that the Radios had been nurturing in Sydney. Melbourne had a more Bowie and Roxy Music aesthetic within some of the punk ranks. At the other end of the scale was the energised traditional rock and roll of Jo Jo Zep and the Falcons and the Sports, much like the UK pub rock scene that predated punk.

That wasn't to say there was no knowledge of the MC5 and the Stooges. The vibrant Carlton scene of the early seventies, key figures of which spawned acts such as Skyhooks, missed nothing.

Jen Jewel Brown (Melbourne writer): 'Lobby Loyde, in the Wild Cherries, then Coloured Balls, co-existed on the same wavelength as MC5. The Stooges also got 100 per cent Melbourne approval rating.'

Mick Harvey, soon of the Boys Next Door, later the Birthday Party and the Bad Seeds, attended the Radios' first showing in Melbourne.

Mick Harvey: 'It was at the Matthew Flinders Hotel in Holmesglen on a Saturday afternoon. I was there with

Chris Walsh [later of the Moodists] and, I believe, Garry Gray [Judas Iscariot and the Traitors, the Reals, the Negatives and later the Sacred Cowboys]. There were around 20 people there. We were the only ones there to see Birdman. They were great at that show—despite the situation.'

The Martini's gig was attended by future Boy Next Door and Birthday Party member Rowland S. Howard, while the date at the Be Bop & Loo Bar was witnessed by a young Nick Cave.

Phill Calvert (subsequent Boy Next Door and later of the Birthday Party): 'It's always, oh, "Nick Cave used to dance up the front at Radio Birdman shows." Well, yes. He did. We all did. When we could dance no longer, we would go to the bar and buy another pot of beer and drink that, and then go back and dance some more.'

Richard Guilliatt (journalist): 'Nick Cave was pogoing down the front and jumped on my foot!'

Garry Gray was already aware of many of the musical roots of Birdman that had inspired Cave's levitation.

Garry Gray: 'Chris [Walsh] and I, and I think Tracy Pew [later of Boys Next Door and the Birthday Party], went to all the gigs and we struck up conversations with the band. I was talking to Rob Younger and we asked him, "What's this fucking awesome song in your set?!" It was "I Wanna Be Your Dog", as well as earlier Stooges stuff that wasn't on *Raw Power*, which was the only Stooges album we had. Chris had got it through the Australian Record Club—it was next to Barry Crocker in the catalogue.

'After one gig, they invited us to where they were staying at the Carotel at St Kilda. They said, "We'll play you the first two Stooges' albums and the first two MC5, and a whole bunch of other stuff." Deniz had one of those portable record players like they had in the beach movies. We had a fucking ball. There was that spirit of pioneering.'

Bruce Milne (Au Go Go Records): 'Back in those days, you thought you were the only person in the world who had heard of the Stooges, and here was a band that was not only well versed in it but were masters of its execution.'

The gig at the Pier Hotel in Frankston was, for Birdman, a rewind to the days of clashing with bouncers at venues in Sydney and one means of transport to the show even attracted the attention of the local police.

Phill Calvert: 'I think Tracy went down there on a scooter and he got pulled over by the cops, because he had Deniz and Rob on his Vespa as well. There was a sort of camaraderie and they were always really super-friendly. Unlike certain other bands, Radio Birdman were always, "We're all in this together. We're part of this same kind of scene."'

In the wake of the tour, Rowland S. Howard fired off a handwritten letter to the Radios fan club, desperate to join.

The Melbourne music press also handed out salivating reviews—among them Andy 'Mort' Bradley, another member of the Townsville and James Cook University connection. He'd moved to Melbourne in 1974 and was roadying as well as writing, sometimes under the pseudonym of 'Supermort'. The large-framed Bradley went to every Birdman gig during the tour, got to know them, and would later move to Sydney and take over as their sound man.

A week after the Radios returned from Melbourne, they had a gig at Macquarie University. For fan George Munoz, the action began long before the show.

George Munoz: 'We all used to wear boots, and if you took off the heel and hammered in nails and put your heel out on the road, it caused sparks. So we were driving along and I shouted, "It's spark time!" So the four doors opened up and we put our heels down, but I didn't look in the rear-view mirror and the police were right behind us. One of them gave us a really hard time, had us against the wall, and saw we were all wearing red Birdman T-shirts. He said, "Are you guys communists!?" "No, we're not!" "You're communists and I hate communists! I'm going to beat you guys up!" And in those days, the cops could!

'He said, "Give me your boots," and he threw them out in the bushes. People had started coming out to see what was going on. So he just gave me a fine and told us to piss off. After the cop left, we went back to find our boots in the dark. "Found one! That's mine!" And we got to the gig on time!'

With their highly anticipated first album still without a firm release date, Birdman once again bucked convention and began working on songs for their second. These included 'Non-Stop Girls' and 'What Gives?'—a Gilbert and Tek tune, inspired at Deniz's end by the Sonic's Rendezvous Band—and 'Aloha Steve & Danno', Rob Younger's debut songwriting effort.

Lee Taylor: 'Rob handed me a folded piece of paper and gave me strict instructions not to look at it until later when he had left. It was his lyrics to "Aloha Steve & Danno".'

Meanwhile, the media was focused on Birdman's very first release, *Burn My Eye*, which was given a glowing appraisal in a three-way review in *RAM* with the Saints *(I'm) Stranded* album and the Ramones' second LP, *Leave Home*. Both pressings of the Radios' effort had sold out a few weeks earlier.

Although Birdman had only a solitary four-song release in the public eye, some had already found deep meaning within the music.

Tim Johnson found himself gently transported by their onslaught of sound. He had been painting since the early seventies and often placed the Radios and acts that had emerged in the punk scene on canvas. Many of these would make their way to the National Gallery in Canberra. Tim also became the band archivist.

Tim Johnson: 'Birdman had a perfectly textured sound, where everything seemed to blend together and produce harmonics. Sometimes the effect of this was hypnotic and created a feeling of euphoria. When I was dancing to this sound, the aural experience gave me the feeling that I was disembodied, and more or less floating in space. I'd want to get closer to the source, so I'd gravitate to the speakers and felt comfortable bathing in the sound, letting it permeate my body.

'This wasn't great for one's hearing, but the whistling sounds I'd experience after were always temporary. I think this is because when experiencing a heightened sense of reality, the thresholds that limit what the body can endure might change. It illustrates the Buddhist idea that the true nature of reality is "emptiness". In the case of Radio Birdman, I was experiencing a kind of self-realisation, a partly supernatural reality on a higher plane, where the physical world was somehow transcended. This is possible in Buddhism, where there are three worlds—body, speech and mind—one of which is sound.'

The impact of Birdman's music on Mark Sisto was in a far more physical realm.

Deniz Tek: 'We were all into the Three Stooges and Mark used to do a few of their moves. One of them was Curly's thing where he would get on the floor on his side, held up by one elbow, and run his legs and spin around in a circle, with the elbow being the pivot point in the centre. One night,

Mark gradually slid over to one of the tables, which had steel legs bolted to the floor and his leg smacked into it. He kept on dancing. After the show, his leg had swelled above the ankle and was turning dark blue. He asked me if it might be broken. I said, "No way, you wouldn't be able to get up and walk on it if it was fractured, let alone dance." Next day he got it X-rayed and sure enough the distal third of the fibula was shattered.'

Fans everywhere had reason to be pain free. In late March 1977, Birdman blasted out before the cameras at ABC TV at Gore Hill in Sydney, for a program that would be called *The Real Thing* during which a number of acts would perform a short set before a live audience.

Pre-performance, the host, 2SM DJ Ron E. Sparks, interviewed Jules R.B. Normington and Johnny Kannis, with Anny Douglass adding an expressive silent commentary.

Johnny Kannis: 'Some of us were offered make-up and I put my hand up! I don't know why because I didn't know I was going to be interviewed. I said to the make-up artist, "Just make me look like Elvis!"'

Normington had been rapid-firing the one-liners at Sparks before the cameras rolled, but switched to monosyllables when filming began.

Jules R.B. Normington: 'In order for him to do his job well he needed me to talk in an interview, so I decided not to! Warwick and I had always had this thing, this grunt speech where we didn't say anything, just grunt, so I thought, "I'm doing that!"'

Shelley Kay: 'That was hilarious! It summed up how different we felt because we were part of a select clique. And we were defining it right in his face.'

Anny Douglass: 'Gosh! What fun! There was so much excitement about that. I just felt really proud of the band. Australia would know who they were!'

The Radios ripped through songs such as the Stooges' 'T.V. Eye', the MC5's 'Kick Out the Jams' and their own 'Descent into the Maelstrom'. It was excellent coverage of them in full flight, with a portion of the time devoted to the wild dancing of the all-important army of fans present.

Doug Lonsdale: 'The cameras kept moving around the whole night and there was no warning. If you were dancing, they'd just knock you over.'

Chris Masuak: 'We took the community with us and the vibe was wherever we went. The event was wherever our fans were. They were as big a part of the phenomenon as the band was. The band was the catalyst and the response was the fans. And it was the same chemical reaction.'

Lee Taylor: 'I remember White Light had put a sign on the door: "Gone to see Radio Birdman." The shop was closed!'

The performance was witnessed by Seymour Stein, head of Sire Records in New York—and home of the Ramones—who was in Sydney to see the Saints.

Seymour Stein: 'I signed the Saints, without having heard them play live. It was a first for me. I promised them I'd come to Australia and see them live within six months and lived up to it.'

During a visit to the Bondi Lifesaver, Alley Brereton gave Stein, who would later sign Madonna, the word about another white-hot act he had to witness.

Alley Brereton: 'I sat down next to him. I said, "Forget about the Saints. You've got to see Radio Birdman."'

A Uniform Approach

Ron S. Peno was not at all amused. With the rise of punk, the musical map was changing rapidly around the world and in some instances would soon make a dent in the charts in stark contrast to the impact of the Stooges and Velvet Underground. The Sex Pistols were about to again make global headlines with the 'God Save the Queen' single, followed by 'Pretty Vacant' with a B-side containing a furious version of the Stooges' 'No Fun'. The Clash's 'White Riot' was already making waves, as was the Damned's explosive first album, *Damned Damned Damned*, which also carried a retitling of the Stooges' '1970' as 'I Feel Alright'.

Iggy Pop, however—although now widely acknowledged as the godfather of punk—had moved in a very different direction with *The Idiot*. Produced by David Bowie, the arty at times near ambient effort was more in keeping with Bowie's work of the time than anything remotely as gloriously room clearing as *Raw Power*, much less the bloodied crash and burn of *Metallic K.O.* One night at the Fun House, Peno of the Hellcats took a stand and destroyed a Bowie record in wild protest.

Ron S. Peno: 'I adored David Bowie. Maybe I was trying to impress Radio Birdman. I think it was a copy of [Bowie's] *Pin Ups* that I shredded, and it didn't warrant that but I was trying to be outrageous. We all thought Iggy had gone disco.

The sands of time and that whole "gang" thing. Destroying *Pin Ups* by Bowie and dissing *The Idiot*, which is one of the classic albums. Speaking of idiots . . .

'I remember John Holmstrom from *Punk Magazine* coming out from America. We met him in White Light and we were starstruck and hanging off his every word. He was like, "I really love *The Idiot* by Iggy," and we were going, "What?!" "Yeah, it's such a cool record, man." And we were like, "But, but, you're John Holmstrom from *Punk Magazine*! The Ramones and the Dead Boys and stuff like that!" And he was like, "Have you heard 'I Feel Love' by Donna Summer?" And we're going, "Oh yuk! Really?"'

By now, Warren Nunn from the Mangrove Boogie Kings had climbed the stairs to the stars and visited the Fun House.

Warren Nunn: 'We turned up at this place that's in our own backyard and there's a whole scene happening we weren't aware of. "Wow, they've got all these babes here! We should be doing this sort of stuff!"'

On the first weekend of April 1977, it seemed the attention of the world—or the bits that mattered—was trained on Taylor Square and the nearby area, with the Fun House hosting the Radios on Friday 1 April, while on Saturday 2 April, the Saints would take its stage. On the Sunday night, both acts would play at Paddington Town Hall, a few blocks east, where Rob Younger had seen—just for something to do—Billy Thorpe and the Aztecs shake the ceiling in the early seventies.

Seymour Stein attended the Fun House appearance by the Birdmen and every effort was made to make the most of his presence.

Lee Taylor: 'They were always going to get a good reception, but we made sure they got a *really* good reception, so all

Seymour would see was everyone going fucking nuts! It was about signing the band, so let's get them signed!'

Both the Fun House audience and Birdman delivered big time with Stein, who, according to legend, was so impressed, he was up and dancing.

Rob Younger and Deniz saw the Saints at the Fun House the following night, as did Stein, but the Brisbane band weren't the sole source of action, courtesy of a now-frequent biker presence.

Warren Nunn: 'There was a big bloke going around standing over people, like littler guys, including a friend of mine, and humiliating them. He tried it on Deniz and Deniz stood up to him and didn't back off. I'm not singing Deniz's praises—I never got on with him very well—but he took charge and I was quite impressed by that.'

Deniz Tek: 'My girlfriend was repeatedly molested by a biker, not a Hells Angel, and I had to intervene. I was in the middle of fighting him and the Angels jumped in, grabbed the guy and threw him head-first down the stairs and into the street.'

While the situation was defused, the broader issue remained.

Mark Sisto: 'I saw the two alternatives as problematic. If they [the bikers] make it [the Fun House] their hang out, there will be the chance of violence, intimidation, theft. So what are you to do? Kick them out? They could react big time to that.'

The joint appearance at Paddington Town Hall by Birdman and the Saints was again witnessed by Seymour Stein. It allowed him to experience the full-bodied thrust of Radio Birdman—in their biggest engagement to date—through a large sound system in a huge room. Audience-wise, it was half-full at best, however Warwick Gilbert's poster, based on the Flamin' Groovies' *Supersnazz* LP, made it seem every bit the event it was.

Johnny Kannis was now an MC at Birdman gigs and came formally attired in white tux and tails for the occasion, while Deniz Tek carried some additional dressing himself.

Deniz Tek: 'My hand was in a partial cast, due to having broken a finger in a fight with a biker at the Oxford. We played hard, wanting to please ourselves and our fans, but also to show the Saints what we were made of. At the time we felt they were kindred spirits, at least musically, and of course we felt somewhat competitive. They were in our neighbourhood. We were not going to be upstaged under any circumstances, whatever it might take.'

Doug Lonsdale: 'I was backstage and Deniz grabbed me and said, "Get out there and introduce the band!" I was drunk and just let out this scream [from the stage] that lasted for about a minute! Then I thought, "What am I doing out here?"'

The unfurling of a new banner carrying the Birdman logo at the back of the stage underscored the pecking order. It was the perfect time and place to make a statement.

Deniz Tek: 'Again, red and black, a cross-reference to the Blue Oyster Cult.'

But there was more. Birdman officially debuted their uniform, clothing that had been worn in varying loose forms at the Fun House, but which, in this setting, had a new authority.

Angie Pepper: 'It came out of a band meeting. I knew where to get inexpensive army surplus shirts, had dyed clothes before and could sew, so I offered my services. Rob came with me to get the shirts and those little Dylon metal tins of black dye. The fabric the shirts were made of resisted taking the dye, despite being dyed several times, so the result was a dark grey, not the solid true black they were going for. Since they were for stage use, where there would be coloured lighting, it wasn't a big issue. I had a machine and could sew, so I sewed on the logo patches.'

Deniz saw the revised presentation of Birdman as something of a move toward reunification after the months of turbulence following his trip to Ann Arbor.

Deniz Tek: 'The new visual approach might have helped temporarily to put us all on equal ground once more. So, when we walked out there on stage that night, we felt strong, united, almost invulnerable.'

Seymour Stein loved the uniforms. He knew the power of such things. The Beatles had one, so did the Who, Paul Revere and the Raiders and many others in rock history—not to mention the Salvation Army. But the apparel held little appeal for Ron Keeley, not least because it was too hot for him to work in.

Ron Keeley: 'I spent far too many years of my life in uniform. I didn't really go for it.'

Some long-time fans were horrified by the overall visual, and what they perceived as a Nazi undercurrent, and walked out of the Paddington gig in disgust. Their concerns were seemingly echoed by the Saints' Chris Bailey, who mockingly thanked the local chapter of the Hitler Youth.

Afterwards, one audience member put their thoughts into action.

Deniz Tek: 'A woman ripped our flag down and tore it, stomped it, while we were in our dressing-room. She was inconsolable. She saw the flag as some kind of Nazi imagery, which of course it was never intended to be.'

Warwick Gilbert: 'This Jewish girl collared me and said, "Do you realise what you've done? The symbol and the flag."

She had memories of the Holocaust and we had people that looked like they were giving Nazi salutes [in "New Race"] and stuff like that. It was sort of tongue in cheek to present it that way, to get a rise out of people. The rage, the shock and the horror on her face really disturbed me. I thought, "I can't really do this."

'It made me think seriously about what I want to put out there as an artist. All you've got to go on is what comes back [from an audience], and I didn't like what was coming back. I felt a bit ashamed to be part of it, actually.'

Catherine Kingsmill: 'There was the chant and the arm salutes and, much to our shame, many of us embraced that without making the connection. I grew up with so many Holocaust victims around my suburb. People with concentration-camp tattoos on their arms.'

Others saw the 'politics' of the Birdmen quite differently.

Damien Minton: 'A lot of people talk about the fascist undertones. It was nothing like that. It was a call and response from the audience to the band and an identification with this "Do it yourself, fuck you" attitude. You're with us or you're against us. It felt like a realignment of what was going on on stage and in the audience. It seemed to be a much more participatory action.'

Toby Creswell: 'There was that garage-nation thing that the Clash were very big on. That whole idea of doing it yourself and being independent and not caring about the industry or whatever it is, but very much responding to community. The politics of that is quite powerful. So the garage aesthetic was very important and I think that was the politics I saw in it.'

Angie Pepper: 'Anyone who would call the guys in Radio Birdman fascists couldn't have known them personally.

They had been treated badly by the industry and the public, and had been given reason to be defensive. They could be aloof, stand-offish and, anticipating disapproval and attack, erected a barrier that they worked behind, together. They certainly weren't fascists . . . they weren't hippies either.'

The other factor at Paddington was the reported presence of the Hells Angels.

Deniz Tek: 'Warwick remembers Hells Angels sitting on the front of the stage. I don't recall that at all. It could possibly be true, but I doubt that we would have allowed that. We maybe could have used their help a couple of years before, when we were being chased out of venues by management heavies, but the crowd at Paddo was all for us. No need for bodyguards there and Angels would have been trouble. I think I would have been in the uncomfortable position of asking them to get off our stage.'

A German film crew are believed to have shot the performance by the internationally rising Saints and were reportedly coerced into documenting some of Birdmen's firestorm with 'New Race', 'Burned My Eye', 'Descent into the Maelstrom' and 'Hand of Law' believed to have been captured—although in the end only footage of 'New Race' survived.

Five Dock crew member Greg Foster feverishly reviewed the night in *RAM*, with the event an awakening for those who weren't already empowered, much as the Sex Pistols' show in June 1976 at Manchester's Lesser Free Trade Hall had been before fewer than 40 people. Each of whom—including Mark E. Smith (the Fall), Peter Hook (Joy Division) and Morrissey (the Smiths)—went away inspired by what they witnessed. Paddington, however, also offered up a choice and drew demarcation lines: Radio Birdman or the Saints.

For Younger, the Brisbane act was a more direct beast than the jukebox of musical diversity he was fronting.

Rob Younger: 'What they did was fantastic, more singular. We had things going in all directions. There's a big difference between the Blue Oyster Cult and Tommy James and the Shondells.'

For others, the Radios' gear change of songs from 'Murder City Nights' to Roy Head's 'Treat Her Right' was a key part of their charm.

Bob Short: 'The thing that most impressed me was almost this formula where Birdman used to play two or three sets a night of a few originals, a cover, a few originals, cover, and it gave it a different mood. Instead of being heavy all the time, there's "Descent into the Maelstrom" and then [Tommy James's] "Hanky Panky". There's a whole bunch of guys going, "My baby does the hanky panky!" and all the girls are doing "the Pony" and "the Swim" [dances]. I always thought it was like a lesson in what's cool. Like, yeah! "California Sun"!

'The songs they played and the songs on the Fun House jukebox and the records in White Light, they were the library, the big library and you'd take books out. We'd have our records and everybody would show each other their collections and we'd learn what those songs were from that. Rob and Charlie Georgees lived in a house together and they had great boxes of monster singles! Everybody listened to fucking singles! Almost to a state of worship. And that's what Radio Birdman were doing on stage; playing these bizarre cover versions between their songs like playing singles!'

Seymour Stein loved what he had seen from Radio Birdman over the weekend. He went to Trafalgar, heard the coming album and met the band. He wanted the Birdmen on Sire and thus beam them out internationally, which, after the lack of interest from the major Australian record companies, was vindication on steroids.

Seymour Stein: 'The Saints were great, but Radio Birdman were even greater. Radio Birdman were one of my all-time personal favourite signings to Sire. I believed that they would find great success worldwide.'

The uniforms continued in a haphazard manner at subsequent performances but soon fell away entirely.

Deniz Tek: 'They didn't last long. As soon as we started seeing copies of them appear in the crowd, we dumped them.'

Rob Younger: 'It didn't really work. And we were never fully committed to it, anyway. Nonetheless, it probably looked better in dark clothing, in any case. Most people do. But it was probably better if we hadn't bothered with it.'

There was, of course, a party after Paddington, as usually took place when the Fun House closed, and no one was ever in the mood for sleep. These post-gig fixtures, which could take place from Five Dock to Tamarama, in the eastern suburbs, were almost as much an event as the actual performances themselves.

Obtaining supplies for these celebrations was a simple process in what was a less complicated time.

Stephen Vineburg (Birdman devotee, artist): 'Everything finished at ten and you had to go somewhere. I remember going across the road to the service station near the Unicorn [hotel on Oxford Street], and they had [containers of] ice out the front and there would be slabs of beer in there. You'd go to the counter and get a beer to take home. You'd been watching these guys on stage and suddenly you're talking to them at a party.'

Brad Franks: 'I remember going back to one, I think it was at Deniz's house, where he was living. I went into the lounge-room and there was virtually no furniture. On the wall was just the poster from the original American pressings of *Raw Power* and a copy of *Kick Out the Jams*, opened up nailed to the wall! And that was it!'

Clyde Bramley: 'We used to have parties at Five Dock and Greg Foster had a huge record collection with a 100-watt stereo system that was huge for the time. It was just one of those places that people came and hung out. It might have been the record collection that drew Rob out there! He was there with Angie Pepper. I ended up having a jam with him and Charlie [Georgees] in one of the bedrooms one day.'

Anny Douglass: 'I'm sure people were relaxed and having a better time before Birdman people turned up. It was kind of like some important people had arrived and you didn't want to do anything that made you look like a dickhead. The most fun person from then was George, the manager.'

Penny Ward: 'Sometimes they [the band] would walk into the wrong party, maybe someone's parents were throwing a party for their 20-year-old kid. You wouldn't know what to make of them [Birdman], because you knew they weren't bikers, but you'd just think, "What the fuck?" [Who are they?] They [everyone] were just waiting to see what they [the Radios] were going to do! Everybody in the room would just stop talking sometimes when they walked in, just because of the clothes they had on.'

Looks, however, were deceiving.

Patrick Bingham-Hall (Birdman devotee): 'This was one of the country's most abrasive, confrontational and loudest bands, at a time when debauchery was almost mandated, yet Radio

Birdman were as good as drug-free, never drank to excess, and were exceedingly polite and respectful towards women.

'The women around Birdman had an elegance to them. They were winsome, gamine, Euro-styled—they weren't sun-bleached blonde. And they weren't groupies, they were feisty, self-assured figures with an intimidating intelligence. They complemented the band and were integral to what they were trying to do.'

The core group even had their own name.

Bob Short: 'They were that most amazing block of women we called "the Fun house Girls".'

Penny Ward: 'I remember the girls who used to harass Angie and me and Anny, and were always on us like, "What the fuck are you doing here? Letting these guys tell you what to do, run your life." A lot of them didn't like girls like us. They thought we were groupies. They didn't understand any girl that would hang with a bunch of men and listen to music like that and not be there under pressure or something.'

Damien Minton: 'Being a young hetero male, the women that would go to Radio Birdman . . . There was a gang of them. They had really tight T-shirts, big leather belts with buckles, tight jeans and Cuban-heeled boots. It was just . . . the sexuality and eros in that room was absolutely electric!'

Ed 'Big Daddy' Roth at the Easter Show

The smell of cattle and fresh scones was a long way from the scent of sweat, cigarettes and beer at the Fun House and the scenes at Paddington Town Hall a week earlier, but at least an appearance at the Sydney Royal Easter Show allowed some exercise in the fresh air. Radio Birdman and the Mangrove Boogie Kings were performing, in a tent set up outside the Poultry Pavilion by 2JJ.

Jim Flowers: 'I had a job selling food and drinks from a truck near the concert area. Birdman suddenly started playing and a lot of farmers and agricultural people drifted by, looking on like it was some kind of city folk's freaky thing. Birdman playing alongside cow and sheep sheds and farmers . . .'

Catherine Kingsmill: 'I'll never forget Deniz said, "The skull crush pavilion!" or something like that and had a can of beer, and he squashed it against the side of his head and kept on playing.'

Warren Nunn: 'The Boogie Kings were the darlings of 2JJ for about three weeks. A handful of our people came and a few of Radio Birdman's fans came. We expected them [Birdman] to be stand-off sort of arseholes, but everyone was very nice. Rob Younger came up, being the gentleman he is, and asked us if we'd like to play at the Fun House. We said, "Yeah, we'll play anywhere!"

'I remember tearing the knee out of my jeans the week after we first played up there, because it was the look! And we started playing songs that suited the Fun House, more like Eddie Cochran sort of stuff. We were accepted, and on the jukebox—the holy jukebox—they had some Dave Edmunds and Flamin' Groovies, which we could relate to, so we weren't totally incongruous. We actually lifted our game a little bit towards heavier music, rather than country, on the strength of the Fun House.'

The anticipation for the release of the Radios' first LP, apparently to be titled *Radios Appear*, had been growing since the *Burn My Eye* seven-inch. The first of the White Light Records handwritten, double-sided A4 flyers in April 1977 carried the news that the album would be available in a few weeks. In a further slight nod to Birdman's shadow over the store's operation, it was also proclaimed on the leaflet that copies of Iggy and the Stooges' brutal farewell document, *Metallic K.O.*, were exclusive to the shop, signed off with the salute from *New Race*.

Mark Taylor: 'We ordered 100 copies [of *Metallic K.O.*] for White Light, and sold them all. The Ramones' first LP and the Stooges' *Metallic K.O.* were crucial influences. They were the petrol poured on the flickering flames that resulted in an explosion of interest in punk rock in Sydney.'

Bob Short: '*Metallic K.O.* was a big deal. I went into an import shop in Wollongong trying to find a copy the day I read about it in *RAM*. It was a time to be dead keen.'

Ron S. Peno: 'I was besotted. I'd never heard an album like it and I was totally influenced by it. Just like, "Wow!" I think all of my live stuff [his stage act] was taken from that record then. It was the opposite of the seventies' live albums—like, "everybody clap your hands!" and drums solos. Abusing bikies and [Iggy] is getting beaten up and comes back on stage, [slurs] "Hi everybody . . ." It was just "Fuck you" to the audience and "Fuck everyone!"'

Rob Younger: 'If someone had played me that stuff before I'd heard the studio material, I probably wouldn't have investigated the band at all.'

The grim central tenet of the recording was increasingly becoming a reality at the Fun House.

Lee Taylor: 'The Hells Angels adopted Birdman as their band. We went to their clubhouse. We were honoured to be there. I know I was. There were banners and there was stuff there from, like, the Cleveland chapter on the walls. It wasn't a doss house, it was fucking great! All of us were on incredibly good behaviour. Look at the [Birdman] logo. I can see why they were adopted.'

Warwick Gilbert: 'We went to the clubhouse. It wasn't great fun. George [Kringas] tried to crack onto one of their girlfriends and they were dangerous guys. They'd bring their bikes into the house and rev them up. It was an ear-shattering noise. It wasn't cool to us. One of them had George halfway up the wall by the throat, so we had to talk him into letting him go and we got out of there.'

Lee Taylor: 'I used to love the fact that they didn't park their bikes in front of the Fun House. They used to park directly on the other side of the road and they could look out the window and see them. That was cool. I'm a big speedway fan. I always love that sort of machinery.'

Deniz Tek: '[The Angels] were anathema to Rob, Pip and I. We weren't terrified of them, but we cautiously gave them a wide berth. Ron Keeley was never the type to want to get near them either.'

Younger relented on one occasion and visited the biker's clubhouse where he naturally made a beeline for a box of records. As he flicked through the contents, Supertramp's *Crime of the Century* LP appeared, prompting an automatic scoff from the Birdman. One of the night's hosts who had been inspecting Younger's foraging efforts from high above declared, 'Fucking great record, isn't it, mate?' The singer was hardly going to disagree.

Ron S. Peno: 'They [the gang] did come up [to the Fun House] a couple of times when the Hellcats played, probably because of our name. It was very difficult trying to say no to their song requests, but we did.'

The irregular donning of Nazi memorabilia by some of the Radios may have aided and abetted this uncomfortable alliance.

Deniz Tek: 'I would love to say that I was perfectly clean and never wore anything like that, but the truth is that I occasionally did. The only things I can remember wearing in public myself were a Maltese cross, which in the sixties we called a surfer's cross, and I loved that [Ed] 'Big Daddy' Roth [American cartoonist and artist] style cultural aesthetic. I also once wore a ripped New Order T-shirt that Ron [Asheton] gave me—it featured a stylised officer's cap with a gun barrel pointing out below the visor. I wore it because I was a huge fan of Ron, and Dennis Thompson, and nobody else had one.

'I wouldn't now display material that confronts or offends others, nor do I approve of it. But in those days, we had no problem with being provocative or annoying. None of this was politically motivated.'

Rob Younger: 'I can see the aesthetic of a smart uniform and the symbolism and all the rest of that. It depends on how many seconds you're going to spend on that before you get into the idea of what does it really represent? And when you're young, you don't give a fuck what old people think. If it's outrageous, you're more inclined to do it. It still hurts a lot of people nonetheless.'

Lee Taylor: 'I use to buy Nazi memorabilia. This is around the gun-shop area of George Street, up towards Railway Square. I bought a repro[duction]. It was a Mother's Cross on a ribbon. Keith Richards was wearing one. But all the other [items] I bought, like an SS tie pin, they were all real.

'We were pulled up by one kid, a guy in the street, and he said, "What the hell are you guys doing? What are you wearing?" We said, "It's just because of the band." We didn't get the way everyone would take it. Of course, it's serious, but we were just being kids. To me, it was important to have those trimmings. And when you think of Radio Birdman too, they were kind of like rock-and-roll soldiers as well.'

Stephen Vineburg: 'Deniz had this brown, leather, army-surplus great coat. The folklore was, if you looked closely, you could see where the German military patch from WWII had been. People wanted to ascribe all these mythic qualities.'

Angie Pepper: 'I was young and foolish enough to not pay much attention to it at the time. In the seventies, if you went to see a band and saw someone wearing SS or Nazi insignia, it didn't mean they were Nazis. It was the stupidity of youth being thoughtlessly provocative. It was a fashion statement that should never have been made.'

Sire

Radio Birdman's licensing deal was done with Sire Records, a major international label and leading light in the new wave and punk scene.

On his return to New York, Seymour Stein sent copies of the *Burn My Eye* EP to major record stores in the USA, and raved about the recently signed Australians.

The broad forward plan was a tour of the UK and Europe, including dates with the Flamin' Groovies, who to many in the Birdman circle were almost deities. In the process, they'd record an album at the legendary Rockfield Studios in Wales, then it was off to America for six weeks of dates with fellow Sire commandoes, the Ramones.

It seemed a rightful reward for all they had battled in Australia, not to mention a nice 'fuck you' to those who had shunned them. And if Sire could successfully handle the Ramones, they most likely had the right mindset to work with the Radios.

The curveball was that the Sire alliance was a bolt from the blue, rather than the result of active courting by the band. For an outfit that never had an overarching strategy in place, it would be an enormous shift away from their proven in-house DIY methods. It seemed likely it would change everything.

Part of that was rethinking the destination of the new songs they had been working on for several months, such as

'Non-Stop Girls', 'What Gives?', 'Aloha Steve & Danno' and 'Hit Them Again'.

Deniz Tek: 'We decided to give Sire a "new, improved" version of *Radios Appear*, which would include the best of the Trafalgar release, the strongest of the new material, plus remakes of a couple of songs. Then we would go ahead and record a completely new "second" album overseas, having cleaned house and released all of what we considered to be the best material that we had.'

It was a situation complicated by the fact that the original edition of *Radios Appear* was still to be released.

The plan had been to issue it through the Wizard label—the home of the likes of Marcia Hines and Hush, which would later issue the Sex Pistols and Buzzcocks in Australia. However, that hit a snag at the eleventh hour and Trafalgar decided to also handle distribution themselves.

Michael McMartin: 'When we did the album, none of the big companies would distribute it, so we thought, "Let's put that on the Trafalgar label, but use the Birdman label and logo—the ultimate independent release!"'

All the while, the increasing crowd at the Fun House was starting to cause issues for some of the faithful.

Kath 'Good Vibes' Kendall (Birdman devotee): 'As the Fun House started to grow from twenty of us to 50 of us to 100, we were really pissed off. The girls didn't have enough space to dance. We were the non-stop girls! The song "Non-Stop Girls" I'd like to think was about us. Once they started playing, there was no stopping us!'

Nor Birdman, with an appearance at the Sydney College of the Arts (SCA) White Bay Campus at Rozelle in early June with the Hellcats opening.

Bruce Tindale: 'The student council were having cheese and wine afternoons under the trees, and we thought, "We can do better than that!" We got [Birdman fan] Patrick Bingham-Hall elected [to the council], and the first thing we did was put Radio Birdman on in the students' canteen! That caused some problems, because someone kicked a door out and that had to be paid for, but it was like, "What the fuck do you expect?" This was the wildest rock-and-roll band in Sydney! And you had them playing in your canteen!'

For Patrick Bingham-Hall, the gig was the first step on a path towards being an internationally recognised architectural photographer, author and publisher.

Patrick Bingham-Hall: 'I took reels of photos and the photos popped up in all the music mags, and—somewhat incredibly—in the *Daily Mirror* and the *Sun*. It all looked so now and so fresh. It was suddenly a thing. And I got paid for these photos, and my name was in the papers.

'I had tinnitus for days. I was only eighteen, just over a year out of high school, and I had organised a gig for what had to be Australia's mightiest rock band. I must have thought I was the new Andrew Oldham [the Rolling Stones' early manager].'

Toby Creswell: 'Someone had obviously told Rob Younger [at the SCA gig], "They're not selling enough beverages," so Rob goes to the microphone and says, "If any of you squares want coffee, it's available up the back." And of course that meant that no one was going to go and buy coffee!'

A week later, Birdman were back at Balmain Town Hall with the Hellcats. They received another near-primal response that seemed exclusive to the venue, with some fans brandishing actual flaming torches, like a scene from *Lord of the Flies*.

Warwick Gilbert: 'Balmain Town Hall was fantastic! I looked out, and in the audience everyone was equally distanced in the hall, trying to shake their limbs out of their sockets. It was an amazing sight, actually. I thought I could recreate that with art, but I don't think it would translate. It was fantastic! And we were the same. It was just that loop you hit sometimes and it just goes where it wants to go. You just tap into that stuff.'

There was also evidence of a change in demographic at Balmain that few saw coming.

Patrick Bingham-Hall: 'I helped set up the amps and then squatted at the side of the stage. The punters at the front were not just the usual bunch of inner-city fanatics. We had some genuine teenyboppers, girls with ringlets and come-hither eye-shadow, who screamed as Rob approached the microphone. "We wrote a song for you, Rob." "I love you, Rob." They threw posies and what looked like love letters onto the stage. Well, this was new.'

John Brewster from the Angels was at Balmain.

John Brewster: 'I only saw them play once. What I liked most was they had a [salute and chant] thing with the audience. I thought, "That's fucking great!" There was a real vibe to that.'

The Radios' much-anticipated LP still wasn't ready for release—a number of rejected test or sample pressings had been dispensed with on a backyard bonfire—although the single, 'New Race', backed with the Stooges' 'T.V. Eye', was out.

Brad Franks: 'I was down at White Light for the launch of the single and Rob was signing the white paper sleeve, and he grabbed mine and wrote: "Senseless noise, Don't buy!"'

Rock and Roll Soldiers

Melbourne journalist Richard Guilliatt had driven to Queensland's Gold Coast when he received word of Radio Birdman's second southern coming.

Richard Guilliatt: 'I just thought, "Fuck! I've just got to see this band again!" I said to my mate, "We've got to go back!" He said, "What???" "I just can't miss them! They're just fucking incredible!" So I somehow convinced him that we needed to drive back to Melbourne, immediately!'

Eighteen hours and over 1700 kilometres later, Guilliatt was being blissfully smacked about by the Birdmen at Martinis.

While he was in transit, the Radios made an impression on other gig goers, after Rob Younger's minimal tolerance was breached, in the wake of some punter commentary from the floor at the Inkerman Hotel at St Kilda.

'Fuck off if you don't fucking like it! Just fuck off!' Rob spat at the small crowd.

Rob Younger: 'They complained to the proprietor and then we got called into the Harbour Premier agency, I think it was. I got a lecture, you know, "You can't do that at a gig, telling audiences to get fucked," and all this sort of stuff. Why not? It was just bullshit. If the audience heckles you, you can heckle them. It doesn't matter. What's the fucking difference? It was familiar territory to us. You know, "You won't get any more gigs through us" shit.'

It was mid-June and the return to Melbourne was dubbed the 'Rock 'n' Roll Soldiers' tour. The eight scheduled dates kicked off at the Be Bop & Loo Bar on 16 June; the Inkerman Hotel at St Kilda on 17 June; the Eureka in Geelong on 18 June; a lunch-time engagement at La Trobe University on 20 June; Martinis in Carlton on 21 June; the White Horse in Nunawading on 22 June; the Station Hotel in Prahran on 24 June, and the Tiger Room in Richmond on Saturday 25 June.

While there were the typical reshuffles, along with the usual complaints about volume and attitude, two bookings, including the Station, would be dumped entirely in the wake of the Inkerman incident. Thankfully, the Radios had again packed their portable record player while Deniz had the opportunity to apply his medical training.

Andy 'Mort' Bradley: 'Two girls were dancing up the front, right in front of Deniz, in bare feet, and they cut themselves on broken glass. Deniz saw this and stopped and waved at me and Johnny Kannis. We helped the two girls back to the dressing-room and Deniz fixed their feet. We found their shoes and then the show continued.'

The out-of-the-ordinary scenes continued at Martinis.

Bruce Milne: 'There were trestle tables down each side of the room, because it was a pizza bar during the day or some nights. Rob Younger took a dive from the stage and slid down one of the tables, smashing bottles and glasses of beer, knocking them off the side.

'The promoter killed the gig and turned the lights on. I think he even refused to pay them!'

That was the least of Rob Younger's problems that night.

Deniz Tek: 'Rob cut his elbow really deep. I said, "This needs stitches," and Rob goes, "I'm not getting stitches," so we just wrapped it up and we finished playing and then I said, "Okay, now you need to go to the hospital." He still refused, so we just washed it out and kept it wrapped up. It took forever to heal.'

One of the highlights of the trip was tearing the roof off the White Horse—the source of the 'Suck more piss!' chant adopted five years earlier by Billy Thorpe and the Aztecs—probably in response to threats from the bouncers and despite another largely apathetic crowd.

A surprising moment came with a last-minute placement on a bill with the Ted Mulry Gang—who had wanted nothing more than for young ladies to jump in their car—at the Tottenham Hotel in Sunshine, as a make-up gig for the cancelled Station date.

Not even TMG's road crew knew Birdman were appearing, thinking a disco would be the support act. But soon the looks on the faces of the brave teens down the front told the story, with Rob Younger doing his best to make the point that the kids weren't in the *Countdown* studio anymore. He used the microphone stand as a projectile and blankly chanted 'Dominance!' endlessly during their version of the Blue Oyster Cult's 'Dominance and Submission'. When the job was done, the band stalked off, leaving their amps screaming with ear-piercing feedback.

Deniz Tek: 'We were hated by that audience, which we liked, and of course played more aggressively, if that's possible. Our visible enjoyment incensed the crowd more. It was no disaster, in retrospect. The crowd had no idea what to make of us, and they didn't applaud or anything, but we were used to that, and to some extent enjoyed making them feel uncomfortable. In fact, I recall that it was a great performance, one of our best ever. We were very pleased.'

Rob (Birdman devotee): 'At the Tiger Room, there was one guy in between songs yelling at the top of his voice, "Louder! Louder!" And we were thinking, "This guy's insane! It couldn't possibly be any louder!" The roof of the Tiger was fairly low and I remember Rob Younger sort of leaning against the ceiling. The full-on-ness of the whole experience was just amazing!'

But something seemed to have altered from the Birdmen's standpoint.

It was most likely a mix of factors. Punk was changing the scene weekly, if not almost daily, and the Radios hadn't received the memo containing the new local unwritten laws. Not they would have bothered to read through it, anyway.

Nick Cave had attended Birdman gigs during their previous visit to Melbourne, but as 'Nicky Danger', he ranted, no doubt provocatively, in line with the times, in fanzine *Alive 'n' Pumping* in 1977, 'I think Deniz Tek is an asshole . . . and Birdman rip off everyone like the Stooges, MC5, Doors, Bay City Rollers, etc. I guess Rob Younger is a good frontman though. I mean that seriously.'

The intellectual side of the Radios with two medical students in their ranks—which was often mentioned in the media—probably wasn't deemed sufficiently anti-establishment by some either.

Deniz Tek: 'The first time in Melbourne we went to a party with Boys Next Door. They were polite. Second time, they hated us, and tried to harass us from the crowd. Hurling verbal abuse because some of us were training to be doctors—"Fucking doctor, fuck off!" Of course, anything that added to the angst factor just made us happier and play harder. No more parties with those guys.'

Birdman's response to this attitude didn't help the situation but some were just confused by it all.

Bruce Milne: 'I've never quite understood where all this [talk of Birdman being outcasts] came from. I think the problem was they were so used to that adulation [in Sydney] that, when they weren't quite getting it in Melbourne, they reacted. My impression was both tours were amazing and people around me were loving it. I don't buy into this thing that's been perpetuated that Melbourne hated Radio Birdman. We loved them!

'They were head and shoulders above anything that was going on in Melbourne, and even when they did the outer suburban universities at twelve in the afternoon—lunchtime gigs—they put on amazing shows.'

Mick Harvey: 'Perhaps they sensed something from some member of the band [Boys Next Door], but there was no general position of disrespect. Perhaps our perspective had changed a bit. But I feel we still respected them enormously as a live band and for their role in the scene.'

Phill Calvert: 'Maybe we had decided, "Well, now we're a band and we're better than you," but we were a different kind of band.'

Nonetheless, Birdman felt they were now fully fledged outsiders and not in the manner they relished back in Sydney.

Deniz Tek: 'Mike stands were again used in self-defence. They are a great equaliser of men, kind of like the Colt six-shooter in the Old West. We got in a fight with [Mushroom Records boss] Michael Gudinski at the TV studios of *Night Moves*, after the band arrived at 1 a.m. and we were kept waiting to do an interview. Then we wouldn't do it unless they showed our "New Race" film clip, which they refused to do. After much discussion, it ended up as a stand-off, with us leaving without doing the interview, being screamed at by the producers.'

Richard Guilliatt's 'Sullen Savagery' piece was a powerful snapshot of the tour.

Richard Guilliatt: 'I have a memory of interviewing them in a motel room and the general air of grumpiness about the stoushes they had had with various people—and just how pissed off and peeved they were by the whole experience.'

Nonetheless, Birdman again left Melbourne having converted more to their cause than they'd repelled.

As they were driving back to Sydney, an article by Red Symons in Melbourne's *Sunday Press* titled 'Radios a band for the birds' reapplied the blowtorch.

The former Skyhook took sneering issue with the outfit's war-like imagery, uniforms, assumed Aryan Nation overtones of the song 'New Race' and what he generally saw as their 'Luftwaffe' allegiances.

To make matters worse, the halo of the Fun House was slipping, as if caught in a slow mudslide.

The once comic instances of the venue's sound system picking up radio dispatches from local taxi drivers now had an unnerving quality.

Radios LP Appears

When Deniz Tek arrived at White Light Records in the first week of July 1977, it was a special moment.

Lee Taylor: 'Rob was always the record collector. Deniz didn't really care about collecting, so you never saw him in a record shop—at least not the places where I worked. But Deniz delivered the album to White Light. That was a big thing. They flew out the door, as Birdman would.'

The store's July stock flyer carried a prominent notice for the release which was available for $5.95, with the band logo stamped in red on the ad.

Radios Appear, the first recording on the Trafalgar label, was produced by John Sayers and Charles Fisher with the cover design again the work of Warwick Gilbert in signature black and red. The brooding shot on the front made the band look almost sinister, with Rob Younger, now one of the most charismatic front men in the country—no small feat in a field dominated by AC/DC's Bon Scott and Dragon's Marc Hunter—doing a thousand-mile stare.

Lee Taylor's back-cover photo of Ron Keeley's upturned drums after a gig at the Bondi Lifesaver was made all the more surreal by the steely tone.

Lee Taylor: 'It's great, isn't it? Mark Sisto said, "Go and take that! That'd be good!" There was just this debris at the end of the gig and, of course, it was a fucking great shot! I was thinking of people [for photo subjects] and so my eye probably really wasn't that good and Mark's was.'

The influence of the MC5 was again spelled out in the credits, which featured Minister of Defence, Mark Sisto, and Minister of Resources, Jules R.B. Normington. And although Pip Hoyle was still on a sabbatical, he played piano on 'Love Kills' and 'Man with Golden Helmet', while Chris Masuak played any other keyboards, such as the raging work at the height of 'Descent into the Maelstrom'.

The *Burn My Eye* EP had been a triumph, but a proper album that sounded more like what many expected was something else entirely. No one had made anything remotely like this in Australia and it marked what was the official coming out of a secret society.

Their collective heart was very firmly on, and within, its sleeve, with the record named after a lyric in the Blue Oyster Cult's 'Dominance and Submission' and the work dedicated to the Stooges. Inside was a near-78-rpm version of Iggy and co's 'T.V. Eye', which morphed from the drawling crawl of the original to a runaway coal train. Iggy's crew were further referenced—along with the MC5—in the lyrics of 'Do the Pop'—as was the title of the Blue Oyster Cult's double live epic, *On Your Feet or on Your Knees*—while in 'Love Kills', the Stooges' endless first LP dirge 'We Will Fall' was name checked.

Rob Younger: 'We paid those bands a lot of lip service and it backfired to some degree, and also it didn't tell the whole story. We made a lot of people aware that there were these great groups around, and that to play really banging high-energy rock can be a lot of fun, and can be something in itself to do. But we narrowed it down a little bit too much. In interviews we didn't talk about all the other things we liked, like the

Velvets and Jan and Dean and James Brown and the Stones. Kim Salmon [from the Scientists] reminded me some years ago that "The first time I met you, all you bloody talked about was Detroit." I felt really embarrassed but I thought, "Yeah, that's probably right. That sounds pathetic."'

Despite that open worship, nothing on *Radios Appear* sounded remotely like the MC5 or any of the Stooges' records.

Rob Younger: 'A lot of people say they're into that Stooges thing and that's where they're coming from, but they never achieve that sort of atmosphere, that aura of menace. There's something that's transcendent about the Stooges. I never thought I was in that league.

'A lot of people still don't get the Stooges, because they don't get why they actually are compelling. They can play the chords and do all the stuff, but not getting [understanding] the records.'

'Do the Pop' was broadly an ode to Iggy Pop's extreme form of dance. It was sparked by a letter from Mark Sisto.

Deniz Tek: 'Mark sent me a poem about Iggy, and I used the general idea to write "Do the Pop", using one line from his poem in the first verse and another line in the second and the chorus. I built the song around these lines that he gave me, changing the idea from a story about seeing Iggy going wild in town, to a song about a new dance craze.

'I don't remember much of what he wrote [originally], but it had the line, "Hey Mr Pop! Whatchu doin' in town," and things like that. "Dives" refers to Mark running and diving—a precursor to stage diving, I guess.'

Sisto's original idea was partially rooted in the antics of a schoolmate.

Mark Sisto: 'It was inspired by John Vogt, a hilarious

prankster of a guy that, on occasion, would tap dance in public. He'd throw in some Shemp [from the Three Stooges] moves too, throwing himself on the ground, slapping himself on the back of his head. We could get him going, chanting, calling out for "Voto rolls".'

Elsewhere on *Radios Appear*, 'Hand of Law', with the rhythmic swing of surf music, was a strong example of the many sources from which Tek drew.

Deniz Tek: 'I took the idea for the riff from the fanfare intro of James Brown, *Live at the Apollo, 1962*. This became the bass pattern, and I mirrored that riff on guitar. For Chris, I had him play the part out of "Pipeline" by the Chantays. Soul meets surf!'

The ocean swell of the Maelström, a passage off the coast of the Lofoten Islands in Norway, was a much darker proposition. It's referenced in *Moby-Dick*, as well as the title of Edgar Allan Poe's 1841 short story, 'A Descent into the Maelström', much loved by Tek. The similarly titled Birdman number included glimpses of Hunter S. Thompson's *Fear and Loathing in Las Vegas*, and the world of fellow authors Bram Stoker and Dennis Wheatley. It was light years from the primal simplicity of the Stooges and closer to the Radios' own rendition of the Stones' 'Sympathy for the Devil' or the Doors' 'L.A. Woman'. It tore to a climax with a screaming run of jagged surf guitar.

Deniz Tek: 'The Poe theme seemed perfect for a song. I had also recently read an interview with Iggy, which took place on a beach. In the middle of it, Ig dove in the ocean and swam . . . out of sight of land! Interview over. So, I imagined that Ig swam out and found himself caught in Poe's "Maelström".

'Man with Golden Helmet', which dated back to Tek's teens in Ann Arbor with Steve Kambly, was also rock and roll on a whole new cerebral level, courtesy of Pip Hoyle's cascading piano solo alone.

Steve Kambly: 'I think the very last line of the recorded version is probably mine. Deniz came up with the music and nearly all of the words of the final version. The original—and I might add rather spontaneous and unfinished version—was a far cry from the recorded version.'

While some fans were only concerned with the adrenalin rush of the band's sound, for others Deniz Tek's lyrics were an otherworldly drawcard all their own.

In 'Hand of Law', for example, he pulled from a jaw-droppingly broad base. Included were references to the Greek gods Phobos and Deimos, the two moons of Mars, the day the Doors' Jim Morrison and Brian Jones of the Stones died, exactly two years apart, two 1970s Detroit street gangs, James Brown, a dream, a line from the Blue Oyster Cult's 'Astronomy', and a connection with 'Hand of Fate' from the Stones' *Black and Blue*.

Mark Sisto's outlook on the world also provided part of the imagery.

Mark Sisto: 'I had been looking at the starry night out at sea. What if this whole scene we see here on this earth is just projected down here? If one of those stars was a movie projector, and all else was just the passive movie screen? What a horror that would be.

'There was this magazine I had brought with me from America, *Despair*. It was hilarious. Some of R. [Robert] Crumb's best. One subsection was Justin Green's "Theater of Cruelty: Th' Kiss-Off", this treasure of a comic. The story was this guy ran this low-end strip club. His main dancer and girlfriend Tanya had vamoosed. He finds her in this cult and on the door was a big hand with an eye in its palm. She opened the door, and holds up her hand and says, "The word is law."'

Deniz Tek: 'It's hard to overstate the importance of Mark in the band's ethos, especially as regards my lyrics of that early time.'

Tim Pittman: 'They are as much a part of the sound of Birdman as the music. The imagery is just fantastic! They produce paintings and/or film images in the listener's mind.'

'Hand of Law', together with 'Man with Golden Helmet' and 'Descent into the Maelstrom', elevated Radio Birdman storeys above all their contemporaries—punk rock and even their heroes.

Rob Younger: 'If the Blue Oyster Cult hadn't been an influence—and I really pushed my feelings for them early on—he probably wouldn't have had songs like "Hand of Law", "Maelstrom", stuff like that. The slightly more epic ones. I think there are things like that [Blue Oyster Cult] in "Love Kills".'

Radios Appear wasn't for the technically faint of heart either, contrary to the three-chord ethos of punk of the time. 'Anglo Girl Desire'—a title Mark Sisto came up with—was a particular mind-fuck.

Bruce Tindale: 'It was really, really clever and really, really hard, strenuous playing. I had to get Chris [Masuak] to show me some of the chords, and it was like, "Holy shit! There's six chords in that song!"'

As had been the case with the *Burn My Eye* EP, a do-it-themselves ethos was applied to the album's distribution process—again from the Trafalgar office and once more with the band heavily involved.

Michael McMartin: 'Rob and I would drive down to Palings, Grace Brothers, and all of the other record stores, and tell them every record was on "sale or return" [basis], as an incentive to get them to stock it. People weren't hearing it on the radio, so they needed to be enticed. We would send out letters, saying, "We notice you haven't got this [record] yet. It is selling. Please get it, sale or return."

'Not a single retailer stiffed us for a single copy. It was extraordinary! It really was. If it didn't sell, they'd at least pay for it and keep it in stock. But we didn't try and put 50 into a store. Some said, "How many should we take?" "Take three." "Okay, if you think that's worthwhile." "Sure is, and when you sell two of them, order another three!" That's where the sales training at Festival [Records] came in. We were sending out parcels to stores across the entire country. It was wonderful!

'Retailers really picked up on the fact that this was one of the first independent albums by people who appeared to know what they were doing—and there was a buzz about the band.'

At White Light it would be their biggest seller and could even be purchased straight from the hands of band members.

John Cotter (Utopia Records): 'Chris brought copies of *Radios Appear* to Fun House and I bought one that night.'

Roger Gold (WEA and Big Time Records): 'I was at Soft Union Records in Balmain when Ron Keeley jumped out of an old Holden and delivered copies, and I bought it.'

Kath 'Good Vibes' Kendall: 'I thought, "Wait until the world hears this!" You might talk about the Rolling Stones, the Beatles, I'd go, "Nah. You haven't heard anything. You haven't heard anything!"'

Brad Shepherd: 'It was exciting to be alive when you heard that music as a teenager in the seventies.'

The media reception was just as enthusiastic, with David N. Pepperell, co-founder of the legendary Melbourne record store

Archie 'n' Jughead's, declaring in *Juke* '. . . to compare them to anything else in Australia is just wasteful . . . the most together unit this country has ever seen has produced the first truly great Australian rock album. This is the future right here for you to have now—this is your chance to not only catch up to the world but to pass it.'

Warwick Gilbert: 'I like the first album. But even that wasn't perfect. It didn't capture the ferocity of the band live. It's a bit mannered, to my way of thinking. I like the savagery of the live band. That's what really set me alight.'

Rob Younger felt that the focus of some on the outfit's interlocking fret firepower diminished their collective virtues.

Rob Younger: 'It all became about this "twin guitar attack", this fucking phrase that kept coming up. Is that all we are? All about two fucking guitars, is it now? Fuck all that!'

Long-time supporters 2JJ continued their push in support of the Radios, usually but not exclusively during George Wayne's program in the afternoon. The station became a gateway to Birdman for many, even those in regional areas of New South Wales.

Steve Abrahall (Birdman devotee): 'With the AM aerial hooked to the flyscreen, on a balmy summer's evening in my hometown of Coonamble [on NSW's central-western plains], the power chords of "Do the Pop" wafted in and out over the static.'

To promote the album, Birdman were again interviewed on air by the station with the quietly spoken Younger always sparkling on his feet, until the day a presenter felt the need to prod the singer over his surname. 'Younger than what?' he was asked. Rob quickly shifted gears. 'Younger than springtime, arsehole!'

Back at the Fun House, the seasons were changing as well. The Gyprock dust that coated every surface was a solid hint. The renovations were progressing according to plan for the restaurant that would take over the space once the band's loose six-month management lease ended.

The strange dark rain inside the room was less easily accounted for.

Catherine Kingsmill: 'When you were at the Fun House you could smoke, but there was a glittery silver stuff that used to be in the atmosphere. Sometimes it would turn dark if it touched your skin. We didn't know what it was. It was like a chemical in the air. I don't know whether it was real.'

Dancing on the Edge of a Volcano

The act of kicking the shit out of the Fun House's jukebox to the point of malfunction would once have been seen as blasphemy of the highest order. Now it was uncomfortably prophetic.

As was Paul Gearside's poster for the Psycho Surgeons' appearance on 30 July 1977. It fed into the attitude behind renaming the venue the Oxford 'Slaughterhouse' for the night, with accompanying artwork that ghoulishly depicted the Surgeons being showered in blood from the audience—a scenario soon to be graphically transferred directly onto Gearside himself.

The success of *Radios Appear*, plus rabid word of mouth, now had punters lined down the stairs of the Fun House and onto the street.

Damien Minton: 'Radio Birdman were apocalyptic, because you'd be on a few Mandrax or uppers or whatever it was, and some beers, and that place would be packed—you'd be lucky to get to the bar—and it would be swirling. And then when they got into that subsonic sound of theirs—this throbbing enthusiasm . . .'

Dare Jennings: 'It was a ritualistic thing, going to these gigs and feeling the power.'

The physical mass of bodies all packed in and dancing as one was taking its toll on the building.

Deniz Tek: 'I was afraid that there would be a disaster, like the floor of the Fun House—with 300 people—collapsing. The building actually shook.'

Kath 'Good Vibes' Kendall: 'I remember the floor starting to move, like a wave, and thinking, "We're all going to fall down and die!" But fuck! What a way to go!'

Bob Short: 'It was like dancing on the edge of a volcano!'

Entry was now $1.50 for the band and that was recycled back into the gigs.

An ad for the Fun House in *RAM* placed its long-standing dress code and attitude on the public record, setting out strict guidelines for those who wished to play in the tiny room. Again, it read like the work of Rob Younger.

WHAT IS NOT WANTED

1. Bands who play shit like Quo, Purple, Queen, Zeppelin, ZZ Top, Bad Co., Ted Nugent (post '72), Bowie. In short, any of the crap one can hear anywhere in this boring burg.
2. Dumb clothing—stage gear consisting of fashion jeans and overalls, platforms, hippie gear (beads, baggy overalls, shoulder bags, etc.).
3. The Equipment Obsession Syndrome—the popular notion that a new expensive brand amp and guitar and monster PA will automatically make a group really 'insane', 'incredible', 'good', 'rock 'n' roll'. Equipment freaks rarely cut it when it comes to actually playing rock 'n' roll.'

On the gear front, sound man Andy 'Mort' Bradley already had enough on his plate.

Andy 'Mort' Bradley: 'The biggest problem [with Birdman] was sheer volume. You had three 100-watt amps on stage for

Deniz, Chris and Warwick. They always had under-powered PA systems and it was really difficult to get Rob's voice out over the top, especially at the Fun House. That was a lot of band!'

A headlining appearance at the Manly Vale Hotel with a fledgling Cold Chisel was a more-than-welcome calendar entry and their first major spot since the release of *Radios Appear*.

Phill Calvert: 'I went to the Fun House and bumped into Johnny Kannis. He said, in a most hilarious sort of commando-type speak, "The men are playing across the water!" What that meant was a bunch of people were all jumping into a car and driving over to the Manly Vale!'

The Birdman way kicked in right from the get-go.

Chris Masuak: 'We had our little vocal PA with us that Rob sang through, and my Trainer six by ten [speaker] column that I brought from Canada. Cold Chisel rocked up and said, "Hey, we've got a PA," and Birdman being Birdman basically told them to fuck off.'

Rob Younger: 'I was sitting at the back of the room with Deniz. I turned to him and said, "These guys [Chisel] are never going to fucking get anywhere!" Like I can really pick it.'

Radio Birdman and their crowd, however, were on, and set at high beam and beyond.

Damien Minton: 'It was Dante's *Inferno*! It was packed and on for young and old, but the great thing about Radio Birdman was they celebrated their audience and you really felt you were part of a movement. That insignia was really something you could identify with, in terms of being a part of that energy.'

Anny Douglass: 'We just went to see Birdman. We went in when they started and left when they finished.'

While some of the Radios faithful didn't waste any time exiting the Manly Vale, it seemed that doubts about the imagery of the band weren't in any hurry to disperse.

Patrick Bingham-Hall: 'Andrew McMillan [*RAM* journalist] sidled up to me after the show and asked if I was comfortable with the militaristic overtones, the quasi-fascist salutes. I never did the salute, not once. It may have been quite innocuous, just teenage war games and Messerschmitt model planes, but it did hint at something psychologically and sociologically unsettling. The legacy of World War II—and in Australia, the Vietnam War—still hung over everything, and that worked both ways. The punters at the venues loved the rock-and-roll soldiers act, but I also wonder how many were turned off by it.'

The main issue of the night, however, wasn't perception, but rather personnel—with Pip Hoyle suddenly rejoining the Radios' ranks.

For Warwick Gilbert, the reintroduction of Pip's keyboards threw the rhythmic make-up of the music, particularly his relationship with Ron Keeley's drumming, out of whack.

Warwick Gilbert: 'I was catatonically bored, all of a sudden. There was no point in me being there playing bass. All that [ghost] sound was immediately gone—there were no spaces. It really did fuck the band over as a going concern and I was embarrassed, actually, to be part of it.'

Gilbert quietly decided to leave Birdman, but the proposed tour of the UK, plus the notion of hitting America with the Ramones, kept him hanging in. However, he had to wait. And wait.

Warwick Gilbert: 'I had no way of getting to England to see my son and that's why I did the European tour. Unfortunately, it was delayed for six months.'

For Chris Masuak, the reintroduction of Hoyle had far greater implications. The young guitarist had initially come into the band on the back of Pip's sabbatical. But while he'd made a vital contribution to shaping the outfit's sound, would there still be a need for him now Deniz's good friend was back in the fold? If so, for how long?

Chris Masuak: 'Hoyle was back on board, so I thought I was out of the band. We'd accomplished something without his involvement. I didn't see the point in it.'

Deniz Tek: 'No one in the band said anything negative about it at the time, but of course, decades later, I found out that Warwick, Chris and Ron were against Pip coming back.'

The ocean of broken glass that covered the floor at the end of the evening at the Manly Vale, crunching under the feet of the representatives of WEA Records, seemed like the aftermath of a battle itself. Despite Cold Chisel soon being signed to the label, the Radios would have been a hot topic back at their office. The talk that someone in the crowd had, for some reason, brought a sword to the Manly gig was a more fitting symbol for what was on the horizon for the Birdmen.

Teenage Shutdown

Deniz Tek was in his final year of medical school when he received a phone call from the Dean's office at UNSW, while on duty at Prince Henry Hospital.

Deniz Tek: 'I was told to get over there immediately. I had no idea what it was about, but I knew it wasn't going to be anything good. Someone had written a letter to the university, complaining that I had given heroin to an underage girl at one of our gigs at the Fun House. The letter claimed to be from the girl's parents.

'There were no witnesses or evidence—just this letter, which the Dean read to me but wouldn't allow me to see. The allegation was utterly preposterous. None of us did hard drugs. Pip didn't even drink alcohol. Of all the bands gigging in Sydney at the time, ours was the least likely to be involved in something like that.

'But it was my word against whoever had written the damning letter. I immediately asked for a meeting with these "parents" and the child, if there was one, to attempt to get to the truth. This was flatly refused. The Dean put the letter in his locked safe and said he would simply wait and collect evidence against me, and if the allegations could be supported, I would be dismissed from the university, and the case handed over to police. As I was leaving his office, he recommended that I quit the band while awaiting final judgment.

'I was thrown completely off my bearings. It hit at the core of my being. To have invested so much time and effort to get within months of successfully completing my degree, then have it all trashed by a lie, was a devastating prospect.

'I was acutely aware that someone was out to get me. I was paranoid, looking over my shoulder, constantly expecting another attack. I called George Kringas, our manager, and we held a band meeting. I told the guys I was going to have to keep my head down for the next few months—no more Sydney gigs—and try and finish university. After that, we could resume our music full bore. They were all understanding and we cancelled our booked dates at the Fun House.'

They didn't know it at the time, but Radio Birdman would never again play the tiny venue. Satellite shows such as an appearance at a Wollongong Leagues Club would be as close as they would get to the harbour city for quite a while.

There was an attempt to frame their absence as a measure necessary to keep the band a cool commodity, rather than being overexposed, which must have seemed hollow given the trials they had suffered to finally get to where they were. In any event, Deniz's loose nickname of Steve McGarrett seemed to become his new tag in interviews. If this was an attempt at disguise it was a flimsy one.

The forced move stopped their momentum in Sydney, their strongest territory, dead in its tracks. The promotional push was now confined to rave reviews of *Radios Appear*, along with occasional TV screenings of the thrilling video for 'New Race' from Paddington Town Hall which included a surprise airing on the ABC's weekday afternoon teen program, *Flashez*.

While Birdman were not able to appear in Sydney, the Fun House was still the place to be to dance to acts like the Hellcats but tensions continued to rise in the crowded room. Any naive romance of the bikers' initial patronage was being replaced by an atmosphere reminiscent of Iggy and the Stooges' *Metallic K.O.*

Alley Brereton: 'When [the bikers] first came to the Fun House, it sort of felt a bit Rolling Stone-ish and a bit outlawish and they were pretty well behaved. Occasionally a few of us would go over to their headquarters on the back of the bikes. But then they started to harass some of the women, and that's when it got out of hand.'

Deniz Tek: 'There was occasional violence—someone would do something or say something and get stomped.'

Kath 'Good Vibes' Kendall: 'We wanted to dance, and it was like, "I don't know if I want to bump his shoulder." It was always so secure with our friends, and the guys used to look after the girls, but it became a bit nervy.'

The original Oxford and then early Fun House crowd also found themselves sharing space with strange newcomers, who had now heard of Radio Birdman and the venue.

Their once-exclusive club had become a diluted, virtual general-admission affair. Newbies in clean, white Birdman T-shirts were arriving after all the heavy lifting had been done by a core group, who had been willing to follow the band into the abyss while wearing a small, round symbol of allegiance.

Bob Short: 'If you didn't have the badge, fuck you! Someone from the band usually gave you one and that was it.'

Tara Anderson: 'The crowd that came in next was from outside the area. They were different people expecting a different band, I think.'

Bob Short: 'In those early days, everyone was essentially some sort of a hippie. It was only when the mob arrived . . .'

Another issue was the behaviour of some in the punk scene who saw violence as an integral part of that culture. One night, Deniz Tek had a knife pulled on him over his selection on the jukebox.

Deniz Tek: 'Punk attracted a few social misfits who focused on violence. Fights began to erupt over silly things.'

At the same time, the fan club was ballooning in popularity. It prompted a change at the top, with its president, Paul 'Cloven Skull' Gearside, stepping aside.

Paul Gearside: 'It got bigger and bigger and in no time I was in trouble from some of the band members, like Deniz and Rob. They were saying, "You've got to get your finger out, because we're getting word that you're not replying to people who've written to you." I couldn't stay on top of it. It got worse and worse, and I said, "I've got to pass it on."'

Meanwhile, Jim Dickson arrived in Sydney from Brisbane clutching a rehearsal tape of his band, the Survivors, with their UK diet of the Pretty Things, the Who and the Kinks. He had previously met an admiring Rob Younger at a local Survivors' gig, but this time made the trip south specifically in the hope of a slot at the now nationally famous Fun House.

Jim Dickson: 'It was *the* place to play. Rob and Ron came over to Greg and Colleen's place at Five Dock. They heard the tape and said, "Yeah, you can play at the Fun House."'

They would never get the chance.

From Camelot to Corpse Flower

The weekend of 12 and 13 August 1977, the Fun House was hosting Johnny Dole and the Scabs on the Friday night and the Psycho Surgeons, Saturday. Radio Birdman, with Pip Hoyle back in the band, were out of town. They had been continuing work on the international album for Sire when the opportunity arose to do two dates in Canberra—beyond the gaze of the academic powers that be in Sydney—with the Hellcats. One was at the ANU and then a second in an ill-suited bar. A trip to the War Memorial was a mandatory part of the schedule.

Ron S. Peno (Hellcats): 'We stayed at Woden and I remember Deniz cooking breakfast and asking, "Hey, Ron, do you like Rotwurst?" Saveloy was about the most exotic I'd had, and here's this American who I was besotted with, saying, "Do you like Rotwurst?" [Ron in a tiny voice] "Yes, Deniz!" He could have said, "Would you like this piece of shit on a stick?" "Yes! I'd love it, Deniz! [tiny shrill voice] It's divine!"'

A large group of the Radios' faithful took the train to the icy-cold capital.

Kath 'Good Vibes' Kendall: 'I had nowhere to stay the first night, so after the gig we slept under the trees in the main park and froze!

'The next night someone in the audience screamed out, "Play some George Benson!" Rob's eyes almost popped out and he jumped off the tiny stage and punched the guy in the nose.

I couldn't believe it! Bob Short was staying at the YMCA and he gave us floor space and put his big black woollen coat over us to keep us warm.'

But as Birdman were heating up Canberra, at the Fun House all that had been festering during recent months had fully congealed into a dark mass during the Psycho Surgeons gig.

Paul Gearside: 'The bikers didn't seem to be obvious to me until that night, and then they were obvious to everyone. I'm not sure if it was the gig where I had an extra-long mike cord and went and had a piss in the middle of a song. I thought, "I'll take it one better than Iggy!" But at the end of "Search and Destroy", someone in the crowd yelled out, "That was a pile of fucking shit!" I said, "If you don't like it, fuck off!" With gusto. But I didn't know who said it.

'These guys came up and said, "Yeah, we'll go, but we'll take you with us!" This bloke just grabbed me, and two of them held me, and a third guy came bursting out of the crowd and kicked me in the crotch. That quick. I was down. Some heavy manhandling and a few punches.'

The reaction of some to Gearside's assault demonstrated the degree to which the atmosphere at the Fun House had changed.

Paul Gearside: 'Someone said into the mike, "Let's hear it for people who can't make babies!" and the crowd cheered! I had my balls smashed in and they thought that was a funny thing to say!'

John Needham had grown up in Parramatta, surrounded by the level of violence that had befallen the singer from the Psycho Surgeons. But having it play out now at the sacred ground of the Fun House was beyond the pale.

John Needham: 'I can remember witnessing that and I never went back. The Fun House to me died on that night.

Everything that was great about that place—the camaraderie, the good times, the freedom of it, the joy—it was just all gone.'

Radio Birdman were advised of the incident by phone and it was curtains for the Fun House: 13 August 1977. The venue ended with the same foreboding air it had when Rob Younger and Warwick Gilbert had first visited in the late sixties.

But the anxiety wasn't over yet. Penny Ward was living with Jules R.B. Normington and their front door was just metres from Gearside's place.

Penny Ward: 'The night Paul was beaten up, I remember going home and being really afraid they were going to come around. That was one scary thing.'

Her fears were well founded.

Paul Gearside: 'I had to get out of my home. The Angels started hanging around outside. They found out where I was. They hadn't finished the job. So I moved.'

Anny Douglass: 'It [the closure of the Fun House] was sad, but I thought it was a business decision by George. I thought he had other plans in the works.'

Deniz Tek: 'I knew that once the Hells Angels started hanging out at the Fun House, its days as a cool venue were numbered.'

For the Radios' faithful, the shutdown of the room—which roughly coincided with the end of the band's loose leasing arrangement—effectively meant being back on the street and out in the general population, where the straight folks went about their numbed existence.

Long Live the Evolution

It wasn't quite as satisfying as ticking off wiping the stage with Skyhooks, but having *Radios Appear* positioned with Boz Scaggs' ridiculously popular *Silk Degrees* in the upper reaches of the Top Ten album chart at a major store in the heart of Sydney was pretty close.

The creation and distribution of *Radios Appear* had changed the game, and before the very eyes of the local industry.

Michael McMartin: 'We had taken the Birdman album to Paul [Turner, WEA Managing Director] and it was, "No, no, no, this won't work . . ." But we then sold 3000 copies. This was a lot of copies, considering that Gold was 20,000 in those days—and all this from our small office. It started to chart and Paul called and just said, "Okay, okay, just bring it over. We'll distribute it."'

Charles Fisher: 'The band came to the studio every day and sat in the front office, addressing envelopes and putting vinyl into covers and putting them in envelopes and running to the post office. Both the band and us at Trafalgar were pretty much sick of it!'

The Australian re-release of *Radios Appear* through WEA, a major label, was effective from 5 September 1977. The media release stated, with no small measure of unbridled seemingly homegrown enthusiasm: 'The combination of an excellent distribution network and (tick one): a) the greatest rock 'n roll record ever; b) the most acclaimed Australian album of the year; c) this boss neato keen platter—will be a surefire winnah!'

There was also a promotion at the time whereby the purchase of an Australian LP entitled the buyer to a free copy of *Long Live the Evolution*. This 2JJ album included live broadcasted recordings, such as Radio Birdman doing 'Burned My Eye' from November 1976, as well as AC/DC, Dragon, Jo Jo Zep and the Falcons, Skyhooks and others.

With the Sire deal ticking away in the background, a planned promotional trip to the UK to lay the groundwork for the overseas tour and the release of the new international LP was scrubbed, much to the disappointment of Rob Younger, who was to be the band's representative.

Rob Younger: 'I had my small-pox injection and I got sick from it. I had vomiting and delirium and then it got called off. I was really looking forward to that, because I'd never been overseas at that point.'

Meanwhile, others had commenced something of their own version of the Fun House but with the likes of Brit roots rocker Dave Edmunds and his *Get It* and later, *Tracks On Wax* LPs hovering overhead rather than the Stooges or the Blue Oyster Cult.

Mental As Anything—another local art-school-based creative collective, with future internationally acclaimed artist Reg Mombassa on guitar—were performing on the pool tables at the Unicorn Hotel on Oxford Street, in a magic scene favoured by many in the Birdman camp, as was the Mangrove Boogie Kings' equivalent at the Albury.

Clyde Bramley: 'I remember going to Darlinghurst on Monday night and seeing the Mentals at the Unicorn and Tuesday nights the Boogie Kings at the Albury.'

Anny Douglass: 'The Boogie Kings were so much fun! The yin to Birdman's yang? You could let your shoulders relax at a Boogie Kings gig.'

Then suddenly, the delay in the Radios taking on the world didn't seem so bad, when they were announced as opening act for Iggy Pop's first Australian tour in November and December 1977. The shows would take in Melbourne, Adelaide, Brisbane and Sydney, with the chance of a date in Perth, plus their own gigs in each city. Deniz Tek's final exams would be over by that point in the year thus placing him out of reach of any potential action from the university. Close to 6000 people a night were likely to attend, in what would be a priceless, if belated, promotional opportunity for *Radios Appear*. And audiences would be primed for the very sound Birdman dealt out, which Iggy no longer seemed to generate quite as furiously, if his most recent efforts, *The Idiot* and *Lust for Life*, were any guide.

His blistering 'I Got a Right' single and the *Kill City* album—the best record the Stones never made—both with James Williamson, would however return Pop programming to its rightful state.

The electricity in the air around Ig's visit was almost visible. The Radios' fan club offered tickets to those who presented the Birdman symbol inserted in the newsletter to the booking office. White Light Records' latest flyer was in Radio/Stooge overdrive, plugging not only the tour, but a new edition of the *Metallic K.O.* LP, with sound quality enhanced. It also declared that in the first quarter of the following year, the Birdmen would unleash a new album.

Warwick Gilbert designed the poster for the dates including modifying the Airkraft typeface which he dubbed "Radiokraft" while Rob Younger was doing a tour prep of his own.

Rob Younger: 'I remember running around this oval near where I was living at North Sydney at the time. I was getting really fit, thinking, "Oh Christ! This is Iggy Pop! I've got to be sharp! I've got to be in shape!"'

Radio Birdman had never been to Brisbane before, and after the announcement of the Iggy visit some local fans took no chances.

Brad Shepherd: 'I camped out overnight in front of the Festival Hall box office in a sleeping bag to get tickets. I put a lot of effort into that!'

With this spring in their step, the Radios headed to Adelaide for the first time on the horrifically badged 'Aural Rape' tour. The City of Churches was a largely unmonitored territory in the pre-Internet age, allowing the outfit to slip in under the radar, with little risk to Deniz Tek's position at the University of NSW. At least, that was the plan.

The South Australian offensive was organised by Patrick Miles, music writer for the *Adelaide Advertiser*.

Eight shows were scheduled between 15 and 25 September, spread across just three venues: the Largs Pier (two nights), the Marryatville (five gigs, including two consecutive Fridays and Saturdays) and the Tivoli.

Sound man Andy 'Mort' Bradley and Patrick Bingham-Hall arrived first, in a rented van of equipment, and went about plastering posters for the gigs on every flat surface in a highly targeted manner.

Patrick Bingham-Hall: 'We took great care to obscure any posters for other bands.'

Birdman hit town and set up at 537 Seaview Road, Grange—a beachfront residence where Jon Scofield was living. He would act as their local driver.

Jon Schofield: 'We had Jo Jo Zep and the Falcons come over every now and again, but there was no in-your-face, powerful rock and roll to be seen in Adelaide.'

That was about to change dramatically. Even the pre-gig sound checks would be an event.

Patrick Bingham-Hall: 'I'd check the microphone levels by reciting lines from "Jabberwocky"—I think that was Chris's idea—I'd sing "Ol' Man River", and occasionally I'd imitate Rob, jerky dance and all, when I was sure he was in another part of town.'

Almost 1000 packed into the Marryatville Hotel on 23 September to see Rob Younger's moves in person, smashing the previous attendance record. The performance, along with interviews with the band, were filmed by the ABC for the *Rockturnal* program. It screened the following year and remains some of the most compelling live Radios footage in existence.

As was the case in Melbourne, a who's who of the local scene were in attendance, including John Dowler, later of Young Modern, Dave Bunney and Giles Barrow, future members of the Exploding White Mice, and Clare Moore soon of the Moodists.

Clare Moore: 'My friends are dancing up the front and I am coolly standing at the back in front of a tall guy, who has his fingers in his ears. I was totally in awe of Ron Keeley. I don't know how he did it. I was desperate to play in a band and was certainly inspired by their performances.'

Jon Schofield: 'The place went ballistic! Quite seriously. It was insane! The Marryatville Hotel is etched in my frontal lobes forever. We were up the front and we all had sore arms after they left from doing the [salute] thing!'

Channel 9 in Adelaide interviewed the band, with the visiting act picking their fave music clips for the *Rock-on-Sunday* program. This was what it was like to be rock stars. However, they had something of a thudding back-to-earth experience at the Largs Pier Hotel, before the remnants of the notorious Sharpie tribes.

Patrick Bingham-Hall: 'The punters were very tough—boys and girls seething with aggro, all with cut-off blue vests and tattoos and close-cropped mullet hairdos. A lot of tension, but we escaped unscathed.'

That was nothing compared to an incident back in Sydney.

Angie Pepper: 'I was home alone at the lower-floor flat in Surrey Street and had just gone to bed, and thankfully all the lights were out. I heard bikes arrive up on the footpath. Then the gate was smashed open and bikers rode down the steps and around the back of the flat. I hid in a corner where I couldn't be seen from any of the windows. The sound of shouting, and bikes revving around the flat, went on for what seemed like about ten minutes. Once I was sure they were gone, I ran up the stairs to the flat above, where a couple lived, and stayed there the rest of the night. There had been incidents involving bikies recently and I was pretty sure we'd been targeted. I don't think I've ever been that frightened.'

The shock waves of the Birdmen pulling more than 2500 people over the course of their Adelaide stay deflated any notion of an undercover operation, with *Countdown*'s Molly Meldrum making mention of the outfit 'causing a storm' in the city as well as Sydney and played a quick grab of the 'New Race' video which he introduced as being titled 'Yeah Yup!'

The Radios' fan club was now run by Roger Westcombe, writing as Satan's Hog, a character from the Blue Oyster Cult's shadow realm.

The band returned to the studio for much of October and continued to work on songs such as the 13th Floor Elevators' 'You're Gonna Miss Me'—which had featured Rob Younger on harmonica for one gig—as well as the MC5's 'Shakin' Street', Bo Diddley's 'Let the Kids Dance' and a surprising version of Kraftwerk's 'Radioactivity'. They also shaped songs like 'More Fun', 'Dark Surprise', 'Iskender Time', '455 SD', 'Breaks My Heart', Tek and Gilbert's 'Crying Sun', and Tek and Masuak's 'TPBR Combo'.

By this point, arch Birdman fan Bob Short had an alternate outlet for his energies, as guitarist in the immediately infamous Filth, fronted by Peter Tillman. These guys left all other alleged punk bands in Australia—with the possible exception of Brisbane's Leftovers—seeming like members of a strict religious order.

Despite recent successes elsewhere, gigging in Sydney was still a no-no for Birdman due to the allegations levelled at Deniz Tek by the university. The void saw the emergence of Johnny and the Hitmen, a loose, often rotating party band of Johnny Kannis, Chris Masuak, Warwick Gilbert, Ron Keeley and Charlie Georgees, and joined by Deniz Tek, Angie Pepper, Clyde Bramley, Steve Harris and Lynne Phillips.

The line-up of Kannis, Masuak, Georgees, Keeley and Gilbert played at Tara Anderson's 21st-birthday party.

While they were out of sight, the Radios were reinventing themselves visually in preparation for the release of the Sire LP. They enlisted legendary Australian photographer Bob King in October 1977 to shoot what would be the cover image. The result was a curious realignment with the uniformed look that had fallen away to the point of near non-existence since its unveiling at Paddington Town Hall back in April.

Had they not been off the radar, an opening slot for Lou Reed—who landed back in Australia in late October—might have been an option. It made for a big weekend for Novocastrian fans, in any event, with Reed appearing at Newcastle's Civic Theatre on the Friday, while on Saturday the Birdmen were at the local university. As had been the case with the Canberra dates, a group of supporters travelled for the occasion.

Bob Short: 'We went to see Lou and then a few of us found a churchyard, and basically dossed out on the steps overnight. Then we figured we stunk after that, so we walked down to the beach, all still in our clothes, and got into the water, and then hung around to dry out, before going onto the uni to see Birdman.'

The euphoria about the impending dates with Iggy Pop—commencing the following month—made everyone more buoyant despite the delayed overseas tour, the loss of the Fun House, the combustive internal friction and the departure of Mark Sisto, who returned home to America. To the massive disappointment of the Birdmen, though, the Iggy tour was cancelled at the eleventh hour. A more significant loss was coming. It was around this time that Warwick Gilbert designed a new poster that was underappreciated—perhaps being too close to the bone—and closed the door on any future artistic contributions from the enigmatic bassist.

Warwick Gilbert: 'That poster was rejected by Deniz, who suggested I do a *Star Wars*–type close-up of the symbol as a spaceship, with all the paraphernalia and plumbing on the outside, in my own time and at my own expense, for free.

'Firstly, Kansas, ELO and Boston had each already done that, with wit and unlimited budgets. Secondly, it revealed zero appreciation and knowledge of the value of what I'd brought to Radio Birdman. So I downed tools and I created no further art for the Tek-led six piece. That final poster was a technical advance for me as an artist at the time, and closest in concept to my Jefferson Airplane Fillmore poster that had inspired the Blitzkrieg poster in 1976. I thought it was my best. Its central motif was an alien craft with a modest Radio Birdman symbol on its flank, drifting across a nondescript landscape with the arse end blown out of it.

'Only in retrospect did I realise that it was my response to being cut out of the creative and financial decision-making process, once I'd served my purpose.'

Deliverance at Altitude

It was as if the spores of the last brutal night of the Fun House had blown west and settled over the Blue Mountains.

Chris Masuak and Patrick Bingham-Hall had decided to drive to the gig at Springwood. Along the way, they stopped off to get some food, only to find they were in another world and not carrying the necessary documentation.

Chris Masuak: 'We got harassed and nearly beaten up by a bunch of yobbos who clearly didn't like us. So by the time we got to Springwood, I was really shaken, really upset and really drunk.'

A local girl took a liking to Masuak when they arrived at the venue; however, it was anything but the beginning of a civic welcoming committee.

Punk rock, or any notion of it, seemed not to have made it past the watery boundary line of the Nepean River, much less this confusing multiracial patchwork of strangers in army-surplus gear, carrying guitars, drums and a strange symbol.

Bob Short: 'That was a fucking disaster! They were like hill-billies! We might as well have come down from fucking Mars! They really went after Jim [Flowers]. It was redneck city out there. "White was going to be right" that night.'

Jim Flowers: 'These guys attacked me and said stuff about me being Chinese, and that they would kill me! I took it seriously and escaped backstage. I was really grateful to the band for protecting me.'

Doug Lonsdale: 'I've still got a scar from that night. I was down the front dancing like a fool, and when I stopped some bloke came up to me. I didn't know what he was saying because there was all this noise, and he punched me. I was that drunk, I didn't feel it.'

Catherine Kingsmill: 'I had my Radio Birdman T-shirt on, and this guy came up and bit me. Just ripped a hole through the back of it.'

The mood was just as black on the stage.

Chris Masuak: 'Keeley threw a stick at Younger, because he was yapping at me, and Keeley told him to shut up and leave me alone. Stuff was starting to seep out by then. The fabric was coming unglued.'

At one point, it seemed as though Masuak had ejected himself from the situation, dramatically taking a swan dive off the metre-plus-high stage.

Patrick Bingham-Hall: 'I took a photo of Chris sprawled at my feet in the middle of the crowd, playing his guitar about 30 feet from the stage. That photo came second in the *RAM* photo-of-the-year competition.'

At the end of the night, the fun really fired up as the band and their friends attempted to get out of the place in one piece.

Warwick Gilbert: 'We formed into a circle like an echidna! The local toughs wanted to kill us. We had to get from the hall to the van with swinging mike stands.'

Bob Short: 'I managed to miss my lift because everybody was just running for their lives to get out of there. I ended up walking. I got to Emu Plains [fifteen kilometres away] at six o'clock in the morning—and was I pleased to see the place!

The band members also made it out alive but some were in no mood to celebrate after the completion of the album for Sire, which despite the early sparks and a sound that had approached the Radios' live attack, had, for them, in the end, flatlined.

Warwick Gilbert: 'The first album promised so much and got everyone excited, and all we had to do was do more of that, but that didn't happen.'

On the other hand, Birdman's stance regarding gigs in Sydney was relaxed, after a starvation diet for fans that had lasted several months. Perhaps counterintuitively, during their absence their audience was now a supercharged beast.

And no one anticipated just how ravenous or demanding a creature it would be.

★

The Birdman machine returned to Paddington Town Hall on Sunday, 20 November 1977. They found a dramatically expanded audience to that at the Fun House, only a few blocks down Oxford Street, just months earlier.

And, similar to the last days of that special space, this was a different crowd. It was a new, darkened legion pulled gravitationally from deep in suburbia, many of whom had only heard about the band and made the pilgrimage to witness for themselves what all the cool kids had been talking about.

Playing to a handful of friends and a few bar regulars at the Excelsior Hotel in Surry Hills just three short years earlier seemed an age ago. Now, the floor of the grand hall was bouncing under the weight of the sea of attendees.

Bob Short: 'We were going, "Fuck! There's so many people!" We couldn't understand what had happened in the course of just a few months. It felt like the world was changing to suit us. It wasn't quite as much fun to be in the audience, because you began losing that thing of space in the room. By Paddo, there was the crush at the front.'

George Munoz: 'It was a different intensity and a little more extreme to me. I didn't go there to dance to "Louie Louie" and sing and dance along to "Surf City". You didn't do that. It was on a different stage and you can't touch them now.'

Rob Younger choosing to wear a provocative black balaclava probably confirmed what many thought they were coming to see.

Rob Younger: 'Not long before the gig, there was an issue of *Time* magazine with a picture on the front of a terrorist, and he had a balaclava. I thought, "I'm going to do something like that for the gig." So I got a black T-shirt and put it over my head. I drew with chalk where my eyes and mouth were, and then took it off and cut out holes. I got quite a bit of flack for it, actually.

'Anthony [O'Grady, *RAM* editor] didn't like it and told me I should have taken it off after a while. I thought, "No," and wore it for the whole gig. It was really hot under that thing. I remember sending a photo to Sire for the artwork of a single that didn't come out and they wouldn't use it.'

Ron Keeley: 'I thought it [the balaclava] was a stupid idea and made the mistake of telling him so.'

The venue was being renovated to accommodate a cinema complex below the main hall. Some overzealous punters—in the search-and-totally-fucking-destroy spirit of the punk scene and/or simply because it was there—gleefully assisted with the demolition work, and more, on the upper floor.

Jim Flowers: 'I think the magic started to dissipate when they began to get big.'

But musically, the occasion was a triumph. Birdman aired a titanic reading of Kraftwerk's 'Radioactivity', which proved that, while the sound of Detroit had a pull and aesthetic, Germany clearly also had its attractions. The Radios shifted the song into a spectral epic of more than seven minutes, with melodic shards of guitar howling through it, a deadpan vocal, and tribal drums.

Deniz Tek: 'We were listening to Kraftwerk a lot. We loved their pop sensibility, and we were delighted that they had shamelessly copped riffs from Brian Wilson's "Good Vibrations". We were fascinated that the pop essence could shine through, despite the soulless, machine-like context. The notion that Kraftwerk might be out of step with the rest of our set never came up. We were always looking for new ideas.'

Rob Younger: 'We only did "Radioactivity" a few times. For some reason it worked and felt fantastic. It's got an awesome beat and riff, that song. It pinned me behind the mike stand, which I dislike. I love Kraftwerk.'

Shelley Kay: 'I thought, "What the fuck are they playing Kraftwerk for?" And all of a sudden, Kraftwerk were cool!'

Jules R.B. Normington: 'Their version of "Radioactivity" was phenomenal! They were just about to go to the next realm. If I could do it all over again, I would have said, "Don't go to fucking England! You guys are just about to branch out into something bigger! Imagine crossing Krautrock and the Stooges with the Birdman sound!" I would love to have seen what would have happened if they'd stayed in Australia, and stayed together, and powered through into something new. That show was something else. It was big. I was excited about it.'

Brad Franks: '[*RAM* journalist] Andrew McMillan got up on the stage when Birdman had finished. This huge, worked-up crowd—and he was like, "Right! We have to seize the moment! We have to march on Sydney Town Hall!" Everyone just looked at him and walked away, of course.'

Bob Short later lent a hand, packing up the stage gear, and was surprised by the attitude he encountered.

Bob Short: 'I was helping George put the big flag away. He thought I was doing it wrong and making a mess of it—like I was shitting on the flag or something—and that took me aback a bit. That was taking things too far.'

Weird Scenes

A second expedition to Adelaide coincided with Fleetwood Mac also appearing in the city. The Mac's ridiculously popular *Rumours* LP was broadly deemed to be a chief marker of all that was bloated and excessive about rock and roll.

Nonetheless, several Birdman members attended their gig at Adelaide Oval. There was even a lighthearted push by some Radios' personnel for George Kringas to organise a visit to their Adelaide base at Grange by Fleetwood's resident pixie, Stevie Nicks.

Deniz and Pip Hoyle would have missed any such appearance—had it eventuated—as they were housed elsewhere with their heads down between gigs with exams coming up.

The Adelaide trip this time was a shorter, but no less impactful, exercise, with bookings at the Paradise Hotel on 24 November, the Marryatville on 25 and Unley Town Hall on 26, where they again played 'Radioactivity'.

Sixteen-year-old Tracey Burgess, later a member of Sydney's Super K with Clyde Bramley, Brad Shepherd and Catherine Kingsmill, saw the Unley gig.

Tracey Burgess (Birdman devotee, designer): 'The room was just completely electric and people were literally climbing the walls—these brick walls. The place was on fire! It just broke me into a million pieces!

'It was a crafted kind of energy and it felt more like an invitation and that's what people were responding to. It was like, "We're here and we're giving out the call, and you're calling back and we need you in it." People felt like they were being addressed personally. It was welcoming.'

John Dowler (Young Modern): 'We supported them at Unley Town Hall. It was Young Modern's first gig. I recall Rob Younger saying something complimentary about my singing. I ran into them later that weekend at a party at a Henley Beach share house. I recall that Johnny Kannis had to be restrained from punching my head in, because I had helped myself to a beer from the fridge.'

Towards the end of the Adelaide dates, another international act, Blondie, arrived in town, and local music journalist Patrick Miles again used his contacts to make some social arrangements.

Chris Masuak: 'We had a little Bird community. Blondie came over and we said, "Hey, let's go for a walk on the beach." And it was like, "Huh?" This New York paranoia thing jumped up. We were just regular guys, we used to go surfing and go to the beach. Like Sundays, we'd go play football in the park together. But Blondie were burgeoning pop stars who came from New York, who had that superiority junkie-chic thing happening. So we went to the beach with Blondie and her band, and tried to get them to play frisbee.'

The two outfits ended up getting along well enough. When Deborah Harry and her band came to Sydney a couple of weeks later, they attended a Radios' party in Bellevue Hill.

After the Adelaide shows, the Birdmen hit Melbourne for three dates. On arrival at one of the gigs, a fan had a cosmic moment.

Rob (Birdman devotee): 'I was playing the Doors' *Weird Scenes Inside the Gold Mine* on a cassette in the car. We were listening to "L.A. Woman" and it's seven minutes long and it took about seven minutes to arrive at the pub. Then we walked into the bar and the first song Radio Birdman launched into was "L.A. Woman"!'

Ron Keeley: 'Playing "L.A. Woman" was like being in the charge of the Light Brigade!'

Their appearance at the Eureka Hotel in Geelong on 30 November 1977 was before only about 30 people, but was documented for what would later be the infamous bootleg *Eureka Birdman*.

Two weeks before Christmas, Birdman were back in Sydney and about to have their final fling in Australia before heading overseas.

They should have rehearsed the Doors' 'The End' for the occasion.

Then the Beast Roared Back

'Who's the prick that threw the cigarette at me?' Deniz Tek demanded of the multitude before him. 'Meet you later! Crush your face!' Birdman had yet to play a note and already the tone of the night was set—almost turning on its head Rob Younger's adage that it wasn't the band, but the audience, that was on trial.

The random patterning of blood on the walls—like some macabre script—along with the crunch of broken beer bottles and wine flagons on the wooden floor seemed to second that motion. Only a brief chant from one small section of the huge crowd for the MC5's 'Shakin' Street' provided a glimpse of fun.

It was Monday 12 December 1977 and Radio Birdman were back at Paddington Two Hall for their second appearance at the venue in weeks, and before an even bigger audience.

They'd officially found themselves straddling the big time, with a ragged honour guard of fans having queued down Oxford Street hours before the outfit hit the stage. This being the band's final gig before they headed to the UK and Europe, they might have expected a warm send-off. Instead, the mood at the previous Paddington engagement had ramped up considerably with fresh recruits, some acting out the Radios' corrosive internal dynamic right before them and directing it back at the stage.

Steve Lorkin (Birdman devotee): 'My father dropped me and a school mate out the front as people were throwing flagon bottles from the first-floor window onto Oxford Street. Not the sort of thing you saw at the Hordern Pavilion or school dances! We were given the choice of turning around and going home, but to me there was no option.'

The explosive reaction to the Birdman flag being lowered slowly at the back of the stage in the minutes before the band came on sent shivers down many spines in a mix of awe and triumph.

Damien Minton: 'By then they understood the dramatics and the dynamic of really, really building up and twisting the expectation and excitement before they got on stage. They completely sucked the oxygen out of the room, before they even walked on. There was just that tense sense of excitement.'

In signature MC mode, Johnny Kannis lightened the mood as he began his usual introduction, 'Hey kids! Let's googaloo! One more time!', before appearing to know something few others did. 'Radio Birdman are over . . .' he announced solemnly, prior to launching into a call-and-response interaction, with the band's 'Yeah hup!' salute. The Radios then tore into a lightning-fast 'New Race', with Rob Younger urging on the pace.

It wasn't long before the night erupted again, and with no security or stage barriers between band and audience, being physically interactive was an option for both parties—especially after one comet of snot too many alighted on Rob Younger.

Bob Yates: 'Some punks down the front were gobbing, and suddenly Rob leaped off the stage and was into it. That big American roadie [Mort] they had was in there, in a full-on brawl. Then Rob jumped back onstage with his shirt ripped, and it seemed to just drive him higher and get the band firing. It was powerful stuff.'

It wasn't the only time Younger had to take a stand. Soon after, someone managed to throw beer into the back of one of Deniz's amps, causing it to malfunction. One punter in the quickly restless jeering crowd didn't take the downtime well.

'Fuck off!' he yelled, to which Younger spat back, '*You* fuck off! We want to play too, you fucking little prick!'

Deniz Tek also climbed into the ring at one point, after a full can of beer struck him in the ear. 'That's really cool to stand back there, where we can't see, and throw a beer can at us. Goddamn chicken shit! You want to come up here and throw it? Come on up here! I'll take you, man! Come on up here!'

Deniz Tek: 'Of course, the guy didn't, but it ratcheted up the tension higher and made me play harder. That show had a serious overload of energy—tensions were sky high. We were just manifesting normally for us. We weren't play-acting. If someone threatened us, we threatened them back.'

Musically, however, the band were in commanding form. They delivered a set that included the new material they had recorded for the Sire album, 'What Gives?' and 'Non-Stop Girls' as well as what would be put on tape at Rockfield in the UK—'Crying Sun' and 'More Fun'—with nods to such foundation stones as the Blue Oyster Cult's 'Transmaniacon MC' and the MC5's 'Ramblin' Rose'.

Penny Ward: 'That was an extraordinary gig, and I remember thinking, "The whole world should be seeing this! They deserve to be on the world stage!"'

Dancing in the crowded conditions was a challenge, however. Some of Birdman's original, more seasoned fans were lost and uncomfortable, both in the mood and size of an audience they didn't know, understand, or wish to be part of. Their band was now popular to a physically intimidating degree, and some, with the assistance of Mort, found a passageway behind the stage that led to the alcoves high up on the side of the hall. There, they could dance more comfortably, well above the mayhem.

Angie Pepper: 'There were some great dancers in Radio Birdman's audience. Penny Ward, Shelley Kay, Anny Douglass, Kath Kendall, among others. By the time they played their last gig at Paddington Town Hall, there was no room at all on the dance floor anymore, and an uncomfortable element of hostility was in the new audience.'

Anny Douglass: 'I didn't really feel connected to the music that night. Who were all these people?'

Frank Cotterell: 'It took me a while to find people I knew. They weren't our band anymore. All these people had come to celebrate something they'd never been to before.'

Paul Gearside: 'What I felt was very selfish, I suppose. Like no one knows who I am anymore, because it was so far removed from when it started.'

Brad Franks: 'It was great to see them playing to 2000 people, or whatever it was, but at the same time that was the moment you lost them.'

Towards the end of the night, the wild freeform performance that had been bubbling up all evening away from the stage lights, fired by adrenalin and whatever other fuels, had gone up a few gears.

Jim Flowers: 'I was drunk, which for some reason meant I started to kick in some windows. A couple of guys objected, so they knocked me out. However, one of my friends fought back and they beat him so badly he was in St Vincent's Hospital for three months.'

Charles Fisher: 'The kids tore Paddington Town Hall apart! I remember walking home on a carpet of glass. They smashed a big hole in the floor, so you could see the floor below.'

Deniz Tek: 'It was chaos! It was like a riot! Speaker columns came down, there was broken equipment everywhere, every window in the place was smashed, and there was a row of cars outside that were completely destroyed. We couldn't even leave the place for about two hours after.

'When we finally did, there was blood smeared all down the stairwell, and I thought, "Gee, it can't go on like this. Someone's going to get really badly hurt or killed." It was scary. I was kind of glad we were leaving to let things cool down a bit here. It was never meant to hurt people or cause violence.'

Warwick Gilbert's concerns back in April at the same venue, with the Saints, had been massively amplified.

Warwick Gilbert: 'It was just shithouse. I didn't want to support something like that. I was there physically, and that was about it. It had gotten too big for my liking.'

Rob Younger, on the other hand, saw something thrilling in the destructive madness.

Rob Younger: 'I always used to think those old rocker shows [in the fifties] where people were ripping up the seats and throwing the arms at the band were great. To actually be at a gig where something like that was happening was . . . quite good! It feels like you're really part of something, if people are actually moved to do that. It's not like you've hired a bunch of people to agitate. People were actually compelled to wreck the joint . . . Have you ever done that? I've never done it. That's gas, to be part of.

'A lot of our gigs had the same essence about them, I'm happy to say. The gigs were more shambolic, more chaotic and anarchic, early on in the piece. People always say that the great bands always seem like they're going to fly off in any direction, that volatility, and we had that. I did enjoy that night.'

The gig was both a closing and turning point, with no return possible from either. The pool of fun, innocence and magic of the Oxford—and later the Fun House—had been drained. Major success, rather than simply survival, now seemed achievable, but at huge cost.

Birdman could have ended at Paddington at their peak, before their fractious internal body clock finally exploded irreparably. The belated Australian release that year of the MC5's near-decade-old *Kick Out the Jams*, along with an upcoming reissue of the Stooges' long-out-of-print *Fun House*, would be their final parting triumph, the grand legacy of a three-year conquest.

But the mission was not yet complete.

At least the earlier allegations levelled at Deniz Tek by the university were now in the rear-view mirror.

Deniz Tek: 'Nothing ever became of the case against me. No supporting evidence ever surfaced. I passed the exams with honours and got my MBBS. I have no idea what happened to the letter. I suppose it is still sitting in a file somewhere.'

Tek left Australia within days of Paddington to prepare for the UK and European tour—the specifics of which still seemed troublingly fluid—and the release of a revamped album for Sire.

Radio Birdman would not appear together again in Australia for almost two decades.

Welcome to the Machine

The first edition of the 'Kingdom of the Radios' newsletter to fan club members—its title another reference to the Blue Oyster Cult and their song 'Dominance and Submission'—was distributed in early January 1978. It opened by discussing the irony of Birdman blasting out a version of the 13th Floor Elevators' 'You're Gonna Miss Me' at gigs, then flying off to court the northern hemisphere for a large portion of the next year.

Deniz Tek's first stop had been LA. He met up with Seymour Stein and was taken to see Sire label mates Talking Heads at the Whisky a Go Go in West Hollywood. Tek's eye-rolling intolerance soon overtook any sense of diplomacy, and he left.

Back in Ann Arbor for Christmas, he met up with John Needham and Mark Sisto, as well as jamming with Ron Asheton, who had a good-luck gift for the Birdman.

Deniz Tek: 'A German Army paratrooper's ski cap. It had a Wehrmacht [army] insignia on it; not SS or specifically Nazi party regalia, but still, it bothered some people, and I didn't have it for very long.

'Ron was an avid student of military history, and collecting German war artefacts was something he did with his dad from childhood. He appreciated the aesthetics of it. He was never aligned with Nazi politics.'

It wasn't the only present from the locals.

Deniz Tek: 'It was a longitudinal cross-section of a foot and ankle joint, encased in plexiglass, meant to be used in an anatomy class at the University of Michigan medical school. This guy named TR was a close friend of the Ashetons. He worked in the lab where they cut up cadavers and made those things. He gave it to me with great fanfare. He sincerely meant it as a valuable going-away gift, symbolising good luck for the tour.

'I felt like it would be impolite to refuse, so I took it. I was concerned about the legality of transporting human remains across international borders, and either John or Mark agreed to keep it in their bag. We had it on the tour for a while, and then it disappeared.'

From Ann Arbor, Deniz, Mark and John drove a van to Philadelphia—a relocation of the vehicle to the new owner—which included a stop at Gettysburg—the site of a pivotal battle in 1863 during the American Civil War—for a visit to the cemetery.

Then it was onto New York by rail. While Deniz was point man in the US, the business for the trip had been taken care of beforehand, via Trafalgar and George Kringas, so apart from overseeing the various versions of the Sire album for each territory, he had an open agenda—and largely on Sire's tab.

That included going to local gigs such as CBGB—and being appalled at the price of a beer—and meeting legendary music-industry figure Danny Fields, manager of the Ramones, the Radios' label mates and soon-to-be American tour partners, although that reported run of six weeks had shrunk to ten days. Seeing the Ramones perform gave Tek plenty of hope for Birdman's international future.

Deniz Tek: 'There was probably the same number of people as we were playing to at Paddington Town Hall the month before, but much less enthusiasm. I figured we'd be playing places like that and hopefully getting an even better reaction.'

Seymour Stein's response to a tape of 'More Fun', recorded at Paddington, was just as promising. Stein felt it was one of the classic teen anthems and a potential hit.

Deniz Tek: 'I wonder how many people—besides Rob Younger—realise that the backing vocal in "More Fun", where it goes "waaa-oooo" sliding into the choruses, was lifted from Pink Floyd's "See Emily Play"?'

The canny Stein probably also had quiet designs on the charismatic Tek as a future solo act.

Of course, there was a catch. For all Sire's enthusiasm, unsurprisingly there was pressure on Deniz to drop his career aspirations in medicine, and focus all his energies on Radio Birdman. No chance. There were also concerns about George Kringas continuing as manager in the band's new and greatly expanded circumstances, although his removal was another non-negotiable for Tek.

But Sire were dead right. This was the big league, part of a vast American industry and the deep end of a corporate pool, where pulling a couple of thousand people as the Radios had at Paddington was little more than standard for reasonably popular acts.

The coolest kids in rock school in Sydney had to re-establish themselves from scratch in a foreign land, and do so under circumstances they would be unable to bend by sheer force of will. There would be no more kitchen-table industry to produce posters and flyers, no hands-on mail-order operation from a single office at Trafalgar; nor a Fun House, 2JJ radio, White Light Records, *RAM* magazine or fan club. Birdman were alone, unknowns in the unknown.

However, the States was a future challenge. Deniz getting to London and meeting up with Kringas and Adelaide journalist Patrick Miles—onboard as a publicist—was a more immediate concern, after confusion over his air ticket.

Needham and Sisto jetted off to the UK without Tek, but on landing at Heathrow had no address to give to a taxi driver, and no names or numbers to call. Thankfully, a saviour was waiting.

John Needham: 'There was a guy with a sign that said "Radio Birdman" or "Deniz Tek", so Sisto goes, "Right, we're the band!" He drove us in to the record company office.'

Back in Sydney, much had been melting in the sweltering summer heat. With Deniz again out of the frame, Rob Younger and Ron Keeley were on a constant collision course that almost derailed the overseas trip before it began. The wounds were sufficiently band-aided for a farewell party at a warehouse in Alexandria.

There, a Tek-less Birdman gathered with friends, including Charlie Georgees and Johnny Kannis, with several playing rotating musical roles in renditions of the Doors' 'L.A. Woman', the Stones' 'Route 66', the New York Dolls' 'Personality Crisis' and the Stooges' '1970'. It was a brief glimpse of simpler times.

Days before the band flew out to the UK, Warwick Gilbert had his bass stolen.

London Miscalling

It must have been someone's idea of black comedy. Radio Birdman travelled 17,000 kilometres to London, only to find the Oz rock boogie that Rob Younger particularly despised had already staked its flag.

Rob Younger: 'I was at a midweek gig at the Marquee to see some shit band, and I had an overcoat draped over my arm. After a while I looked down and there was a ring where the lining was starting to burn. I looked at the guy next to me and he had his cigarette hanging over me, and I said, "Mate, you've set fire to my jacket! Hey . . . you're Lobby Loyde, aren't you?" And he goes, "Yeah," and then just looks back at the band.'

Younger and the remainder of the Radios had arrived in late February, a few weeks after Deniz Tek finally touched down, and something already felt off.

Despite Seymour Stein's enthusiasm, there was little appetite for any spend on promoting the coming single, 'What Gives?', that was to open Birdman's UK account. In fact, everything involving funds seemed a struggle—from securing living expenses to the rental of equipment for the tour. Deniz and George Kringas took their concerns to the top of their local record company, Phonogram, only to be told the label was no longer distributing the records of Sire.

Suddenly, it all made sense: no one gave a fuck, because there was no requirement to do so. Miraculously, George negotiated with Phonogram and secured enough finance for the tour, although there would be limited if any budget for promoting and distributing the already pressed Sire LP, which was to have been strategically released in late March. It was the initial wave of what would be a brown tsunami.

The all-important and notoriously critical British music press had already savaged import copies of the 'New Race' single, with *Sounds* declaring in December: 'Wallaby-rock and it's worse than the Godawful Saints . . .' Others in the English media followed suit.

Timing wasn't on the Radios' side either. The UK had had its fifteen minutes of punk-rock fame, the fall of which was best characterised by the Sex Pistols' recent split after a disastrous US tour.

The culture had moved on and Birdman neither looked nor sounded like the creature into which the scene had morphed. Had their English campaign begun six months earlier, as originally planned, the landscape would have been very different. But now they had their backs to the wall, in freezing temperatures and in a foreign country with little money. It was a situation which drip-fed a combustible liquid on the Radios' constant internal simmer.

Fan club members back in Australia had been advised their heroes would do a month of unheralded gigs on arrival in the UK, a disastrous strategy that, thankfully, was dumped in favour of the Anglo Strike tour. Initially, this was scheduled to be just six dates across London: 8 March at the Rock Garden, 10 Hope and Anchor, 16 Nashville Rooms, 17 Rochester Castle, 19 Nags Head and 21 Hope and Anchor.

RAM's 1977 poll results should have put something of a spring in their collective step, given that the Radios were stamped right across it, with Deniz Tek taking second place in the best guitarist list, ahead of AC/DC's Angus Young in third.

Ron Keeley: 'I was voted Australia's second-best rock and roll drummer. Or maybe it was in New South Wales. Or Darlinghurst. Which would be weird, because as far as I know I was the only rock and roll drummer in Darlo at the time.'

The outfit were named second in Album of the Year, with *Radios Appear* beating the hugely popular Dragon. Birdman were also third in Best Group, ahead of Split Enz.

But it was cold and distant comfort in London, where they didn't even have the uniforms as talking points.

Warwick Gilbert: 'Seymour Stein was disappointed when it wasn't Nuremberg in England. He said, "What happened to the uniforms?"'

Nonetheless, they opened the tour with typical power and resolve at the Rock Garden at Covent Garden. *Sounds* saw it differently, with a damning review printed two months later, firmly establishing the tourists' lowly place in the pecking order of the UK scene from the outset.

Meanwhile, the 'What Gives?' single made its way into the light—seemingly only in the UK—with some high-powered live footage to go with it.

Warwick Gilbert: 'The guy who filmed the first Paddo Town Hall [gig] with the Saints made a clip of "What Gives?" from the lip of the [Paddington] stage in front of Rob, to promote the single in the UK. That one captures Radio Birdman way better than *Radios Appear*. It was shit-yer-pants exciting stuff!'

But the hard-driving song was again cannon fodder for the British media, with the *NME* stating it was 'very tame', while *Melody Maker* decreed that it 'gets nowhere fast'.

However, on the upside, *NME* deigned to publish a substantial piece on the band. Although, unfortunately, they opted for the cringeworthy headline of 'Never Mind the Cobbers—here's Radio Birdman', and the subhead 'Australia's one decent band, says our man in the outback', it did feature name checks of the Psycho Surgeons, the punk pit at the Grand Hotel in Railway Square, and Johnny Dole and the Scabs, in what was basically a profile of Sydney punk. So far so strong, until it mentioned that in their early days the Radios would 'smash guitars during the acoustic numbers in their set'. There was some good news from *Sounds* as well, with a review of the white-hot Hope and Anchor gig finally spotlighting the Birdmen's live act in local print. On a low-budget tour with little to no advertising, this was essential in getting the word out.

Meanwhile, in America, Sire were shooting for the stars and wrote to Jack Lord, who played Steve McGarrett in *Hawaii Five-O*. A copy of the new album was enclosed, with Lord advised of the song 'Aloha Steve & Danno', and that Deniz Tek had adopted his screen character's name as his alter-ego. A photo shoot with Lord and Tek was requested, for possible placement in magazines such as *People*, as well as the music trade papers, to tie in with the proposed US tour and potential release of 'Aloha' as a single. Nothing came of the ask, but there would be other opportunities.

The next UK date was at the Nashville Rooms and saw Mark Sisto offering a corrective strategy to the individual spitting at Rob Younger.

Mark Sisto: 'He was a big guy and I thought, "Fuck, what am I gonna do? Ask him? Please?" So I went up behind him, sort of cupped my hand and smacked him on the ear, and grabbed some of his hair and said, "No one spits on this band!"

Rob didn't like that. He thought I was "wrecking the vibe", acting like police or something. Oh, okay, next time I'll let it go. I risked my neck to do that. But okay.'

Alley Brereton was in London, having left Australia in July 1977, and had seen much of the UK punk scene up close. She hooked up with her favourite band, only to find herself in Sisto's sights one night.

Alley Brereton: 'There was some guy hitting on me all the time and he gave me the shits, so I threw a beer at him and Sisto threw me out of the gig!'

The gig at Rochester Castle was another killer and Birdman deservedly won an encore. Maybe the trip would be worth it, after all.

Then came a hammer blow from Australia. An article in *RAM* by Anthony O'Grady, cuttingly titled 'Whatever Happened to Radio Birdman?', talked up the outfit's considerable impact, but also seemed to deride them for going overseas and for their part-time schedule, and questioned their future. It was like a partial obituary.

Deniz Tek: 'It seemed like a massive betrayal.'

That night, 20 March, Birdman appeared at the infamous punk-rock pit the Vortex, before another audience desperate to interact.

Mark Sisto: 'Someone was spitting at Pip and I just stood between them. But there was the alpha dog who had a Mohawk hairdo and all his sidekicks. And there was all this back and forth with Rob. It was a terrible mismatch. He'd shout some insult and Rob would just slam him verbally and shame him in front of his crew. It was hilarious!

'Some beer was splashed about and splashed back, and I think Rob threw an empty beer can. The next thing, this guy had a long-necked beer bottle and he whipped it really hard and it just missed Deniz's and Rob's heads. And I thought, "Well, there's so many of them, you can't run." That is to say, with the impossibility of retreat, I attacked. I belted him on his jaw. He collapsed, then I put his sidekick in a headlock with my thumb up his nose.'

Deniz Tek: 'It was very confrontational, that gig. It was sort of like what you imagine the [Iggy and the Stooges'] *Metallic K.O.* gig might have been like. I put my guitar down to go help Mark. It was like a saloon fight in an old Western movie!'

Rob Younger: 'There was shit at the Vortex but it was due to my stupidity, throwing a bottle at a heckler, hitting him on the leg, and him pegging it back, just missing Deniz's head. I was an idiot. Worst night of the whole tour. I don't remember if Sisto was even there.'

The next day, the mood was dark and the band met to discuss the incident and in a nod to Mark's ranking in the Birdman inner sanctum, a vote had to be taken, with the majority result seeing Sisto given his marching orders.

Deniz Tek: 'Chris and I supported Mark, and the rest voted to boot him off the tour.'

Mark Sisto: 'I said, "Don't worry about it. I'm out of here!" The next day I headed off to Paris, and then Spain, and then returned to Australia.'

The loss of Sisto, the Radios' bulletproof, eternal 'on switch', and close friend and muse for Deniz Tek, removed a major cornerstone from the brotherhood, at a time when they needed a bond more than ever.

Deniz Tek: 'The band was coming apart at the seams. The Vortex split it further.'

But, as always, the strength of their performances kept their heads well above the water line. At their return to the Hope and Anchor on 21 March, their final date before heading to Rockfield to record, they received an unprecedented three encores.

The *NME*, frustratingly, saw the gig very differently, stating in a tiny review, '. . . their load of staggeringly dull rock numbers, played with next to no enthusiasm . . .'

Thankfully, a near half-page piece in *Sounds* titled 'Invasion of the Birdmen' was far more complimentary. Not that it impacted on sales of the Sire LP, as it was sitting gathering dust.

Deniz Tek: 'The album didn't get past the warehouses. It didn't get distributed into stores because of the dispute that Sire had with their distribution. People were coming up to us, saying, "You guys are great! When are you going to record something?"'

Worse, their North American tour with the Ramones in the second half of the year was in jeopardy. The way things were going, the band mightn't exist by that point, anyway.

Crying Sons

The sheep would stare, blank eyed, through the windows of the building in rural Monmouth, Wales—opposite Rockfield's Studios—as if fascinated by the car-crash theatre playing out inside. The facility had hosted Black Sabbath, Mott the Hoople, Dr Feelgood, the Flamin' Groovies and Queen, and somehow a three-week booking in the name of Radio Birdman remained on the books. It was quite a place: a 24-hour-a-day facility, with excellent accommodation, a large banquet table, maids, and a stereo that was pumping long into the night. For Birdman, there was also some of the old camaraderie and they staked their flag. The address would soon, however, become Arsenic Manor.

Deniz and Rob had wished to jointly produce the new LP. This proposition was seen by some as a further entrenchment of the all-powerful three-way alliance of Tek, Younger and manager Kringas. In the end, Deniz alone got the nod for the job, which all but guaranteed the input and counsel of Rob Younger. At least that was the perception and what seemed a continuing shut-out of the rest of the band.

Deniz Tek: 'The band voted for me to produce, in place of Charles Fisher. George thought we couldn't afford to bring him to Rockfield, since we had lost our label support. I accepted the role—there was no musical challenge I wouldn't take on.'

Warwick Gilbert: 'It was a miserable time. I didn't like being told what to do.'

The original material that had been worked up in Sydney in the second half of the previous year was put on tape, with 'Alone in the End Zone' and 'Hanging On' constructed in the studio, as was Pip Hoyle's instrumental, 'Across the Stones', later retitled 'Alien Skies'. Warwick's 'Crying Sun' particularly stood out as a potential hit single, but instead would characterise the shitstorm of the Rockfield experience.

Deniz Tek: 'Part of my job as producer was to make sure that everything that needed to be done got done, in the limited time we had. I wrote up a schedule of milestones that we needed to reach, including finishing the backing tracks, the vocals, the instrumental overdubs, and the mixing. The mixing was scheduled for the final week.

'I was going to mix the album with [studio engineer] David Charles, but I wanted anyone who was interested in certain songs to attend, so I posted the mixing schedule. Ron attended a couple of sessions for songs where he was concerned about the drums. I don't recall anyone else showing up. I knew that Warwick was very much invested in "Crying Sun", as was I. I fully expected him to attend the mixing session and provide input. He didn't, and David Charles and I went ahead with the mix that day to stay on schedule.

'On the last day, I asked everyone to come to the studio and listen to all the mixes. When we listened to "Crying Sun", Warwick said nothing, and walked out. Didn't say a word to me. It might have been possible to do a remix, and I would have pulled an all-nighter to get it done, but he didn't communicate anything.'

'All the months we rehearsed that song, played it at Paddo, recorded a version at Trafalgar—and zero communication about how he would have preferred it to be different.'

Warwick Gilbert: 'It sounded great when the engineer mixed it. I couldn't believe it! It sounded like Booker T. & the M.G.'s, something great with the organ. Then when they botched the [final] mix, I thought, "Fuck it, I'm out of here!"'

By this point, eye contact was almost non-existent between some parties, 'conversation' just single words. Everyone reacted to everyone else's reaction and the situation spiralled downward.

Rob Younger: 'Rockfield was poisonous. It got worse.'

Deniz Tek: 'I was cast as an outsider in the eyes of the band, when I could have been a stronger advocate for unity and cohesion. I just wanted to get the job done—I was totally focused on the music and nothing else. In retrospect, maybe we should have had Charles [Fisher] come and produce, but by then it would have been like rearranging deckchairs on the *Titanic*.'

Charles Fisher: 'I was very disappointed I didn't go to Rockfield with them, but that was the decision they made. They fell apart at Rockfield. I like to think, if I'd been there they wouldn't have.'

With the album completed, on 20 April the Radios hit the Nags Head again, the tiny Red Cow in Hammersmith, where AC/DC had made an early breakthrough almost two years earlier to the day, the legendary Marquee Club, and then a third show at the Hope and Anchor on 28 April.

Some bonds were not so easily completely broken and two days later Gilbert and Younger were among the 100,000 strong crowd at Victoria Park for the 'Rock Against Racism' gig, which featured a headlining performance by the Clash.

Warwick Gilbert: 'We walked through the streets with the crowd. I thought the Clash weren't much. I didn't think they were as good as us, actually.'

Several members of the Birdman faithful in Sydney were just as indifferent when a shipment arrived at White Light, containing import copies of the UK single 'What Gives?'. The title, they felt, said it all.

Chain-Smoking in a Munitions Factory

A night at the famed Paradiso in Amsterdam at least provided some lighthearted relief from the gut-grinding and increasingly personal UK and Euro campaign.

Warwick Gilbert: 'The local promoter invited us along to see Van Halen. Rob and I met the promoter and Bob Geldof outside and went in.'

Rob Younger: 'The best part was when David Lee Roth moved to stage right, below a balcony, positioned with a light trained down on him. He was exhorting the crowd with a raised fist, singing, "I'm on fire! I'm on fire!" Someone above him poured a beer onto his head. He was furious. I'd have given whoever it was a medal.'

When Birdman appeared at the venue the night before, the small crowd were light years in attitude from the energised audience of the Fun House.

Ron Keeley: 'There were two guys with glass display cases, selling every kind of hash you could imagine. The gig was full of people lying on the floor, stoned out of their heads. Not the sort of crowd for us, really.'

Doing a show on their own in Amsterdam hadn't been part of the original plan. The slow death of the all-important American tour with the Ramones mid-year had finally been pronounced, but the dates with Sire label mates the Flamin' Groovies were proceeding, with the first in Paris on 2 May.

After that, the pairing hit Brussels, where the Groovies' Cyril Jordan fell while grasping a bottle and cut a tendon in his hand. Impending dates between 4 and 15 May were dumped.

While in Europe, the Radios decided to do what they could, gig wise. After the Paradiso, they returned to London for a few shows, including a second crack at the Nashville and another round at the Marquee, this time to a growing support base.

Robin Wills (the Barracudas): 'I remember being at the front of the stage, shouting out for "King of the Surf", because [Wills's band] the Barracudas were playing it. They played it and then [he called for] "Don't Look Back" by the Remains and they did that too! They were the greatest high-energy bar band you've ever seen!

'I do remember being quite shocked, because in the audience there were these guys with jean jackets with the sleeves off, with the Radio Birdman patch at the back. They must have been Australians who came over [to the UK], and they were doing [this salute] along with "New Race". Standing behind this guy putting his fist up, I was thinking, "Is this a new movement?"'

But an unforeseen circumstance had emerged. Countless acts back in Australia had traditionally plied their trade, and built a following, by criss-crossing the nation in a car or van. However, apart from concentrated trips to Melbourne and Adelaide, for Birdman this was a whole new experience. With the hell of Rockfield spiking their guts—on top of all the long-term annoyances and overhanging grievances—for the first time they were now squeezed into a nine-seat Kombi for hours and hours each day, in a foreign country, with minimal, if any, money. What could possibly go wrong?

Strangely, everything. Everyone got on everyone else's nerves all the time. So, while the Birdvan back in Sydney had been a carriage for a measure of camaraderie, this vehicle would be dubbed the 'Van of Hate'. To ratchet up the friction further, one of the tapes on high rotation inside was the recording from Rockfield, and thus a constant reminder of the three-week nightmare. Another by Kraftwerk didn't quite act as a psychological flotation device either.

Rob Younger: 'We'd been given a couple of Flamin' Groovies' T-shirts for the tour, with "Radio Birdman" in little print at the bottom. There was only two of them, so we had to toss a coin to get them, and Deniz and I won them. The reaction was like it was staged with double-sided coins or something. That stuck with me.'

The dates with the Groovies were scheduled to recommence on 16 May at Leicester University Students Union, with local promoter Ed Bicknell, the manager of a soon-to-break act called Dire Straits, handling the tour.

Two gigs in Manchester were next: the first, a killer, the second less so. *Sounds* sneeringly slammed one of the shows, adding further fuel to the argument of some back in Australia that the band had failed to stand up in the UK.

A schoolmate of Rob Younger, Glenn Rafferty, was in line outside one venue and an amazed Rob ushered him inside.

But Manchester, like the Vortex gig, would be a turning point, when Ron Keeley, in a bid to make some space in the van, asked Birdman insider John Needham, who was travelling with the band, to make his own transport arrangements. Needham, troubled by the situation unfolding around him, anyway, grabbed his belongings and departed. For the next year, he would travel across the world. His seat in the van was left vacant. After Mark Sisto's departure, Deniz was less a second close aide and confidante.

Deniz Tek: 'I happened to get a copy of Sven Hassel's book *Comrades of War* and read it in the van. It really resonated with me. Guys that got slung in prison camps because they deserted or ran off to avoid being in the German Army, then getting sent to Russia on suicide missions. They hated the Reich, and existed only for each other and to try to survive against terrible odds in the worst possible conditions. When they had the opportunity, they ambushed and killed SS. I had never read anything like it. I drew some parallels with the band's situation at that time—obviously not on the same spectrum, seriousness wise. We weren't dying, but our band was. It was how I felt.'

'Aloha Steve & Danno', with its surf-music influence writ large, was the first Australian single from the Sire version of *Radios Appear*, arriving in May 1978. It could have been a huge hit, even in the middle of winter in Oz, but the Birdmen were on the other side of the planet in the process of imploding.

As always, though, they were still turning in strong performances, as they did at Leeds. The gigs continued in Liverpool and Birmingham. The arrival of the Sire version of the *Radios Appear* LP this late in the tour was just cruel. Much of the internal bitterness was about an end that now seemed inevitable.

Warwick Gilbert: 'I wasn't talking. I kind of shut down internally. I think the loss of the band really destroyed me, because I'd kind of bet everything on it. I'd dropped my art career and everything for it, and then . . .'

Gilbert immersed himself in the safety and security of art, just as he had as a kid. He kept a diary of the van tour and pointedly drew a crying sun.

Warwick Gilbert: 'I just made notes and wrote poetry. I did little sketches and things. A couple of ideas for paintings. Surreal-type things. I did one called "Strained Relations", which I think I'll do again. It's a really good image influenced by Dali, and that kind of summed up the band. It's two people kind of devouring each other on the beach. It was an interesting image. One was a clown and one was a business guy.'

He also designed a bass-drum head with an image of a string of individuals backstabbing each other, with the words 'Radios disappear' underneath. Cleverly, from a distance it looked like a smiling face. Warwick's artistic outpouring wasn't well received.

When Birdman were dumped from the bill of the big show with the Flamin' Groovies at London's historic Roundhouse on 11 June, it was yet another blow—but they could barely summon up any disappointment. The final three dates that were to follow were also cancelled.

That just left the home stretch. It began at the Friars at Aylesbury—where 'world cup footy in Aston hall' was third on the bill—and Croydon's Greyhound, which had recently hosted Siouxsie and the Banshees and the Fall, and which saw the Australians billed as 'Radio Bird'. Gigs followed at Cardiff, Brighton, Plymouth—just weeks after an increasingly dominant AC/DC, and days after Split Enz—and Swindon. Finally, on 10 June 1978, they arrived at the College of Further Education, Oxford, or Oxford Polytechnic.

The End

It was only right and proper that Radio Birdman's final performance in the UK was at another Oxford and witnessed by many of the band's original inner sanctum, including Angie Pepper, Penny Ward, Dare Jennings and Jules R.B. Normington.

And the curtain was brought down in the same manner it had originally been raised.

Jules R.B. Normington: 'Radio Birdman played rock and roll that was totally honest and totally committed. The earth moved at just about every gig they played. Even at their last gig, they never lost it. The Oxford was one of the best they ever did. And it totally went off, because it was uni students. The whole place went nuts.'

Deniz Tek: 'I wrote the set list to sequentially reflect the stages the band had gone through in the prior four years, as a gift to our pals. We played covers that we hadn't done since '74 or '75. We really put our hearts into the gig. I would characterise it as bittersweet, rather than disappointing.'

Ron Keeley: 'That was one of the tightest, hardest, fastest gigs we ever played. We came off stage and I don't even remember saying goodbye to anyone. We just went our separate ways.'

Rob Younger: 'I can't recall any particular feelings either way at that point. I knew it was all over for the band, that's all, but no big deal.'

Just days after the Oxford, the opportunity of seeing Iggy Pop in London at the Music Machine was too good to miss, even for a warring tribe.

Pop was appearing with three-quarters of the Sonic's Rendezvous Band—including former Stooges' drummer, Scott Asheton, and MC5 guitarist, Fred 'Sonic' Smith—as his backing.

Deniz Tek: 'I had met up with pals Fred Smith and Scott Asheton earlier that day. They gave us VIP passes for the whole band, and we had a great vantage point on a balcony level, just to the right of the stage.'

Warwick Gilbert: 'We went to the sound check and Deniz took Fred's old Epiphone guitar along, and Scott Asheton came up and was wearing a Birdman badge. Deniz took the Epiphone over to Fred, and Fred took it out of its case and stood it against his Marshall stack. Then he backed up to the lip of the stage and just went down on his haunches and stared at it.

'I swear you could sense, you could feel, the music of the MC5 and its history in the air. He did that for some minutes. It was really eerie. Then he walked over and picked up that guitar and all hell broke loose. He got this sound—it was incredible. And I looked across at Chris and Deniz and their jaws were agape.'

The performance of the Iggy-led band elicited similar reactions.

Rob Younger: 'It was the most spinechilling experience I'd ever fucking seen by one performer. Incredible! Some people can put a lot of energy into a gig and be graceful. Iggy did that. He was positively balletic, poised, wild—all of that shit. Wonderful. Our band had never been capable on putting on that show. Wouldn't have come close.'

Chris Masuak: 'To me, watching "Sonic" [Smith] was the single most important lesson I ever got as a guitar player. Seeing Sonic with Iggy was the first time I saw how much higher the bar was. I was at the front of the stage, taking photos. Iggy was right in front of me and Sonic was just over to my left. Iggy saw me and was kind of mugging for me, and I took a number of spectacular shots of him and Sonic.'

Rob Younger: 'Masuak took some great photos. Amazing! He got up the side where few people were allowed, and down on the stage.'

Afterwards, Rob and Deniz went to dinner with Iggy and the Rendezvous guys.

Deniz Tek: 'Fred really wanted to buy that [Deniz's] guitar back.'

Iggy, himself, however, soured the divinity of the evening's earlier performance, taking Rob to task over his Flamin' Groovies' T-shirt, for some reason, and didn't endear himself to the female friends of the Radios in attendance. Meanwhile, Chris and Warwick were incensed that no one thought they too might have wanted to hang with several major architects of Birdman's sound.

Still, the overseas venture had been anything but a disaster. Birdman had gone to the other side of the globe as a barely recognised quantity and, despite losing the backing of their record company almost from day one, put in any number of powerhouse performances worthy of their reputation back in Australia. It was just that they were doing so at the wrong time and place.

Alley Brereton: 'People didn't dance in London like they did in Sydney. It was a very symbiotic relationship at the Fun House and that's what drove everybody—but that didn't happen in England.'

Ron Keeley: 'We were singing songs about cars and girls and surfing to a bunch of skinheads and tattooed punks. Half of them had probably never seen the sea and, to them, the idea of driving a 455 SD [Pontiac Firebird] was just out of cuckoo land.

'We played some pretty good gigs. But I look back now with some sadness, because of all the angst and aggro. It was a bit of a mess in lots of ways.'

Rob Younger: 'There is an uninformed view which stuck to us, one which many were quite pleased to go along with, that we fucked up completely. It even had us returning to Australia after a few shows, humiliated. We spent four months in London.

'We just got some bad press at crucial times. The Hope and Anchor, I think it was—the third time we got three encores! Three! People went ape shit! The next thing, we get this scathing review about how shit we were, and how everyone was leaving in droves! We did good gigs at the Marquee. We did two there—the first one, especially. The place was fucking packed and we killed it. We did lots of good gigs all over the country. And a few shit ones.'

Deniz, Rob, Angie Pepper and Jules headed to the US in different directions, while the rest of the band returned to Australia.

The broad future plan for Birdman was to dress the wounds, fill the roles of those departing and press on.

Ron Keeley had already given notice, and the writing seemed very clearly on the wall regarding Warwick Gilbert.

But with the movement of other personnel, the continuation of Radio Birdman was no longer an option. Pip Hoyle, on his return to Australia, relocated to Newcastle for his medical career, and Chris Masuak, still just twenty years old, decided, as much as he enjoyed the early camaraderie and the power of Birdman music, to back his own talents and instincts with the Hitmen.

Chris Masuak: 'It was so extraordinarily brutal and treacherous and nasty that I didn't want to be around that anymore. They'd lost my trust. They had surprisingly shown Warwick, Ron and myself that we and our friendship were worth nothing to them.'

The very elements that fired the outfit seemed unlikely to sustain it in the longer term.

Rob Younger: 'I'd say the band, due to its personnel make-up, had an inbuilt obsolescence. Despite various members latterly referring to some "brotherhood", it was never really like that.'

Alley Brereton somehow bumped into Younger in New York a month or so after the final UK gig.

Alley Brereton: 'I was at an opening of a new dance club downtown, and there was Rob. "Hi! How you going?" He said, "I don't know what you're so happy about." I said, "Why? What's wrong?" He said, "You didn't read the paper today?" I said, "What are you talking about?" He said, "About the war they've just declared." And I remember I left there, it was about 2 a.m., and walked two miles up to the paper shop outside Gem Spa on St Mark's Place, to look at the headlines and see what the fuck was going on. There was absolutely nothing happening. It was like this joke or a metaphor.'

What Radio Birdman created was so special, an existence-changing lifeboat, that simply moving on wasn't an option.

Hitmen, Professors and Things

Chris Masuak wasted no time with the Hitmen's first gig—with Fun House regular Steve Harris in tow—taking place at the Rex Hotel in Kings Cross, just weeks after Birdman's UK tour ended.

Other shoots were emerging, with the Professors, featuring Radios devotees Stephen Vineburg and Bruce Tindale also making their debut, and creating their own version of the Fun House, complete with a jukebox, in the process.

Stephen Vineburg: 'We lived at 65 Abercrombie Street, Chippendale, and the pub down the road was the Royal Oak Hotel. One day we went in and said, "Next Saturday, we want to take over the back room and put on a show there." Anyway, hundreds came and the next Monday they got about ten calls from other bands, asking if they could play there. We called it the Royal Oak Au Go Go.

'When Rob Younger returned from overseas, he came to see us [the Professors] at the Captain Cook Hotel. I think he had mixed feelings about us covering [Birdman's] "Murder City Nights".'

Another act that had its roots very much in the Fun House was the Things. Arch Radios fan Damien Minton was a member, and they appeared at the Royal Oak with a set that included the song 'Mandraxed Watching Hellcats'.

Climbing the stairs to
The Fun House daddy
Gonna have fun with
The Hellcats mummy
Have to let go with
Mandrax sissie
So if anyone calls
Tell 'em I'm on the floor

It was just the start of a flood of Sydney bands shaped in partial or deep homage to Radio Birdman over the coming years, a feat AC/DC never conjured up, despite their enormous success.

In June 1978, Birdman themselves materialised—at least in recorded form—when the Sire 'overseas version' of *Radios Appear* was finally released in Australia. Bob King's shot of the band in uniform on the cover against a white background was a long way from the mysterious photo that stared down the world on the original LP.

The inside sleeve featured a collage of Patrick Bingham-Hall photos including some from the volatile performance at Springwood.

Tone-wise, the accompanying Sire biography was battle ready. Signed off by 'Steve McGarrett, Temporary Minister for Information, World Affairs Desk, Radio Birdman', it read like a political manifesto, yet stated the Radios were 'allied to no political party'. It began with the almost self-defeating declaration to a new market that 'Radio Birdman is the name of an obscure international rock and roll band', and was peppered with references to 'fighting units', 'soldiers', 'mercenary' and 'attack'. It further spoke puzzlingly of their stance on the punk and new wave scene and attempted to explain that there were two versions of the *Radios Appear* album.

That such a document made it onto Sire letterhead, allowing an unproven investment to frame themselves in such a manner, particularly in the then highly conservative American market—where even AC/DC still had their struggles—was stunning.

The issue of the two editions of the LP was further vexing, particularly in Australia. The mixing of older material and new was not without precedent, with the first records by both AC/DC and the Angels packaged as compilations for the international market, but neither were commercially available in their homeland. Not so this time.

Some early copies of the Sire record carried a prominent 'caution' notice, via a sticker on the cover, in an attempt to explain the contents. To many of those who had worshipped the original debut album, this entire episode was a major 'What the fuck?' (A publicist is probably still waking in the middle of the night screaming.)

The record did have plenty of high power but lacked the amp hum and grit of the original. There was more of a tough pop edge and colour, with new songs like 'What Gives?', 'Non-Stop Girls', Younger and Tek's 'Aloha Steve & Danno' and 'Hit Them Again', which Deniz had written with Ron Asheton back in Ann Arbor in late 1976. However, a faster, far more concise version of 'New Race' was slightly jarring, like the Stones reworking 'Satisfaction'.

Patrick Bingham-Hall: 'I was in the studio when they recorded that sped-up version of "New Race". I asked why the hell they would want to do that. Chris Masuak and Johnny Kannis quickly closed me down . . . like, "Don't say anything!"'

There were also omissions from the original LP.

Deniz Tek: 'I was never very fond of "Monday Morning Gunk", a holdover from TV Jones days. I was happy to dump that one. "T.V. Eye" always worked well live, but the recorded version wasn't great, so we replaced it with the 13th Floor Elevators cover ["You're Gonna Miss Me"].'

Warwick Gilbert: 'I hated that [album]. All except "You're Gonna Miss Me". That sounded like Radio Birdman. That was one take. That was great. It [the Sire version of the LP] was a real step backwards. A great shame. I was really pissed off, because most people couldn't tell. They just saw Radio Birdman.'

Deniz Tek: 'I think in retrospect that [record] was probably not a good idea. I don't think it's any improvement on the [original] black one. The black one should have been number one and we should have done a whole new one for number two.

'At the time we wanted the world to have the best possible record, and there were things we knew could have been better. We didn't have any semblance of a long-range view. Everything was for the immediate moment.'

Meanwhile, cassettes of the Rockfield sessions were circulating—to much teeth-grinding from the band—among the faithful in Sydney, with a track list that read: 'Smith and Wesson Blues', 'Death by the Gun', 'Closin In', 'TPVR', 'More Fun', '455 SD', 'Do the Moving Change', 'Breaks My Heart', 'Dark Surprise', 'Iskender Time', 'I Will Not Give In', 'Alien Skies', 'Burned My Eye', 'Didn't Tell the Man', 'Crying Sun', 'In the Endzone', 'I-94', 'Crying Sun reprise'. Many of the Radios' early points of reference were also up and about again. The Stones found a new lease of life in 1978 with *Some Girls*, while former New York Doll David Johansen offered a powerful solo statement, as did fellow ex-Doll Johnny Thunders with

So Alone, while his earlier project, the Heartbreakers' *L.A.M.F. (Like A Motherfucker)* continued to resonate. Lou Reed stunningly hit his artistic stride with *Street Hassle*, the Dictators followed the *Manifest Destiny* album with their third effort, *Bloodbrothers*, while former Amboy Duke, Ted Nugent, went off all the charts in every respect with the million-decibel, bare-chested frenzy of *Double Live Gonzo*.

Despite their US tour being dumped, word of the Birdmen was spreading across America and Canada with a mid-teen Duff McKagan, later of Gun N' Roses, falling for them, while future comic giant and Toronto resident Jim Carrey was said to be president of the Radios' Canadian fan club.

After the Maelstrom, *Pebbles*

The crowd at Paddington Town Hall was largely present for Midnight Oil, but there was also a contingent for the Hitmen, in the opening slot, back at the great hall which the Radios had left in ruins the previous December.

With Warwick Gilbert joining Chris Masuak on guitar, former Saint Ivor Hay on drums, Phil Sommerville on bass, and Johnny Kannis out front, the Hitmen were now firmly on their feet, with energised versions of the Sonics' 'Strychnine', the Remains' 'You Got a Hard Time Coming' and the Flamin' Groovies' 'Shake Some Action', along with the impressive songs of Gilbert and Masuak. For those who'd missed seeing Birdman, or just wanted to relive something of their spirit, the Hitmen would be the next best thing over the coming years, with the outfit—in various configurations—a strong going concern for decades to come.

The spectre of the Radios hovered over more than just Paddington Town Hall and the Oxford in nearby Taylor Square. They also hung above the magical few Pitt Street blocks from Hay to Bathurst, which took in the Civic Hotel and record stores such as Ashwood's and Martin's.

Radio Birdman however weren't the only ghosts who walked that stretch.

Phantom Records arrived in Pitt Street late in 1978, established by Birdman associate Dare Jennings, who had taken over the stock of White Light Records. Initially, Lee Taylor and Rob Younger were both behind the counter, with the contrast between Younger's softly spoken presence and his raucous legend taking some getting used to.

When the singer was putting together a sheet of new releases with Taylor, his sharp wit kicked in for a slogan for the store.

Lee Taylor: 'Rob, off the top of his head, just wrote: "The big beat in the heart of the vinyl jungle."'

Dare Jennings: 'The attitude was critical. Without the attitude, what did we have?'

By reputation alone, Younger was intimidating, which didn't make for an ideal sales assistant for those seeking the new Little River Band record.

Toby Creswell: 'There was no way you were going to buy an uncool record from Rob Younger!'

Along with the Record Plant where Frank Cotterell was behind the counter, Phantom would become an institute of rock and roll knowledge in the city and help facilitate a major catalyst in the scene: the first of the instalments of the sixties' garage compilation *Pebbles*. Like *Nuggets* before it, *Pebbles* drew back a curtain on a sea of obscure American bands, long forgotten and out of print. Despite the deliberate false lead of being from 'Kookaburra, Australia', the series originated in America. The initial four volumes would soon create a unique subculture in Sydney's inner-city scene of bands playing sixties' garage punk, pop and psychedelia.

Pebbles was the ripened harvest of the education program first prepared by Radio Birdman and White Light, along with the efforts of individuals such as Jules R.B. Normington, Lee Taylor, Mark Taylor, Clyde Bramley and Jim Dickson.

Rob Younger: '*Pebbles* is the music that really influenced rock and roll in Sydney at the end of the seventies. It wasn't the Stooges or the Dolls, or any of that stuff. It was *Nuggets* and *Pebbles*. *Pebbles* volume one was a fucking cracking record!'

Clyde Bramley: 'Everybody that I knew basically was collecting singles and all the second-hand stores and St Vinnies right across Sydney were hunting grounds. We'd drive for miles and miles to find a sixties' single.'

Brad Shepherd: 'I remember my friend, Bruce Anthon, who worked at Rocking Horse [Records in Brisbane] and was the drummer in the Survivors with Jim Dickson, he dropped this nugget in my lap one night that was an epiphany to me. I was so excited about Birdman and the stuff that had immediately influenced them, like the Stooges and the MC5, and then Bruce casually says, "You ought to get into the stuff that those guys were into. Like Question Mark and the Mysterians." "What are you talking about?" And I've been excavating ever since, effectively.'

While *Pebbles* was a collection of singles, one lone seven-inch—the sole recorded output of Deniz Tek's musical muses, the Sonic's Rendezvous Band—was also making a sizeable impression. 'City Slang' was five minutes and seven seconds of prime-cut Michigan muscle on Detroit's Orchide label. It was mono on one side, stereo on the other, both to be played at LP rather than single speed, with a frantically hammering piano by both Fred Smith and Scott Morgan somehow audible above the roar.

There were no pictures of the band on the sleeve and the lyrics seemed to be an impenetrable alien dialect, adding further to the strange mystical power around the song and even its title. While in time it became the inner city's version of 'Smoke on the Water', initially it felt as if 'City Slang' had almost singlehandedly refocused the post-Birdman 'Detroit' scene in Sydney.

Michael Gethen (Birdman devotee, photographer): '"City Slang" was akin to achieving a state of religious ecstasy. It's a great example of the beauty of music in numbers; the chord progressions are mathematically precise.'

Brad Shepherd: 'I remember hearing "City Slang" for the first time in Rocking Horse Records. Typically, on a Friday afternoon after school I would wander into town, and Jim Dickson manned the counter. He was like, "You guys have to hear this!" I couldn't believe it! That's the best song I've ever heard! Everything you liked about that kind of music, but better.'

Pebbles and 'City Slang', along with the ghost of Radio Birdman, were the musical well from which central Sydney drank for the next few years.

Visitations from the Other Side

Mark Sisto always seemed destined to have a shark's fin protruding from his back. It was all part of the realisation of his dream—or perhaps prophesy—at the Manly Vale Hotel years earlier. It was late 1978. Sisto had returned to Australia and was fronting Deniz Tek's first post-Birdman outing, the Visitors, with Pip Hoyle on keyboards and Ron Keeley on drums, along with gun for hire Steve Harris on bass.

Both Pip and Deniz had been living and working in Newcastle, and for Tek more fun had morphed into none at all.

Deniz Tek: 'The workload of an [doctor's] internship in those days was very intense. Also, we were thrown in the deep end, often placed in life-and-death situations without adequate experience or back-up. The learning curve was very steep. In addition to daily work, I was on duty every second night and every second weekend. That added up to frequent 100-plus-hour work weeks.'

The doctors got a number of Tek's intense new songs into shape.

Deniz Tek: 'I believe that some of those songs, such as "Miss You Too Much", "Sad TV" and "Journey by Sledge", were derived from the deep trauma of the recent Radio Birdman break-up.'

When it came time to provide that material with a vehicle, Tek, at a critical juncture in his musical career, went with instinct and deep faith, choosing Sisto as singer. Mark had never actually fronted a band proper, but Tek knew his friend had a strong voice, plus an aura that was almost an entity in itself.

The decision to re-bond with Deniz was a simple one for Ron Keeley.

Ron Keeley: 'Playing his numbers filled me with a kind of fierce joy . . . and that was enough.'

The Visitors made their debut at Sydney's Stagedoor Tavern on 27 December 1978, supported by the Lipstick Killers, led by Psycho Surgeon Mark Taylor and former Filth singer Peter Tillman, who was soon to become one of the other truly commanding front men on the scene.

Sisto dressed for the occasion in his shark-finned shirt.

Anny Douglass: 'I had a sewing machine. He was really clear on what he wanted. It was bloody fantastic when he wore it on stage!'

Songs like 'Brother John'—a hallowed tribute to John Needham after he left the UK tour in 1978 for a global trek—the apocalyptic 'Disperse', which Sisto delivered via a loudhailer, and 'Hell Yes' were aired, with a version of 'Hyacinth House' by the Doors slotted in nicely. They rounded out the night with Radio Birdman's 'Descent into the Maelstrom'.

Mark Sisto: 'It [the band] was an unexposed roll of film.'

★

'What did you buy?' Rob Younger asked, as usual, from behind the counter of Phantom Records in mid-1979 when the author walked in. After I handed over the bag, Younger pulled out a copy of Motorhead's *Overkill* LP. He inspected it and flipped it over, saw the photos of the individuals involved, then passed judgement. 'They look like our roadies!'

'Our' was the singer's new outfit, the Other Side. He had planned to join forces with Jim Dickson, now a free agent after the demise of the Survivors who'd recently appeared on the *Lethal Weapons* 'punk' compilation album, along with the Boys Next Door and others. The problem was that Big Jim was up in Brisbane and without a phone, so letters were the sole mode of communication. When he finally made it to Sydney and knocked on Younger's door, he was given the news that Clyde Bramley had been recruited for the bass spot, along with former Hellcats Charlie Georgees and Mark Kingsmill, on guitar and drums respectively.

The Other Side made their debut as the R4M Quartet with the Visitors at the Civic Hotel in Pitt Street at the end of February 1979. Their moniker an obscure reference to a piece of equipment on the aircraft on the cover of the Blue Oyster Cult's *Secret Treaties*. Mysterious name or not, the gig was no confidential matter, and a line of punters stretched down from the first floor of the Civic and along the street. The strange name was short lived.

Rob Younger: 'I went cold on the idea. I'd developed an aversion to the militaristic imagery Radio Birdman employed early on. "The Other Side" represented more to me, in the sense that it was suggestive of "us against them".'

The outfit's bio drew a further, seemingly pointed line in the sand stating that they were 'not ambassadors for some shitty subculture'.

Governed by Charlie Georgees' masterful guitar playing and led by the re-energised Younger, the Other Side, like the Hellcats, was a virtual jukebox of cover versions, including

'Sonic Reducer' by the Dead Boys, 'I Got a Right' by Iggy Pop and James Williamson, 'Time of Day' by the Remains, the Chocolate Watchband's 'Don't Need Your Lovin'' and along with such surprises as 'True True Lovin'' by Cliff Richard & the Shadows.

Rob Younger: 'Mostly it was just like the fucking Rats all over again. I wasn't playing with Deniz any longer, so it was back to doing covers. I started writing songs but they weren't very good. A couple of them maybe I thought at the time were okay, but they weren't, really.'

Michael Charles (later of the Lipstick Killers): 'Rob Younger's penetrating vocal delivery of the Animals' "I'm Crying" stays with me to this day.'

Angie Pepper had stepped out as well, fronting the Passengers, who made their glowing debut in mid-March 1979, also at the Civic, on bassist Jim Dickson's birthday, with Fun House goers Jeff Sullivan on guitar and Steve Harris on keyboards.

Bob Yates: 'Rob Younger was in front of me at the Civic, watching the Passengers, and I was fascinated with the cool way he kept time with his leg, sort of bending his knee and tapping his heel down to the beat. A sort of nonchalant way of doing it.'

The magic of Tek's Visitors had hardly gone unnoticed by Younger either. In fact, no one saw their qualities with greater clarity. Particularly as he was not working with Deniz post-Radios as he had originally expected and now the Visitors had these amazing songs that weren't passing his lips.

Rob Younger: 'My bedroom was above where they first started rehearsing in Fitzroy Street. I was quite jealous of Mark being able to step in and inherit all these songs, and he did a fucking good job of them too, a really good job. I thought,

"This is great! Here's a guy who's never sung with a band in his life, and it sounds way fucking better than what I sound."

'I thought it was a new stage in his [Tek's] writing. Some really good songs in a short space of time: "Life Spill", "Journey by Sledge", "Sad TV", "Living World", "Brother John".'

The Visitors did a particularly memorable performance at the Governor Bourke Hotel at Camperdown in the first week of April. Mark Sisto's appearance was again out of the norm, wearing only black shoes and socks and Speedos, with his skin entirely painted black. Some thought he was naked.

It wasn't his only radical action that night.

Stephen Vineburg: 'Sisto jumped off the stage and landed on one of those round bar tables—I don't know how it didn't tip over—and he started doing that James Brown dance-type thing while they played "Sweet Soul Music".'

George Munoz: 'I used to have this Ford Capri and I put a little PA system inside the bonnet. Mark Sisto started doing that song "Disperse", while we were driving through Darlinghurst. People were coming out to see what was going on.'

In the second half of June, the Visitors, the Other Side and the Lipstick Killers appeared at Flicks, an old movie theatre at Manly—the venue home to some overzealous bouncers—before a large crowd. There was trouble before Deniz even entered the building.

Deniz Tek: 'Angie and I arrived and a couple of guys came out of an alley and confronted us. I can't remember what they said exactly, but it was abusive toward Angie. I spoke up to defend her, aggressively, and the fight was on. No major damage on either side, cuts and bruises, and torn clothing. My adrenalin level was sky high, though, and I recall that night was a really good one for the band.'

Things were going well for the Other Side—at least until they opened for Rose Tattoo at the Bondi Lifesaver, and ended up brawling on stage with Tattoo's road crew over an audio dispute.

Rob Younger: 'After maybe four songs I said, "Well, we can't play unless you give us some sound [on stage]." A voice came through the PA from the mixing desk, "You can't fucking play anyway!" All this sort of stuff. Right, okay, fuck you! So I threw the mike on the ground in disgust, because I knew basically they were sabotaging our gig. Then I just got king-hit from the side. I remember them [the Tattoo crew] knocking over Charlie Georgees' amp and pushing people about. People left and got their money back.'

George Munoz: 'I was standing next to the mixing desk, and all of a sudden this guy took out a metal bar from the console and ran to the stage. I thought, "These are my friends! And you guys are doing this? Fuck that!" So, with my mate, we started disconnecting all these leads. We went to the PA and disconnected that as well [so Rose Tattoo would be unable to play next], but that wasn't enough for us. We said, "Let's go and burn their truck down!" We picked up some papers, some newspapers, and had some matches, and started looking for the truck. It had been there all fucking day but now it was gone. Police wagons turned up. An ambulance came because some guy threw a bottle through [a sheet of] glass, and a girl was on the other side, and she lost an eye that night.'

Meanwhile, the Hitmen had signed with WEA and released a single, Chris Masuak's 'Didn't Tell the Man'. They'd already had several dates opening for UK punk tourists the Stranglers under their belts. Later, they added supports for Tom Petty and the Heartbreakers. It was the beginning of the band's attempted crossover into a much broader, more suburban audience than Birdman had embraced or had been able to access. Slowly, they'd lose their inner-city appeal with that expansion of territory.

Hopes of Radio Birdman as a main event making a comeback were never far from mind and rumours surfaced of $3000—a sizeable fee for the day—being offered to each member for three reunion shows, one in Sydney, Melbourne and Adelaide. Any reformation was however never going to be simply about the money. Theirs was a fabric not so easily repaired.

Iggy Pop kept the flag flying in their absence. He arrived in Australia in July 1979 to promote his *New Values* album and, while he didn't do any gigs, his appearance on *Countdown* more than made up for it. After host Molly Meldrum attempted an interview, a shirtless and clearly wired Pop performed 'I'm Bored', terrorising the normally adoring studio audience, kicking both at them and the cameras, and finally flinging his microphone stand. The punk prince finally delivered the high-diving act so many had expected for so long.

Comrades of War

The pre-release publicity for the movie *Apocalypse Now* was gearing up as the return flight of Radio Birdman was somewhat miraculously scheduled for Sunday, 5 August 1979, at the Stagedoor Tavern in Sydney.

With Birdman under the name of Comrades of War, the title of Sven Hassel's pivotal novel, the occasion would also mark the bowing out of the Visitors who, as their name indicated, were never going to be a permanent fixture. Thus, the night was billed as the 'Death of the Visitors Party', with the Hitmen also appearing.

Deniz Tek: 'The Visitors and the Hitmen were doing a show at the Stagedoor, and so why don't we get Radio Birdman back together? For some reason we thought, and I don't remember exactly why, we can't call it Radio Birdman. It was supposed to be a "secret" reunion, which of course everyone knew about.'

The fact that Chris Masuak, Warwick Gilbert and Ron Keeley chose to be involved only 14 months after the horror UK experience spoke volumes about the powerful allure of the band.

Warwick Gilbert: 'It was just trying to reignite the flame, I guess. The Hitmen certainly didn't satisfy my [musical hunger] . . .'

Mark Sisto and Johnny Kannis were in for a much bigger night than they had anticipated.

Rob Younger: 'I remember talking to Mort, our mixer, and he was having a moan about playing Kraftwerk through the PA. I had reservations about doing it [the Birdman reunion] but didn't know what to do about it. I went with Clyde Bramley. I was still really pissed off with Ron and Chris, because of the band break-up, and I didn't like the association with Kannis or any of those people anymore.

'We had the Other Side going, and I remember Clyde saying to me, "If you play with these guys, I'm not going to have anything to do with you." I said, "You're right. I shouldn't be doing this. But you shouldn't be here either." So we fucked off.'

Deniz Tek: 'We had a packed room waiting for us, and we had to go on without him, so Kannis, Mark and myself shared the vocal duties.'

John Needham had just arrived back in Australia from over a year in South-East Asia and India, and was aware from letters from Deniz that Tek had written the Visitors' 'Brother John' in his honour. What he wasn't prepared for was the royal treatment that was planned at the Stagedoor.

John Needham: 'I saw Deniz and Sisto a few days before the show, and they said they wanted people to carry me onto the stage! I was horrified. I said, "If that happens, I'm not going." It didn't, thank God.'

After strong sets by the Hitmen and the Visitors—their twelfth and final appearance in a nine-month life—Sisto and Kannis, with no prior rehearsal, took to the stage again with a Rob Younger-less Radio Birdman as Comrades of War.

The outfit tore through a ragged but powerful set that included a swag of Birdman and related material, including 'I-94', 'Hand of Law', 'Smith and Wesson Blues', 'Man With Golden Helmet', unreleased songs like 'Hanging On' and

'More Fun' while roaring to a close with 'New Race', an epic take on the Door's 'L.A. Woman' and finally, 'Descent into the Maelstrom'.

Mark Sisto: 'A high-powered dragster! Like going from a 750 BMW to a 900 Kawasaki. Pulling "G"s, holding on, as opposed to rolling through bends. Very exciting, big crowd, big reaction. It showed me just how different the Visitors were to Radio Birdman. A remarkable ability of Deniz to make such a style shift.'

Within weeks of the Comrades of War gig, the Other Side drummer Mark Kingsmill defected to the Hitmen. It was the ultimate indignity to Rob Younger, who had long seen that outfit through a dark prism. Worse, the Hitmen almost immediately landed a prized opening spot for a now-rampaging Cold Chisel on their Set Fire to the Town tour, as well as a slot on *Countdown*.

By September, there was an ad on the wall at Phantom Records seeking a drummer for the Other Side, who was into 'rock and roll savagery'.

I endlessly badgered Younger, who was still working in the store, for an audition. He finally relented, only for me to bomb spectacularly. At least I did so in a cool place—Studio 20 in Darlinghurst, Radio Birdman's old rehearsal space.

Ron Keeley eventually and rightfully landed the job, despite his tense history with Younger. However, it was Clyde Bramley who had to broker the deal.

Clyde Bramley: 'I was persona non grata with Ron after the Comrades of War show, but then we needed a drummer for the Other Side. Rob said, "Why don't we try Ron?" But he said, "You'll have to go and talk to him!"'

Ron Keeley: 'Why the Other Side? I really don't know. But with Rob, I knew I was guaranteed high-energy rock and roll, which is what I liked above all. Our repertoire was all cover versions, so there was no scope for arguments over arrangements. And after the Visitors, I was at the top of my game, so Rob had no cause to complain or spit the dummy.'

A subsequent Other Side gig at the Bondi Lifesaver was witnessed by Rick Nielsen from Cheap Trick, who were in Sydney at the time.

George Munoz: 'He was jumping around, dancing. I was standing next to him and he was really having the time of his life!'

Several months after the incomplete Comrades show, Rob Younger was listening to the Doors' post-Jim Morrison effort, *American Prayer*, and seemed to receive a reassuring message from the grave in 'Curses, Invocations'.

He had long admired sharp, well-executed writing and hearing Morrison's free-flight verse, albeit over a noodling jazz background, seeming to state that the occupation of Birdman was, in the late Door man's estimation, a less substantial life pursuit than a wordsmith cosmically indicated that perhaps Younger's decision back in August was the correct one.

Rob Younger: 'It's a wank, but it felt like a personal message or something. [Laughs.] It really took me aback.'

By October, the Passengers had said farewell and Angie Pepper joined Deniz Tek in Detroit, although a sense of Tek's homeland continued to hang over central Sydney. Related or not, Dragon released a single called 'Motor City Connection', while in the real thrill of the year the Lipstick Killers issued the thumping single 'Hindu Gods (of Love)'/'Shakedown U.S.A.' on their own label, Lost In Space Records. It was produced by

Deniz Tek, with Steve Harris on keyboards along with some studio input from Rob Younger. The Psycho Surgeons single 'Horizontal Action/Wild Weekend' the previous year came in handmade sleeves covered in cow's blood from a country abattoir and sounded just as primal. The 'Hindu Gods' seven-inch however was all class from its opening eastern guitar motif and could have sat comfortably on the *Nuggets*' compilation. It made the Killers stars in their realm and officially raised the bar for all future DIY recordings.

Eureka!

It was the unique typeface that stood out first, then the stark red-and-black colour scheme, and finally the virtual facsimile of Warwick Gilbert's Rock 'n' Roll Soldiers poster for Radio Birdman's second tour of Melbourne in June 1977. It was a sealed copy of *Eureka Birdman*, the bootleg live album, and came complete with a red logo jacket patch, all for $5.95 from Martin's Records in Pitt Street.

Documented—as the title implies—at Geelong's Eureka Hotel on 30 November 1977, the sound quality was poor and there were technical issues—an almost instrumental version of the Stooges' '1970' after Rob Younger's vocal mike gave out—but the LP was a blazing statement, showcasing the enormous forward thrust of the Birdmen in full flight.

Perhaps of greatest significance for fans was the inclusion of unreleased songs like Chris Masuak's 'Death by the Gun' as well as Deniz Tek's second teen anthem 'More Fun', along with their version of Bo Diddley's 'Let the Kids Dance'.

The release was not only after the fact for the Radios, but for the fan who'd made the recording. The back cover was 'dedicated to Nick Mondon, Rock 'n' Roll Soldier, '50–'78'.

Rob (Birdman devotee): 'My mate Nick used to take his cassette recorder, an old National Panasonic, to gigs and just sit it on a table and press record. The Eureka came out really well.

Then about three or four months later, Nick died in a bizarre swimming pool accident.'

The lighting was allegedly faulty and thought to have electrified the water. Nick was found on the bottom.

Rob: 'We wanted to do something to remember him by. So we thought, "We've got this fantastic tape . . ." It was the full gig and we weren't going to fit that on a single LP. So I picked out what I thought were the essential tracks, plus the ones that hadn't been recorded, like "Let the Kids Dance", and supplied the tape to [the manufacturer] Charlie the Bootleg king.

'A week or two later, a couple of boxes roll up with copies of the record in plain white sleeves. I had a mate who worked as a screen printer. He did the artwork for the cover, which was the Rock 'n' Roll Soldiers poster modified, and used some of my photos for the back cover. The pic on the back looks like one shot, but is actually Rob and Deniz combined to look like a single shot.

'We also got some red material and printed a whole bunch of patches, and cut them all up and put one in every record. From there, I'd take them around to the record shops. There were only ever 500 copies. We didn't do it to make money. We did it for Nick. If Nick had never passed away, the record probably would never have been made.'

Keith Glass (Melbourne's Missing Link, co-founder of Archie 'n' Jugheads Records): 'Rob Younger came in one day when I wasn't there and threatened to punch my head in, because he thought I orchestrated the release. Not so.'

As for the Other Side, by early 1980 the unit was no more. Seemingly burned out by the ongoing tension between Rob Younger and Ron Keeley, an opening slot for Cold Chisel at the Comb and Cutter at Blacktown in Sydney's west was both a surprising opportunity and their last stand.

Younger continued quietly penning his own songs, including the near-biographical anthem of alienation, 'Born out of Time'.

Rob Younger: 'I wrote it on Clyde's bass. For a while there, I thought I got it from [Fleetwood Mac's] "Tusk". But many years later, I realised, the bass line which the rest of it is written around—although the song doesn't sound like it—is similar to the Shocking Blue song "Eve and the Apple".

'I was in my bedroom at Bourke Street, Surry Hills, writing on an acoustic guitar. I was just hacking away. I'm a shit guitar player. But I wound up having six, eight, maybe ten songs that no one had ever heard.'

As part of the Rock Legends series, the Mercury label had begun reissuing long-out-of-print albums in Australia, which similarly had been in the wrong place at the wrong time. These included the New York Dolls' *Too Much Too Soon* and, most significantly, the first local issue of the Velvet Underground effort *The Velvet Underground and Nico*, thirteen years after it was first unleashed in America.

But while the Velvets were no longer totally unknown in Oz, few knew much of Australia's sixties' punk heritage. This situation changed significantly, both locally and internationally, with the release of the first of four volumes of *Ugly Things*, a compilation put together by Glenn A. Baker on the Raven label. The sounds of the Missing Links, the Black Diamonds, the Creatures and the Atlantics on the record had a huge impact on the local sixties' garage scene, which was already feasting on the *Pebbles* series.

It suddenly seemed as if the ground was opening up to a hip past, with even commercial Sydney radio occasionally plugging 'Creature with the Atom Brain' by Roky Erickson from sixties' arch acid gobblers the 13th Floor Elevators, whose 'You're Gonna Miss Me' had been dealt with by Radio Birdman.

Phantom Records had expanded to a record label, under Dare Jennings and Jules R.B. Normington, kicking off with the Passengers' single, 'Face with No Name/Girlfriend's Boyfriend', followed by 'Cool in the Tube' by the Surfside 6—even though there were seven of them—including Chris Masuak's brother, Gregg, and Toby Creswell—and the Flaming Hands, fronted by another figure from the Birdman circle, Julie Mostyn, with Jeff Sullivan and Steve Harris, and their single, 'I Belong to Nobody'.

With the Civic Hotel just a block away down Pitt Street, and often an outlet for artists on the label, Phantom was perfectly placed in a number of respects, a cool, accessible alternative to the major record companies of the time.

Up in Brisbane an act was making a racket very much in Radio Birdman's image. Fun Things—with Brad Shepherd on guitar, piano and lead vocals, and brother Murray on drums—issued a blistering four-track EP that hit Sydney, in particular, like a plastic explosive in mid-1980. With a telling opening track, 'When the Birdmen Fly', and other scorchers such as 'Lipstick', they were the real deal, despite still being at high school.

Brad Shepherd: 'Long before we recorded "When the Birdmen Fly", we had a long discussion about, "Should I rewrite those lyrics, because you know what people are going to say?" I discussed this with my brother Murray and [bassist] John Hartley and it was, "Nah! It's gotta be the Birdman!" They were a revelation to me.

'That record would never have existed without Radio Birdman—either by direct influence, or by them being the conduit whereby I discovered the New York Dolls and the Stooges and the MC5 and the Blue Oyster Cult.'

Rob Younger: 'The Fun Things' record is fabulous! When I heard it and learned it was by these guys in their early teens, I considered giving the game away—seriously. It was accomplished, assured and powerful. I was a bit jealous, actually. Young upstarts.'

Like *Pebbles* and the 'City Slang' single, the Fun Things' EP helped inspire a number of bands in inner Sydney that had sprung up around a rehearsal studio at Day Street: Room 101, the Most, the Playboy Lords, ME262 (later Trans 262) and Trans Love Energies, which morphed into Slaughterhouse Five and then the Fifth Estate. It was another tier of a movement inspired by Radio Birdman, and underpinned and empowered to varying degrees by John Sinclair's book *Guitar Army*. One of the chief fire starters of that movement in Australia was about to step well outside his comfort zone with some youngsters himself.

Alone with You

When the Sunnyboys officially debuted in August 1980 at Chequers in central Sydney, with the Lipstick Killers, ME262 and Trans Love Energies, the city's who's who were in attendance, with Rob Younger front and centre in the packed house.

Had it not been for a change of heart, the former Birdman would have been up on the Chequers' stage.

In early June, Rob had been approached to front the new outfit for arch Radios fan Richard Burgman along with Peter Oxley—both from the Shy Impostors, who had been led by another Fun House regular, Penny Ward.

The emerging band's sparkling songs were created by Oxley's eighteen-year-old brother and gun guitarist, Jeremy. Younger was known as an intense figure on stage and off, but his first and enduring love was pop and singles, and these guys had both in spades. He rehearsed with them several times, working on songs like 'Alone with You' and 'I Can't Talk to You', and even tackled some of Rob's own efforts, including 'No Next Time', 'Sun God' and 'Born Out of Time'. But a crossroads moment arrived on two separate fronts.

Rob Younger: 'Eventually, I dipped out of it, and I just said they'd do a lot better if I wasn't there. I baulked when the name "Sunnyboys" came up. It suited them but I didn't feel like it was going to suit me. I just thought, "They don't need me. He's a guy [Jeremy] with a great voice, songs, and plays the house down, and he writes all the stuff. What am I doing here?" I've told them over the years that they owe their career to me, because if I hadn't left, they'd be fucking nowhere. The world can thank me for that too.'

The Sunnies' enormous promise was in clear view that night at Chequers, and they were quickly snapped up by Phantom Records. The label had just issued the Visitors' four-track twelve-inch. The tracks 'Brother John'—perhaps Deniz Tek's finest-ever song and guitar solo—'Life Spill', 'Journey by Sledge'—with Angie Pepper singing harmony—and 'Hell Yes' made for an extraordinarily strong snapshot of the band's brief existence.

Rob Younger: 'It just sounded cool, assured, especially on a record that was all done live virtually, and I think the vocals are just one take. This is a record that's done in an afternoon.'

Jules R.B. Normington: 'It was meant to be an entirely different cover. Deniz and Sisto and I were in a bar in Ann Arbor one time, watching Gang War [former New York Doll Johnny Thunders and MC5er Wayne Kramer] play. We were at a table and it was round with a walnut pattern. If you look at a walnut pattern, sometimes it looks like skulls and stuff. We must have been pissed, because it looked like it was moving, and Deniz said, "That's got to be the cover for the Visitors' record!" I took a photo of it.'

The defunct outfit were now scattered around the world. Mark Sisto was in the US Army and training in Alabama to be a chopper pilot, which would see him stationed in West Germany for the next three years. He was still pinching himself about his experiences in Sydney.

Mark Sisto: 'I was in an army barracks, one of thousands of shaved-head GIs. Guys would ask me, "What was it like in Australia?" I said, "If I told you the truth, it would make me sound like an outrageous liar." Could it have really been that good? Maybe it was all a dream.'

Ron Keeley was living in the UK with his partner, Chrissie Doyle, while Pip Hoyle had a medical practice in regional New South Wales and Deniz Tek was working at Detroit Receiving Hospital, the primary trauma centre in Michigan.

Deniz Tek: 'As a foreign-trained doctor, in addition to taking more exams I had to complete a year of work in a hospital to get full licensure in the US. I spent all of that year working insane hours as a resident doc.'

And in the city that, in 1974, had had the unenviable title of America's murder capital, and was still very much in the mix of contenders.

Deniz Tek: 'We were getting at least four or five gunshot wounds every night in the ER.'

Respite, typically, came in the form of music.

Angie Pepper: 'On the rare occasion Deniz had a few days off, we'd drive to Ann Arbor where his parents lived and visit Ron Asheton. We were close friends with the Asheton family, and Ron and Deniz enjoyed playing together as often as his gruelling schedule would allow.'

That included jamming with the former Stooge in Destroy All Monsters at Bookie's Club. It was just a few minutes' walk from where Deniz and Angie were living, and getting on stage with Tek's musical touchstones, the Sonic's Rendezvous Band, to blast through 'City Slang', was another vital and grounding outlet.

But as insanely busy as the former Birdman was, he was looking to expand his professional horizons immeasurably by returning to his dream, as an eight-year-old, of being an astronaut.

Deniz Tek: 'I began to reconsider it seriously when they started up the space-shuttle program, and it became known that they needed doctors to be mission specialists on spacecraft. I started the application process but was told that my medical degree wasn't going to be enough. I would have had to go back to university and get at least a four-year engineering degree as well. That was going to be too much.'

Rob Younger, meanwhile, reteamed with Clyde Bramley in what would be a studio-only project with Bruce Callaway, John Hoey and Ken Doyle. A single, 'Face a New God/Waiting World', would emerge on Roger Grierson and Stuart Coupe's Green label under the name the New Christs, with Younger credited as Rowdy Yates. The singer certainly had a stride that wouldn't have broken the surface of a body of water.

Tracey Burgess: 'I kept seeing Rob everywhere up at the Cross. He's got that smooth gliding walk. He never swings his arms or anything, and he had the denim jacket with the embroidered tiger on the back.'

The Hitmen had reshuffled slightly, with Warwick Gilbert now on bass and Tony Vidale taking second guitar, next to Chris Masuak. The outfit were even deeper into a territory that Radio Birdman never wished—or were unable—to straddle, working most nights of the week on the regular gig circuit with a power set list that opened with 'Dancing Time', before kicking into 'Kill City' by Iggy Pop and James Williamson, with strong original material such as 'No Clue', 'Wings of Steel', 'I Am the Man' and 'Cold December'.

Former Fun Thing Brad Shepherd landed in Sydney from Brisbane in late 1980 with a returning Ron S. Peno, looking to secure work for their band, the 31st. Shepherd rapidly became the new rock prince in harbour town and began living a Radio Birdman fan's dream—firstly, rehearsing with Rob Younger and Clyde Bramley, and then being headhunted by the Hitmen to replace Tony Vidale.

Brad Shepherd: 'It was like winning the lottery!'

The smile on Shepherd's face was only eclipsed by the glow of the Phantom label, which issued an incandescent four-track seven-inch EP by the Sunnyboys. It made the inner city sparkle and soon the outfit lit up the entire country.

Artist Tim Johnson had got to know another young Sydney act, the Celibate Rifles, whose singer, Damien Lovelock, had witnessed Radio Birdman at the Bondi Lifesaver.

Tim Johnson: 'When [Rifles guitarist] Kent Steedman was still a school student, he used to turn up at my place and copy all the Radio Birdman tapes I'd been collecting.'

In the background, moves were quietly under way regarding some other recordings, with Trafalgar to release the album Birdman had recorded in the UK in 1978, a clean tape of which Deniz Tek had squirrelled away.

Deniz Tek: '*Living Eyes* was from a line in the song "Time to Fall". That concept, of eyes alone lying on the surface of a frozen planet, having to witness all of eternity, came from a sci-fi novel I read. The eyes were conscious and living—immortal, even—but couldn't move or do anything except witness.'

A perfect pair of those windows to the soul had long been hidden in plain sight.

The Living Eye

Angie Pepper had returned to Australia from Detroit in October 1980 when her visa expired. She was accompanied by Rob Younger to the photographic studio of Patrick Bingham-Hall to discuss artwork for the shelved Radio Birdman album.

Patrick Bingham-Hall: 'Rob and Deniz wanted me to try and come up with some kind of moody mix and match, using low-key chiaroscuro images of the band members, maybe with existing shots, maybe with new. I said to Rob, "We might as well start with you," and arranged to meet in my studio one evening.

'I got Rob to stand in front of a black backdrop with a stark light raking across his profile. He was a photographic model beyond compare—he knew what I was up to, and his expression and composure needed no direction from me. There was this fabulous moment when the light shone through the iris of his right eyeball, and I said, "You can't believe this! Wait till you see this!" I processed the film and made a print of the eyeball moment. It was as I'd thought. I had honestly never seen that done before, and I have never seen it since. Rob was suitably blown out. The next I heard, that photo was to be the front cover. A purely aesthetic triumph for me.'

Rob Younger: 'My original intention was for it to be a photo montage, à la *Fun House* or the Doors' first LP. But WEA seemed to think the one of me alone looked fine by itself. I think they just didn't get it or couldn't be fucked trying to make the idea work.'

But how to promote the coming record? Radio Birdman didn't exist and weren't about to magically materialise, as the Comrades of War exercise had proved. Angie had a thought.

Angie Pepper: 'Ron and Scott Asheton had told me they wanted to visit Australia. I had the idea to get Ron and Scott over and put a band together with Radio Birdman members for a one-off music venture. I knew the chemistry would be great, as would the music, and that there was an Australian audience who would love to see a band made up of Birdman and Stooges members.'

Pepper pitched the idea to Deniz, who was still in Detroit completing his medical residency.

Deniz Tek: 'I rang Ron [Asheton], and asked him if he and his brother [Scott] could do it. Ron was very enthusiastic. Scott backed out—I don't know why. Ron said, "You know, we should really get [the MC5's drummer Dennis] Thompson. He's just like driving a Ferrari. Trust me, you'll love it." Of course, we said yes. I love Thompson's drumming.'

It was all set, and Trafalgar again got behind the project.

Tek arrived in Australia in January 1981, his training concluded, just as AC/DC were about to storm through the country with new singer Brian Johnson and the globally successful *Back in Black*.

Deniz was free from professional responsibilities until the middle of the year, when he would commence the US Navy Flight Surgeon program, which would see him crossing the oceans as part of his duties. To blow off some steam and trial some songs he'd been writing, he teamed up with Angie in the

Angie Pepper Band, including Clyde Bramley, Ivor Hay and Steve Harris.

The *Living Eyes* LP was released in March 1981, almost three years after it was recorded in the UK, with the WEA record company bio amazingly mentioning the infamous illegal Eureka bootleg.

Tek had no problem with Rob Younger alone staring down the world from the front of the album.

Deniz Tek: 'The cover art was a surprise to me when it came out—Rob's face! But I thought it was excellent and appropriate—Rob being the "front man" and all. It was a very strong cover and carried the vibe of the record.'

Rob Younger: 'I quite like the cover, but at the time I was definitely concerned about being the only band member depicted. Since the band had broken up acrimoniously, I didn't particularly care who might be offended, apart from Deniz. As it was, no one seemed too concerned, or at least I didn't hear about it.'

The cover was designed by Rob, Angie Pepper and Warwick Gilbert, with Gilbert's stunning inner-sleeve art including a carpet of skulls, harking back to the Radios' scorched-earth demise during the recording.

Warwick Gilbert: 'It was just a collage of the Mexican Day of the Dead. And I thought that was appropriate—the grinning in death, the band.'

Deniz Tek: 'It is an incredible piece of art, reminiscent of Picasso's *Guernica*.'

While the record sounded quite different again to what had first been created at Trafalgar in Sydney, there were plenty of riches on show, including the towering 'Crying Sun', with its namecheck of Mark Sisto, 'Alone in the Endzone', and its stunning guitar solo by Chris Masuak, plus '455 SD', a bow to a high-powered Pontiac.

There were also songs that seemed to reflect the mood and circumstances under which they were recorded, such as the brooding 'Time to Fall' and the crackling 'Hanging On', with its searing guitar theme.

Deniz Tek: 'The lyrics [of 'Hanging On'] were written shortly after the disastrous gig at the Vortex punk club in London. The theme of a besieged tribe was certainly inspired by events happening in and around the band at that time.'

There was a lightheartedness, too, in several other tunes such as 'More Fun' and 'Iskender Time', with its nod to John Needham.

Deniz Tek: 'Iskender's was a Turkish restaurant. As a band, we often met there, had a meal and discussed band business. They had two locations. The chef/manager and his son were big fans—they had the "New Race" single on the jukebox and played it whenever we walked in. They took pride in me having Turkish ancestry.

'Needham would often meet us there, and at that time he was working at Gladesville Psychiatric Hospital as a nurse.'

Equally buoyant was 'TPBR Combo', an abbreviation of tuna peanut butter on rye from *Zap Comix*.

Deniz Tek: '"TPBR" came from a Justin Green comic, "Th' Kiss-Off". And much of "Crying Sun" came from another Justin Green comic. We used to read a lot of strange comics, and had no qualms about recycling ideas.'

Toby Creswell: 'People took the band very seriously, but if you actually look at the songs and what they were about, there were two about sandwiches. They were about having fun, cute girls, and all that kind of stuff. It's not doom and gloom.

It's really in that garage-band surf tradition of hot-rod songs and things. People used to go on about how it [Birdman] was fascist, and it wasn't fascist. I mean "More Fun" is not a fascist song. Or "I-94". I think that got a bit lost.'

For some reason, 'I-94', 'Smith and Wesson Blues' and 'Burned My Eye'—now retitled 'Burn My Eye '78' and with new lyrics—from their first EP were included, again tinkering with the past, rather than moving forward from it.

Deniz Tek: 'When we got to Rockfield, we didn't have enough new songs for a second album. We would have if Pip's song "Alien Skies" and Chris's two songs "Death by the Gun" and "Didn't Tell the Man" were included. None of those three made the cut, and so new versions of the three [*Burn My Eye*] EP tracks, re-recorded at Rockfield, were used. We thought this was a reasonable compromise, as the EP had only been released in small numbers in Australia.

'If I had it to do all over again, *Living Eyes* would have had the new songs that appeared on the Sire *Radios Appear*, plus the newer tunes. We would have had plenty of material.'

Rob Younger: '[*Living Eyes*] is coloured by the time we spent there—the antipathy involved with the band breaking up.'

Warwick Gilbert: 'It reminds me of Deniz's solo material, but with us playing on it. A rotten experience.'

The Ride of the Valkyries

Donnie Sutherland's Saturday morning music program, *Sounds*, had long featured guests who hadn't slept and nodded off on camera, sometimes with cigarette in hand; or maybe they were still under the influence of whatever from the gig the night before. Rob Younger was wide awake and seemed seconds from openly dying of boredom. His burning contempt radiated from televisions across the country, and even the sunglasses hanging limply from the collar of his T-shirt had an ice-cool disdain. It was early April 1981 and Younger was in the frame to discuss a one-off Australian tour 'event'.

The media release for the April/May venture, which was titled New Race, was stamped with the Radio Birdman logo and announced that the Stooges' Ron Asheton and MC5's Dennis 'Machinegun' Thompson were teaming with Rob, Deniz Tek and Warwick Gilbert from Birdman. Pip Hoyle was also expected to be involved.

Initially, the dates were to kick off in Coffs Harbour on 22 April, and then take in Brisbane, Sydney, Melbourne, Adelaide, Canberra, and back to Sydney.

Gilbert was still in the Hitmen, who had just released a third seven-inch, the cracking 'I Don't Mind', backed with a version of 'Rock 'n' Roll Soldiers' by Ron Asheton's New Order. But he wasn't a happy Hitter and so the lure of the Birdman siren again, plus the opportunity to work with Asheton and Thompson . . .

Talk of New Race, coupled with the Radios' three-year-plus absence, saw *Living Eyes* hit the 2SM Top 50 album chart, in a list that included *Back in Black*, the Police's *Zenyatta Mondatta*, John Lennon's *Double Fantasy* and Dire Straits' *Making Movies*. What's more, it was a rising 'bullet performer'.

Early rehearsals involved Michael Charles.

Michael Charles: 'Deniz asked me to drum until Dennis Thompson and Ron Asheton arrived. I willingly obliged. That was a huge thrill for this new kid on the block, and for a drummer, more so, playing alongside Warwick Gilbert.'

The American pair touched down in Sydney in the first week of April, probably still pinching themselves. While Asheton had the Destroy All Monsters outfit, the career of neither had exactly been on a rocketing trajectory since the demise of the MC5 and the Stooges. Now they had jetted to the other side of the world to perform with the members of a hugely popular local band deeply rooted in the music they had created.

Rehearsals initially saw some minor head-butting for domination, but Asheton and Thompson were entering Birdman's space, turf that had been torturously cultivated. Ron Asheton was a close friend of Tek, but this was about reputation.

Deniz Tek: 'They were the ones joining *my* band, as I saw it, and they were the ones who had to deliver the goods.'

Ron Asheton: 'It felt like guys I'd been playing with for a while. We only had five days to practise before we played our first gig. It was amazing that a group thrown together that fast could come up with something that tight.'

The artwork for the tour naturally fell to the talents of Warwick Gilbert, including the creation of the lettering and band logo.

Warwick Gilbert: 'I got that from *Apocalypse Now*. One of my favourite movies. I did the "H bomb" and then *Apocalypse Now* lettering and applied that to New Race.'

At Gilbert's suggestion, Wagner's 'Ride of the Valkyries', which had featured spectacularly in the movie, was played over the PA to herald the band's entrance on stage each night from the opening gig.

The power the New Race outfit wielded was astonishing as they roared through tunes by Birdman, the Visitors, the Stooges, the MC5 and Asheton's Destroy All Monsters. The band-penned 'Columbia', inspired by the first of the NASA space-shuttle fleet which had just taken its maiden flight, was also included.

New Race wasn't an updated edition of Radio Birdman, but a new high-octane beast entirely, with Thompson's drum work more attacking than the swing of Ron Keeley, and Ron Asheton's guitar around Deniz differing considerably from that of Chris Masuak. And it was all through a considerable sound system, rather than the band's own small rig—as was the case with Birdman—with a six-man road crew that included Gabor Bunda, a schoolmate of Deniz's from Ann Arbor.

For the first time, several former Radios were on a level playing field with the rest of the country's music industry.

For audience members, it was all totally surreal. The Birdmen alone had a real mystique. Seeing them on stage alongside two underground rock and roll icons in a Stooge and an MC5er—and at their local pub, not in the untouchable, barely visible distance at the Hordern Pavilion—was like having the New York Dolls perform at your 21st.

For the diehard Radios fans, as well as for those who'd missed the band the first time, it was utter nirvana.

Tim Pittman: 'Almost as soon as Birdman broke up, there was a whole new audience waiting. People like me who were too young to see them the first time around. Double J fans, surfers, teenage punks—the great unwashed. The New Race tour was full of them.'

Ron Asheton: 'Deniz always told me how much Radio Birdman and the people that followed them were Stooges and MC5 fans, so I expected it to be good. The tour was maybe better—everything was sold out, almost. It was like massive crowds. If it was a place that held 2000, there would be that many people. My thing was, "Hey, now I know what it feels like to be in the Rolling Stones, to be so well received by everybody."'

Dave Laing saw the Prospect Hill Hotel show in Melbourne.

Dave Laing (Birdman devotee): 'New Race was my first opportunity to see something Birdman-related live. Having never previously seen Rob Younger in the flesh, my most vivid memory is him walking out on the stage—V-neck black pullover against translucent white skin, and that long hair offset by a bit of mascara. He looked like the real deal—a genuine ghoul, and in a world of suntans, a real freak. He was perfect. I didn't bother with the bar. I was pushed up front of the stage and I remember the sound as a shitstorm of noise and chaos, with that piercing tone Ron started perfecting in Destroy All Monsters cutting through. His playing really brought something different—an extra threat of violence—to Deniz's material.'

In Canberra, of course, a trip to the War Memorial was mandatory for military heads Ron Asheton and Deniz Tek, and photos were taken.

At times on stage there was conflict, too.

Rob Younger: 'I remember throwing the mike stand about as usual, and Ron Asheton had a big moan to me after the set, and said, "I've been through all that with Iggy, man!", and this sort of shit. He was nearly getting hit with the mike and he didn't like that, but I thought, "Oh really? A bit wild, is it?"'

Tim Pittman: 'The Sylvania Hotel show [in Sydney's southern suburbs] was easily one of the best gigs I've ever seen. Loud and wild and teetering on the very edge of being out of control. I can still recall the rumble of the bottom end as the intro to "455 SD" came thundering through the speakers, the crowd moving as one like a massive ocean current, lifting me off my feet and transporting me from one side of the room to the other.

'It was actually kinda scary too, as the floor was literally acting like a springboard, bouncing up and down from all the energy, making me wonder whether we were all about to go crashing through to the foundations beneath. At one point, Rob tossed the microphone like a lasso around his head, firing it out into the audience before *thud*, it hit the unsuspecting target—poor sod—and dropped to the floor. Masuak joined them on stage too, which brought added kudos. For me, it was everything Birdman's legend had promised and more.'

During the run of Sydney dates, New Race appeared instore at Phantom Records, and a party was arranged at Campbell Street, Darlinghurst, where Clyde Bramley, Richard Burgman, Brad Shepherd and Doug Lonsdale were living.

Brad Shepherd: 'I was in the Hitmen at the time. We'd been out playing shows and I came back home and Campbell Street, between Taylor Square and Crown Street, was just buzzing with people spilling out of our house. And Ron Asheton and Dennis Thompson were there among these people. It was just a surreal experience. Dennis Thompson was telling me stories about the blokes in the MC5, and he was still cranky about things that had happened. Ron was very friendly.'

Chris Masuak was at each Sydney gig he was able to attend, and got on stage again at Sgt Peppers and Selinas.

Chris Masuak: 'They were a great band. I was more interested in seeing Ron Asheton and Dennis Thompson than my old bandmates. Standing next to Ron Asheton on stage was incredibly inspiring. That was just wonderful!'

There were probably those who felt that the entire exercise was just an extension of the alleged fascism of Radio Birdman, particularly given the band name. They wouldn't have been calmed by a pre-performance incident at Selinas.

Warwick Gilbert: 'As we walked across the suspension bridge, above the crowd to the stage, to the stirring strains of Wagner, Ron Asheton stopped and turned to the audience, so we stopped too. Then Ron clicked his heels together and gave a perfect Nazi salute with utter and complete conviction, to the horrified looks on the upturned faces below. And I thought, "Oh, fuck!" I felt really ashamed! Ron had a Nazi fetish, but could be the kindest guy.'

By the second week of May, the New Race tour was all over. They'd pulled approximately 16,000 people—the equivalent of three sold-out nights at Sydney's Hordern Pavilion—and packed many of the country's regional and suburban beer barns that just six years earlier had been alien, enemy territory for Radio Birdman.

In that sense, New Race was Birdman's belated coming of pub age, their triumphant final arrival in pub land, shoulder to shoulder with the deed holders such as Midnight Oil, the Angels and Cold Chisel.

Ron Asheton: 'It was some of the best times I'd ever had playing anywhere, and that includes even in Stooges' days. Thompson and I didn't want to leave. I was going to get married just to stay there to work some more. That's how much we loved it.'

Brad Shepherd: 'New Race were as exciting as anything I've ever seen in my life. It was really important to me. As exciting as seeing the Clash at the Hammersmith Palais, Slade at Festival Hall, Black Sabbath or anything.'

Deniz Tek: 'It was really great. Sort of healing of relations between me and Warwick, and it was good to be playing with the guys again. Chris even joined us for some of the shows. It was a good time for the band to heal wounds.'

Keeping New Race alive beyond the tour had logistical and geographic issues, however, not to mention Tek's own professional circumstances at the time. But at the very least, they finally made it to the cover of one of Australia's major music magazines with a three-page feature in *RAM*—something the Radios never achieved in their original lifetime.

The Iceman

While Deniz Tek was on sea deployment with the US Navy, Angie Pepper attended a US Marine Corps Officers Ball in Honolulu, and found herself dancing with the central figure in what should have been a big hit for Radio Birdman.

Angie Pepper: 'It was a very formal affair, men in dress white uniforms, women in long gowns, and Jack Lord [from *Hawaii Five-O*] was a special guest at the event. He danced with several of the women there, including me, and was very generous with his time—gracious and polite. We sat and talked for a little while and I told him about Radio Birdman's "Aloha Steve & Danno" tribute song. He was unaware of the band or the single, and asked if I would send him a copy, writing his address on my program.

'It was a very surreal experience. Driving myself home from the Coral Ballroom in Waikiki, I felt like I had borrowed someone else's life for the evening. The next day. I sent him the single.'

After the New Race tour, and following some further dates and recording with the Angie Pepper Band, Tek had returned to the US—with Pepper following a few months later—readying himself for his place in the US Navy Flight Surgeon program in Florida. From there he joined the air wing of the Marines in Hawaii, initially looking down at the world from beneath the rapidly swirling blades of a helicopter, and then watching the ground below rush past at high speed from a jet.

The naval move had multiple benefits. Tek had always wanted to contribute socially with medicine, and now could also fulfil another desire: to be strapped into fast, sleek, ultra-cool aircraft, the airborne equivalent of the muscle cars he loved. A combination of F-4 Phantoms and his role as a Marines' flight surgeon would be the former Birdman's professional life until the end of the decade.

Being at sea as part of his service shaped a future for Deniz, as well as a nickname that was very much in character. It would also provide Hollywood with a storyline.

Deniz Tek: 'During my first shipboard deployment, we were out at sea for six months. I got the reputation for being too serious. Actually, I have a good sense of humour, but sitting in the wardroom for meals, with the same bunch of guys every day for months on end, is no different to being in the van with the band, driving for eight hours a day between gigs. I thought my call sign would be "Doc", since that's what everyone was already calling me, anyway, but I ended up being christened "Iceman", usually shortened to "Ice".'

It was a work/life situation far removed from that of his one-time combatant Nick Cave. With the Birthday Party now workers in Satan's boiler room, Cave was wildly out-Detroiting what Birdman ever did, turning the human-volcano sound of the Stooges' *Fun House* LP into a lurching, mangled roar on their live recording, *Drunk on the Pope's Blood*—'16 minutes of sheer hell!' as the cover declared. It included a version of the Stooges' 'Loose', which they later expanded into a full set of material by Iggy and his buddies at Melbourne's Crystal Ballroom.

★

As the old saying goes, 'You can take the boy out of the Birdman but you can't take the Birdman out of the boy . . .'

Chris Masuak and Brad Shepherd were on stage at the Comb and Cutter Hotel in western Sydney, tuning up before the Hitmen's later performance. But all their efforts were drowned out by the music the DJ was playing. Masuak took it for as long as he could, before striding purposefully to the microphone: 'Fuck you and all you stand for!'

The release of the Hitmen's self-titled debut LP on WEA in mid-1981—with famed producer Mark Opitz, whose CV included AC/DC, the Angels and Cold Chisel—was a major advancement for the former Birdman members. But there were still axes to be ground.

Chris Masuak: 'That first album was quite an achievement. A tight fucking band! But the record company really didn't know what to do with us. We still had that attitude we had developed in Birdman, and we were always a bit of a victim of that, because it gave the press and the industry the chance to get back at Radio Birdman. So we copped a lot of bullshit from journalists, from industry people, from disgruntled ex-girlfriends—whoever didn't get a chance to take it out on Birdman or were too chicken shit.'

In the second half of the year, Warwick Gilbert gave notice of his intention to leave the Hitmen and return to animation.

Tony 'the Kid' Robertson from Brisbane's the 31st stepped in during their Australian dates opening for American 'Born to Be Wild' legends, Steppenwolf. The Kid was home.

The Hitmen's roll forward continued with a support spot for the Clash at Sydney's Capitol Theatre in February 1982, while Rob Younger stayed chatting in the foyer.

The First and the Last

Radio Birdman had battled wild accusations of Third Reich affiliations for much of its latter-day career. The publicity for the New Race live album, *The First and the Last*, sparked further spot fires that had to be quickly extinguished.

The promotional poster was a view from the back of what appeared to be one of the Nazi rallies in Nuremberg in 1933, showing a sea of helmeted soldiers, with a red Birdman patch caught on barbed wire added to the foreground.

Released in September 1982, and titled at the suggestion of Ron Asheton after the book by German World War II fighter pilot Adolf Galland, *The First and the Last* was all horse-power and sonic brimstone, recorded at Selinas, Sgt Peppers and Manly Vale Hotel in Sydney and the Crystal Ballroom in Melbourne.

Chris Masuak's guest spots on 'Columbia' and the MC5's 'Looking at You' from Sgt Peppers and Selinas were included, and he and Pip Hoyle were among the special thanks in the credits.

The record wasn't an exact document of what New Race delivered on their Australian tour, because Rob Younger, ever the perfectionist—and by far his own toughest critic—decided to take action, as he was not exactly delighted with his vocals on the original tapes.

Rob Younger: 'If I had sounded great, I would never have touched it. But I didn't want to put out a shitty-sounding record, all for the sake of authenticity. I was really jumping around, so I was off mike and all of that [during the recording], so I redid my vocals. There's no live vocals by me on that record. I don't like my own singing, anyway. Deniz wasn't in the country. If he had been, it would have been a whole different story.'

Deniz Tek: 'I was back in America by the time they got around to mixing it, and without telling me, Rob redid all his vocals. Because of the way it was recorded, my backing vocals had to be eliminated too, so they got Clyde Bramley to sing my parts. I was furious!'

Clyde Bramley: 'They just needed somebody, with a different voice to Rob, to come in and do some backing vocals. If you listen to them, they're not very good! But it sort of fitted in for the live atmosphere of it.'

Deniz Tek: 'The original vocals were great! You can hear the live vocals on the Revenge Records releases [*The First to Pay* and *The Second Wave*], which were mastered from a reference cassette copy of rough mixes of all the recorded shows. Ron [Asheton] sold his copy to the French label for $500.'

Ron Asheton: 'They couldn't get enough copies [of *The First and the Last* album] to keep it in stock in Ann Arbor.'

John Needham had now started Citadel Records to which Rob Younger would be strongly linked as producer.

Its first release was the Minuteman single 'Voodoo Slaves'/ 'I Wanna Be Your Minuteman', in September 1982, both written by Needham and produced by Younger. The band included some of the key figures in the early Radios camp, with veteran fan Doug (Dug) Lonsdale on vocals, Needham on guitar and Clyde Bramley on bass, a role Alley Brereton had filled in the outfit's early days.

That seven-inch would be added to the swag of local releases by Phantom and other labels, by bands such as the Passengers, the Visitors and the Lipstick Killers, that Jim Dickson, former Passenger and towering oracle of the Sydney scene, took to a thrilled Europe in the days before strong distribution networks. The Minutemen effort hit France like the best kind of bomb, capitalising on the word of mouth from Birdman's 1978 Euro tour and the release of the Sire edition of the *Radios Appear* album. It helped spearhead a new scene on the continent.

The Radios themselves continued to have an impact locally. In October 1982, WEA released a record titled *Soldiers of Rock 'n' Roll—An Audio Documentary of Radio Birdman*, which was narrated by the velvet tones of Dragon's endlessly charismatic Marc Hunter.

It was a strange venture, more like a radio program, with grabs of interviews with Dennis Thompson and Ron Asheton, as well as giving voice to insiders including Paul Gearside, Felicity Surtees and Jules R.B. Normington. It featured music from the MC5, the Stooges, the Pink Fairies, Birdman, New Race and, curiously, the Angels. The only member of Radio Birdman to be included in the project was Chris Masuak.

Rob Younger: 'I listened to it once and thought it was appalling.'

Incredibly, the cover art was strikingly similar to the Nazi rally image used for the promotional poster for the New Race album.

Rob Younger: 'Warner Brothers came up with it and they thought it was alright and we didn't.'

Fifty or so copies were circulated before it was withdrawn. It was then reissued with a plain white cover, with the same cumbersome title and the Radio Birdman logo.

The Hitmen weren't having an easy time either, with hopes of securing Ron Asheton to steer their second effort, *It Is What It Is*, dying on the vine. Worse, after the album was completed, Brad Shepherd moved on to settle in an up-and-coming band called the Hoodoo Gurus, where Clyde Bramley was already placed.

Pre-dating the arrival of the pair, and prior to a name change, Le Hoodoo Gurus had issued their first single, 'Leilani', on the Phantom label.

Pressing on, the Hitmen landed a spot at the Narara Festival on the NSW Central Coast early in 1983, on a massive bill that included INXS, Cold Chisel, the Angels and Men at Work, before a peak crowd of almost 50,000. They would then take a hiatus, with Johnny Kannis leading the soul-revue outfit, Night Train.

Rob Younger kept his hand in, drumming as 'Sticks Younger' in Sydney outfit Coupe de Ville at the Leichhardt Hotel, as well as a party gig with the Tim Johnson Band, in which Rob played some bass and sang Dylan's 'Wicked Messenger' and the Velvet Underground's 'Venus in Furs'. He was still working on his own songs when the opportunity arrived to back them out of the garage and onto large stages.

The author, then writing for *Juke* magazine, rang Younger for comment on the rumours that were circulating.

Rob Younger: 'You seem to know all about it. What are you calling me for?'

For Christs' Sake!

Amid the excitement that greeted the announcement that Iggy Pop was finally to perform on Australian soil in June 1983 one individual was more thrilled than most.

Rob Younger: 'I got a call from Charles Fisher [at Trafalgar] saying, "If you can get a band together, you can land a support for Iggy." I thought, "Fuck, that sounds interesting. I'd love to do that!"

'The Hitmen weren't playing much and I was on fairly good terms with most of those guys at that time. I'd been seeing a bit of Chris, for some reason, so I asked them if they were interested and roped in [Celibate Rifle] Kent Steedman as well. We did about four rehearsals.'

Chris Masuak: 'Kent came on board which I wasn't really greatly pleased about, because I was sick to death of all that quasi-Detroit posturing, and I thought, "Oh fuck, not another Deniz Tek wannabe!" But we endured.'

They became the New Christs—Younger, Masuak and Steedman, with Tony Robertson on bass and Mark Kingsmill on drums—a name which already had some minor currency, after the earlier 'Face a New God' single.

Any mention of Radio Birdman, however, saw Younger quickly slip into bristle mode. He very firmly preferred the focus be on the right fucking here and now, rather than what once was and could have been.

The 'Robert Younger'–produced double single, '25th Hour', by the heavily *Pebbles*-influenced Lime Spiders, with Warwick Gilbert on bass, was released just weeks before Iggy's arrival in the country.

The tour opened at Sydney's Capitol Theatre over two nights on 28 and 29 June. The Christs spectacularly upstaged the overly wired Punk Godfather from the outset on both occasions.

Rob Younger: 'That was the first time I felt a little personal satisfaction from playing music. We were in front of at least 2000 people each night and with just my own songs that had never been played to anyone before, and we killed it! I could write these songs and play them to all these people, and they were fucking digging it? I couldn't believe it!

'We did a few covers as well. "Did You No Wrong" by the Sex Pistols, or alternately [Roky Erickson's] "Creature with the Atom Brain", I think. The first night I think we opened with "Face a New God" and "Return of the Spiders", the Alice Cooper song from *Easy Action*, the second. And I'd never played a stage that big before. The band acquitted themselves really well. I just remember the idea of getting away with it. That really, really thrilled me!'

On 16 July, the tour reached the Sylvania Hotel. Johnny Kannis was on his way to a Night Train gig further south, and saw the signage for the Iggy and New Christs show.

Johnny Kannis: 'One of the last things I remember is driving past the Sylvania Hotel on the way to Corrimal Leagues Club.'

The car crash that followed minutes later was horrific. Kannis, Steve Harris and Lynne Phillips were seriously injured, with Johnny hospitalised for months and Steve Harris concussed for three years. The Hitmen seemed finished, permanently.

On the other hand, the Christs were really firing.

Chris Masuak: 'The band was, as they say, a well-oiled machine, and we could go wherever Younger took us. A fantastic live band. An extraordinarily great band.'

This didn't go unnoticed by the former Stooge, whose own outfit was anything but, and at one of the Tivoli gigs in Sydney he joined the Christs on stage.

Rob Younger: 'Iggy got up with us to do "Search and Destroy". He was supposed to sing but his mike wasn't working, so I just took over and performed the whole thing, while he danced around. The crowd seemed happy enough; after all, his dancing is as good as his vocalising. We were all pretty wired. I could simply have handed Iggy my mike, let him do it, but that hadn't occurred to me. No one chipped me about it later either, called me an idiot, a wanker—nothing. Iggy seemed happy enough about the whole affair.'

Chris Masuak: 'Iggy was just in awe of us. I would put forward the proposition that the best gig he did [on the tour], and the best time he had, was onstage with us. Him and Younger were on the stage, bashing it with their fists!'

After the tour, with the Hitmen out of action following the car accident, the Christs continued on, but in time Kent Steedman had to return to the Celibate Rifles. White-hot Lime Spiders' guitarist Richard Jakimyszyn stepped in.

Two bristling later singles for Citadel—'Like a Curse' and 'Born Out of Time'—would have a sizeable impact in Europe, with Chris Masuak's scorching solos remaining virtually intact in live renditions of the songs since.

Chris Masuak: 'We could do anything. A very good example of that is "Born Out of Time", where he [Rob Younger] is actually leading the band. We're playing that live in the studio and you can hear him ring leading the proceedings. We could segue from song into song into song, and follow him, because we knew what to do.'

Deniz Tek, meanwhile, although still fully professionally engaged in the US Navy, had fired a quiet shot with the single of '100 Fools', backed with Pip Hoyle's 'Alien Skies' from the 1978 Rockfield sessions. It was the opening round in what would be, for Tek, a long, highly prolific and varied solo career that would include several dream collaborations, as well as touring extensively in his own right.

'100 Fools' was part of a barrage of Citadel releases that would telegraph a scene to the world: 'Crying Sun/Gotta Keep Movin'' by New Race, the Screaming Tribesmen's 'Igloo', Angie Pepper's 'Frozen World', and 'Out of the Unknown' by Died Pretty, the spell-casting-and-catching new outfit for former Hellcat Ron S. Peno. Rob Younger was initially the unit's drummer, and went on to produce their sparkling early work, including their debut LP, *Free Dirt*.

By early 1984, Johnny Kannis was back on his feet, although still very much carrying the impact of the car accident. The Hitmen then returned, with Richard Jakimyszyn joining Chris Masuak on guitar, in what was to be a final goodbye tour.

But that stripped the New Christs bare of personnel and saw the demise of Rob Younger's outfit, although by that point it was being torn by old polarities, anyway. Nonetheless, Younger felt deserted, and this just as an offer of doing an album in the UK presented itself—combined with the chance to back up the strong reviews of the 'Like a Curse' single in France and the UK with some gigs. For the second time, Younger had lost out to the Hitmen, an outfit he had long viewed with contempt. He downed tools for the next few years.

Melbourne fan Dave Laing, who later ran the Dog Meat and Grown Up Wrong record labels, came to Sydney to witness the Hitmen's farewell dates. Laing was stunned by the post-Birdman world he found in the harbour city.

Dave Laing: 'I went to record shops like Phantom and the Record Plant every day. There was nothing like them down there. You could count the number of people in Melbourne who knew [the Sonic's Rendezvous Band's] "City Slang" on the fingers of one hand. The second and third Dictators albums, and the DMZ album, were fifty-cent records, if they happened to show up in the bargain bins. No one knew who the Remains were.

'The Hoodoo Gurus, the Lime Spiders, the Celibate Rifles, all toured a bunch, but it all felt like something brand new in Melbourne. The Lipstick Killers never played here, nor the Visitors, the Other Side or the Passengers, and the Hitmen had pretty much given up on Melbourne. The early eighties' Sydney scene, as inspired by Birdman, just seemed like another planet.'

The Hitmen's sweat-drenched final curtain would be documented on the blazing *Tora Tora D.T.K.* LP. After their last bows, Chris Masuak joined the ranks of the Screaming Tribesmen, with Mick Medew.

The Hoodoo Gurus by now were beginning to enjoy mainstream success in Australia with their first LP, 1984's *Stoneage Romeos*, which rang out like an offshoot of the *Nuggets* and *Pebbles* compilations. It was also enthusiastically received on the American college circuit. Mark Kingsmill of the Hellcats, the Other Side, the Hitmen and the New Christs would join on drums.

Radio Birdman's flame of influence continued to ignite to varying degrees a host of Sydney bands such as Ballistic

Therapy, Howling Commandos, Melting Skyscrapers, Mutated Noddies, Conspirators, Mushroom Planet, Spectre's Revenge, Psychotic Turnbuckles, the Eastern Dark, Decline of the Reptiles and Hard Ons.

And the counterculture that had fired Birdman in Australia stepped further into the light in September 1986, as former New York Doll Johnny Thunders toured Australia, with ex-Sex Pistol Glen Matlock and another Doll, Jerry Nolan. They didn't pull anywhere near the crowds New Race did, but the presence of these alternate-universe demigods in such out-of-town spots as the Seven Hills Inn, deep in western Sydney, and Wollongong's Cabbage Tree Hotel was still something from a wild dream.

Deniz Tek was high above it all, quite literally. He and his colleagues were being watched.

The Need for Speed

Deniz Tek: 'I was in a Marine F-4 Phantom squadron, VMFA-212, with the call sign "Iceman". A couple of researchers from the *Top Gun* movie production team hung around the squadron for two weeks, taking notes. Then when the film came out, there was an Iceman in it. They officially deny any intentional reference. My old aviation buddies all call me "the original Iceman", and some say I was more like the Val Kilmer [Tom 'Iceman' Kazansky] character than he was himself! I was happy with the call sign until the movie came out. That ruined it.'

Nonetheless, the Iceman tag would follow Tek well beyond his flying days. So, too, Angie Pepper's voice had trailed her, alighting on the ears of Arif Mardin, producer and arranger at Atlantic Records, who'd guided such names as Aretha Franklin and Dusty Springfield.

Mardin had been at school in Istanbul with Deniz's father, so when the Birdman was in New York City for a toxicology mini-fellowship at Bellevue Hospital, his father encouraged him to reach out to his old classmate.

Deniz Tek: 'I gave him a cassette tape of Angie. I was keen to see what he thought of her voice and delivery, and he was impressed. He said she had "a most special voice", and was considering signing her.'

But at the time Pepper's priorities were twofold and iron

clad: being a mum and providing support for Tek during his medical residency training.

Back in Australia, the New Christs had been born again. Former member of the Passengers with Angie Pepper, Jim Dickson arrived back from the UK in the second half of 1985. He had auditioned for punk band the Vibrators, and fittingly joined English rock-and-roll master historians, the Barracudas. He'd also bumped into the Who's Pete Townshend, who grumpily asked if Jim had a cigarette.

Dickson felt he had unfinished business with Rob Younger. He persuaded the singer to get back on the horse and form the band that should have been in 1979.

The pair would be joined by guitarist Charlie Owen and drummer Nick Fisher, on their first album, *Distemper*. It was a mix of bristle with a sprinkling of gold dust courtesy of the guest keyboards of Louis Tillett.

Over the coming years, and through a number of differing line-ups, the Rob Younger–led New Christs with Dickson a stalwart would make numerous highly successful sweeps through Europe, including a slot on a major Spanish festival with Alice Cooper. They'd also be the long-term musical vehicle for Younger that allowed him to sharpen the stagecraft he'd previously learned by trial and error.

Rob Younger: 'With Radio Birdman, I was just trying to figure out how to do stuff for quite a while, and I never really felt on top of the game.'

Evidence of the local impact of the Stooges was reflected by a tribute record to the Detroit act on Melbourne's Au Go Go label. The brainchild of David Laing and Bruce Milne, it was titled *Hard to Beat*, and featured a range of acts from across the country including the Celibate Rifles, Adelaide's Exploding

White Mice, Hard Ons, ME262, Melbourne's Seminal Rats, Adelaide's Raw Power and Johnny Kannis.

All the while, the myth and legend of Radio Birdman themselves continued to evolve, a hunger fed by the issuing of their official works to date, including the New Race project, and more in the 'Under the Ashes' box through WEA in December 1988. In doing so, the Radios were given a level of commercial respect usually reserved for the likes of the Stones or the Doors, and something that had never been afforded to their heroes.

Au Go Go also reissued Iggy and the Stooges' long-out-of-print *Raw Power*, by which time early Birdman fan Rick Grossman—who had done time in Matt Finish and the Divinyls—replaced Clyde Bramley on bass in the Hoodoo Gurus, joining his old friend Mark Kingsmill.

Deniz Tek, now an emergency medicine specialist, also had a change of professional circumstance. In late 1989, he departed the Navy after nine years having travelled from the upper reaches of the Arctic Circle to the Persian Gulf, Haiti to the Philippines. It was a considerably larger stage than either the Fun House or Paddington Town Hall.

He and his family moved to Billings, Montana, where his skills were applied in a local hospital.

The regrouping and reconfiguring of the Hitmen by Johnny Kannis and Chris Masuak as Hitmen D.T.K. would be a bridge, not only for Tek's musical re-entry, but also Radio Birdman's return.

So It Begins . . .

Several members of the Ramones were side of stage as the New Christs ripped through their paces at Sydney's Hordern Pavilion. It was January 1991 and one of the party pointed to Rob Younger and nudged singer Joey Ramone: 'That's the *Hawaii Five-O* guy.'

While the Christs were firing, Deniz Tek hadn't played for anything but a few laughs, and to keep his hand in, since the New Race tour a decade earlier.

That was until some old comrades who were in the Lone Star State reached out. Hitmen D.T.K. were recording what would be their *Moronic Inferno* album in Houston, Texas, at the legendary Sugar Hill Studios. The sessions were engineered by Andy 'Mort' Bradley, former sound man for both Radio Birdman and the Hitmen. Mort's CV would later include two Grammy nominations in the classical-music realm, as well as working with acts as diverse as Beyoncé and Destiny's Child and Willie Nelson.

Chris Masuak: 'Every time I went to Canada to visit my folks, I would catch up with him [Tek]. When we went to record *Moronic Inferno*, I said, "Well, why don't we invite him down?" It was relaxed, and [we] had a good time. I think it inspired him to strap the guitar back on.'

Deniz Tek: 'It was an opportunity to get back in the studio

after a long lay-off, reconnect with Chris, and also to meet up with Mort.

'[The 13th Floor Elevators'] "You're Gonna Miss Me" was recorded at Sugar Hill. Mort had the original four-track master, along with countless other treasures in the tape archive vaults there. Truly mind blowing!'

Tek greatly enjoyed the studio experience, and later, back in Sydney, joined the Hitmen for the kick-off of their 'Moronic Inferno' tour, most notably at two packed-out nights at the Annandale Hotel on 16 and 17 November. Tek's appearance saw the corner pub transported back to the wildly jubilant mood of Paddington Town Hall in late 1977. With Pip Hoyle and Mark Sisto also taking part, such Birdman fodder as 'Do the Pop', 'Hand of Law' and 'Aloha Steve & Danno' were aired with an epic closer of 'L.A. Woman'.

Both performances were filmed and witnessed by Deniz's old friend Ron Asheton, and Niagara of Destroy All Monsters, who were about to tour Australia as Dark Carnival, with Hitmen D.T.K.

Against a background of the Velvet Underground's eardrum-melting second effort, *White Light/White Heat*, finally being available in Australia, almost a quarter of a century after it was unleashed in America, Tek had the bug again. He went on to make his debut solo album, *Take It to the Vertical*, at Sugar Hill, with Chris Masuak, drummer Scott Asheton and Angie Pepper, as well as Dust Peterson—a chopper-pilot buddy from Deniz's squadron—on bass.

An Australian tour was organised for August/September 1992. Pip Hoyle was added on keyboards, while Rob Younger took in several shows from the audience—further steps towards a Radio Birdman reunion.

The biggest date was in Sydney at the Hordern Pavilion, with the Rollins Band, Hard Ons and Kim Salmon and the Surrealists. The surprise was Scott Asheton. The once ultra-cool individual with the movie-star looks was barely recognisable under a baseball cap, unwilling and uncomfortable during an interview by the author. He wasn't rude or difficult but it was almost as if he had been instructed to stand in for the real Scott Asheton.

In any event, the album and tour marked a new beginning for Tek. Two years later, the Deniz Tek Group came into being, with the Iceman joined by Kent Steedman on guitar, Jim Dickson on bass and Celibate Rifle Nik Rieth on drums. The subsequent album, *Outside*, included Pip Hoyle and Chris Masuak, while Pip, Chris and Rob Younger appeared on Tek's *4-4 Number of the Beat* recording the following year. The allure of being around other Birdmen once more, despite major differences in the past, clearly was a powerful gravitational force.

These associations, and Radio Birdman's standing, were further bolstered by the pairing of silverchair and You Am I's Tim Rogers at the ARIA Awards in late 1995 and their delivery of 'New Race'.

Tim Rogers: 'I was perennially in awe of Rob Younger, so I took it seriously and tried to keep my head down and just play. But I busted an A string, I think, in the first bar and the whole guitar just popped outa tune. I was frozen in embarrassment. For years I couldn't look at Deniz when I'd run into him, let alone Rob. Ugh!'

Tek subsequently recorded the anthem with silverchair in New York, an experience that slightly altered his own approach to the song.

Deniz Tek: 'It morphed a little bit after I heard the silverchair version. I liked the way he [Daniel Johns] sang it.'

Thousands across Australia were about to be too wildly delirious to notice any change.

We Kept You Waiting?

By mid-evening, the area was barricaded off for safety reasons. The merch tables had been jostled and bumped all night by the tidal movement of humanity at Selinas in Sydney's eastern suburbs, but the increasingly violent shunting of the benches threatened to pin someone against the wall and cause serious injury.

It was January 1996 and several thousand had gathered to witness the return of Radio Birdman after almost two decades of legend and myth gathering in the wilderness.

And they were being toasted with the enormous venue's third-highest-ever beer intake. Not bad, given the benchmarks previously set by heavyweights the Angels and Midnight Oil.

Getting into the venue was a struggle and, once finally inside, there was a further battle to move in any particular direction. For one punter, entry alone was proving to be particularly difficult. His challenges associated with motor neurone disease were mercilessly pounced upon by some members of the new Radios army, who were doing their best to display just how far the band's audience had moved from the safe realm of the Oxford and early Fun House.

Mark Sisto: 'I'm outside and I hear these guys mocking someone. Amongst all the laughter and insults, I heard, "I was in Birdman." "Yeah, sure you were, mate! Which one were you? Deniz Tek? Ha! Ha! Yuk! Yuk!" It was [former Rats and early

Birdman bassist] Carl Rorke being cut down by these hoons. Why didn't I put these guys straight? I hate myself for that. I grabbed him by the shoulders. "Carl! Mate! Long time! Wait here, I'll get you a pass." I dash inside, go up to the dressing-room, and we went down and brought him up.'

Much had blossomed in Radio Birdman's absence. Died Pretty, fronted by Ron S. Peno, were beloved, with 1991's *Doughboy Hollow* their majestic pinnacle. Although defunct—at least, at the time—the Sunnyboys, with guitarist and Fun House dweller Richard Burgman, were mainstays on commercial rock radio. The Hoodoo Gurus (with long-time manager Michael McMartin, who steered Birdman's early career at Trafalgar), featuring other Oxford attendees Rick Grossman and Mark Kingsmill, as well as arch Radios fan Brad Shepherd, were nothing short of Oz rock royalty.

Original associate Dare Jennings, who printed the first Birdman T-shirt, had now founded the global-reaching Mambo clothing line.

There had been growth amongst the band as well. Chris Masuak was no longer a teenager and had almost two decades of touring and recording in the bank, with the Hitmen, the New Christs and the Screaming Tribesmen, as well as studio production. Rob Younger had honed his stagecraft in the New Christs and remained in demand to shape the recordings of other acts. Deniz Tek had a vibrant solo career.

But few ever expected a full and proper Radio Birdman reunion. It had long been in the way-too-fucking-hard basket. Few acts on the planet had ever held a torch of internal animosity quite as high as the Radios, much less gone on to shape that fire into a near art form. In the end, everything fell into place with minimal use of heavy earth-moving equipment.

The process began in early 1995, when the Deniz Tek Group were in Sydney to record as well as take part in Australia's Big Day Out festival. Also on Tek's agenda was delving into some history after seven boxes of tape materialised from Rockfield Studios in Wales containing the *Living Eyes* sessions from 1978.

Deniz Tek: 'John Foy [from Red Eye Records] contacted Rockfield owner Kingsley Ward to see if the original *Living Eyes* masters still existed. Kingsley found the 16-track tapes in a shed, boxes covered in mould. He was doubtful that they could be resurrected and was happy to give them to John, who had the tapes couriered back to Sydney. John gets total credit for retrieving those tapes.

'The band assembled at Trafalgar, now Electric Avenue, under the new owner and chief engineer Phil Punch. This time it was all of us, including Warwick, minus Ron. We listened to the tapes and had our photo taken. The first time all were in the same room at the same time since 1978. Rob and I remixed the album, along with the outtakes, with frequent input from Chris and the others. By that time, Rob and Chris both had extensive experience as producers.'

The home of much-loved godfather of the scene, Jim Dickson, became the Radios' HQ during the process with Big Jim's curries—made famous during his stint at the Petersham Inn in Sydney's inner west—the social lubricant and adhesive.

In late 1995, the Red Eye Records label reissued a fresh version of *Radios Appear*, along with an expanded edition of *Living Eyes*, to a market hungry for the band so many had heard about, but very few had actually seen. That too was being addressed.

Deniz Tek: 'John Foy was with [Big Day Out festival co-owner] Ken West at one of my solo gigs around that time at the

Annandale. Rob got up to sing a few songs, and there was a bit of magic in the air, and the crowd went off. Apparently, Ken West was impressed. He reportedly asked John, "What would it take?"'

Foy took this interest to the band, who then appointed long-time associate John Needham as their manager. Needham did the initial negotiations for the national BDO gigs, by far the biggest concert date on the Australian music calendar.

Deniz was back home in Montana when the call came, with an offer for Radio Birdman to be part of the Big Day Out, which was to include Rage Against the Machine, the Prodigy and Nick Cave with the Bad Seeds.

Deniz Tek: 'Chris Masuak happened to be visiting and was staying at the house. I said, "Hang on, lemme ask Chris." "Hey, Chris, John [Needham] is on the phone. Do you want to get the band back together and play the Big Day Out?" Chris said he would. We gave the thumbs-up, and went from there.'

Rob Younger: 'I was quite happy to reform in '96. Well, with vague reservations. I harboured no great bitterness at that point, so it wasn't a wrench particularly to reunite. We called it an experiment, if I recall, like a social experiment—interpersonal relationships being what they were at the end of the previous incarnation.'

Warwick Gilbert: 'I was a director at Disney by then, and thought, "Shit, yeah! I'll play the Big Day Out!" I'd forgotten all the rubbish and assumed everyone had grown up. I thought it was a nice way to kind to cap things off. It was great to see everybody.'

Chris Masuak: 'My way of thinking was this was a nice way to bury past hatchets and make things okay, and it seemed that's what it was.'

Ron Keeley, who had been in the UK for the previous fifteen years, had already been ushered back into the circle by Deniz, who'd invited him to one of his gigs in Paris. There, Keeley ended up back in the driver's seat behind the drums.

Ron Keeley: 'I think it was actually an audition to see if I could still do it. And I could.'

The drummer had always had a soft spot for anything that involved Tek, so when Deniz contacted him about the reformation he was straight in. But he had to address two issues as a matter of some urgency: buy a drum kit and prepare himself physically.

Ron Keeley: 'The first thing I did was sign up to a gym.'

After locking down the Big Day Out appearances, next was arranging national concert dates around their BDO commitments. A major fan of the band, and founder and director of concert promotion and artists management company Feel Presents, Tim Pittman, made his move.

Tim Pittman: 'I got in touch with John Needham, who gave me 24 hours to make an offer, as Premier Harbour [booking agency] were also bidding. Since I was due for surgery that day for a cruciate medial ligament tear in my right knee, I had to prepare and then make the offer via my hospital bed. Another patient heard me making the pitch and introduced himself as Rodney, the former monitor engineer for the Hitmen—small world, huh? I secured the deal with John the next day, and found our first crew person, all in one short hospital stay.'

The venture would include Big Day Out appearances across the country, as well as the Radios' own shows—with Wayne Kramer from the MC5 as the main opening act—in Sydney, Wollongong, Newcastle, Brisbane, Gold Coast, Canberra and Melbourne.

Rehearsals began, and for Warwick Gilbert there was a moment of sheer euphoria when Pip Hoyle was unable to attend for one session and the 'ghost noise' ambience that had entranced the bass player during the Blitzkrieg era in 1976 materialised once more.

Warwick Gilbert: 'We just rehearsed as a five piece and, *bang*, there was that sound again! And I thought, "Holy fuck!" All these years later and it was exactly the same. It was just fucking awesome! Without Pip blocking the spaces, it left room for the guitars to feedback and breathe. Those two guitars kind of swooping around on the edge of feedback. That was just bloody glorious, and it suited the name too, Radio Birdman. It was like jets or something, sirens, and the bass and drums went straight down the middle.

'It didn't really get captured on record—to my disappointment—but that flying, that feedback, was phenomenal.'

The first appearance by the returned Birdmen was an invite-only affair at the Manning Bar at Sydney University, but every major fan around the country seemed to be in attendance.

'We kept you waiting?' Rob Younger coolly teased in his opening remarks.

Ron Keeley: 'I was incredibly nervous. Could I really do it? So I thought, "I'll do everything I used to do." So I had some Jack Daniel's and smoked a joint. Now I hadn't smoked a joint for eighteen bloody years! And it was like the first time. You go, "Whoa! What's happening?" Getting behind a kit after that was really quite scary, but we got through it.'

Alley Brereton, who'd been present at Birdman's first-ever gig at the Excelsior in Surry Hills more than twenty years earlier, was at the Manning Bar to witness what was once the unthinkable.

Alley Brereton: 'I couldn't believe Radio Birdman were playing again. I nearly felt like crying. Everybody from the Fun House was there and they played so fantastically well. It wasn't some crappy reunion. It was still full of fire and spit and venom and out there. I just thought it was the greatest show ever!'

Brad Shepherd: 'It was more a relief to me, that I wasn't disappointed. I didn't know if they were still going to excite me the way they did when I was a teenager in Brisbane in the seventies, but they were thrilling.'

While everyone in the room danced the night away to the point of heat exhaustion, coupled with facial cramps from smiling for hours, one individual was unimpressed by it all.

Rob Younger: 'After that [gig], I thought, "This isn't going to work." It just didn't sound very good. It wasn't very powerful. The overall cohesion of it and force of the band was really light. I'd played in the New Christs, probably three line-ups by then. The first couple of them were really powerful—much more powerful than Radio Birdman were then. I'd experienced something far more thrilling. But we rose to the occasion.'

The tour proper commenced at an overly packed Narrabeen Sands Hotel in Sydney's northern suburbs on 10 January, before 1200 rabid fans. The summer heat hit the constantly-in-motion Ron Keeley particularly hard, with the battery of lights bearing down on him adding to his woes.

Ron Keeley: 'The lighting guy stuck a rack either side of me, and I sent a message back, "Turn the bloody lights off, or I'll put a stick through one of the cells." He did for a while, but then turned them back on, so I put a stick through one of the cells. He turned them off then.'

Chris Masuak, who had never shied away from volume, had quickly made his presence felt on stage. Perspex covers were made for his amps that allowed the sound to breathe, but tempered his fierce decibel output.

Chris Masuak: '[The complaint from the band was] "Masuak's too loud!" Okay. I'm in a rock and roll band, playing through a 50-watt Marshall [amp] with two speakers covered, angled away from the band.'

The protectors were soon discarded, but volume remained an issue and territorial disputes regarding the guitars also arose.

A string of big-room engagements followed, including Waves in Wollongong and Selinas before 2500 people, while their appearance at the Sydney leg of the Big Day Out on 25 January saw the Birdmen perform inside the Manufacturers Hall at the Showground. It was the same stage on which the Stones had appeared just over 30 years earlier to the day.

At the Palace in Melbourne, Wayne Kramer joined them on stage for an encore as the 2000 people in attendance pinched themselves.

Ron Keeley: 'Everybody had a turn to solo, and he [Kramer] turned to me and gave me the nod and I just shook my head, because it was "T.V. Eye" played at a ferocious pace. Probably the fastest we ever played it.'

Dave Laing: 'It was so wild and so crowded that, when I bought two cans of beer at the bar, by the time I'd made my way back across the room, both tins had been crushed flat against my chest.'

An appearance at the Melbourne BDO, followed by two nights at the Metro in Sydney—playing to almost 2500 people—then festival slots in Adelaide and Perth two days later on 4 February closed the reunion run.

The stats were impressive. All but one of their headliner gigs was sold out, with Birdman the biggest draw of the side shows associated with the Big Day Out.

However, while some of the old camaraderie had been in the air, there were also the customary sparks and acid burns, with Rob Younger's expression during a joint interview with Chris Masuak for Channel V in Perth seeming to tell something of the story.

Rob Younger: 'The Big Day Out gigs were fun. The band played really well for a time—better than I ever thought. But it eventually turned to shit . . .'

Chris Masuak: 'It was very apparent early on it was not going to be an adult reunion. It was going to go back to the same dynamics, and the real purpose of the reunion was simply to get some people back in the game on their terms. But I was determined to tough it out.'

A Spanish Axe and the ARIAs

The commercial to promote Nike Air sneakers during the 1996 Atlanta Olympics was a thrilling meeting of art and commerce, with Iggy and the Stooges' 'Search and Destroy'—from 1973's near universally ignored *Raw Power*—the soundtrack.

Iggy Pop: 'It was a real kick to see the athletes doing those things to the music and to hear our sound portrayed in that sort of a venue because for so many years I was shut out.'

Radio Birdman's days of being shunned were also over and they had just done a live-to-air broadcast from Melbourne's Triple R, as part of their 'Caught in the Act' program before an invited audience. The session was later released as the *Ritualism* album on their own Crying Sun label.

Fast forward and they were playing at the Mudslinger festival in Perth in January 1997. Evan Dando from the Lemonheads, one of the other acts on the bill, expressed his awe after witnessing the Radios' performance, to which Chris Masuak responded with words to the effect of 'It's easy when you're good'.

On the face of it, the remark was nothing more than a declaration of the band's self-belief. Yet the statement by the guitarist was deemed a cardinal breach of protocol.

All the while, between Birdman commitments, Deniz Tek's drive and tireless work ethic saw him embark on a string of other projects, such as Dodge Main—with MC5er Wayne

Kramer and Scott Morgan from the Rationals—as well as join the Sonic's Rendezvous Band at their reunion gig in 1999, at the Magic Stick in Detroit, with Tek in the honoured slot of the late Fred 'Sonic' Smith who died in 1994. Their songs from the Radios' repertoire were among the best received, as was the case in New York with Scott Morgan's Powertrane before a packed crowd.

Deniz Tek: 'We came back on with Ron Asheton and did half-a-dozen Stooges songs, and it was "New Race" with Ron that brought the house down.'

When in Sydney for several solo gigs, Tek looked as though he'd been digging the injured from the rubble of that building collapse.

Lee Taylor: 'He had this wad of stuff wrapped around his finger and was in pain. I said, "How the hell did you play with your finger like that?" He said, "I made up for it with wildness!"'

Warwick Gilbert wasn't feeling remotely as inspired. His initial hopes for Birdman with the 1996 reunion had evaporated.

Warwick Gilbert: 'It was unworkable for me as a bass player, and uninspiring for me as an artist. But it didn't matter—the brand was up and running, all my graphics were in place, and the tenfold audience couldn't tell the difference. Remarkably, neither could the band, so I left.

'I'm just grateful it happened at all. It was life-changing. It's just such a shame. It [the Blitzkrieg five piece] was an extraordinary band. You just knew it was the best. You didn't think it, you knew. I didn't stop missing it.'

Scene veteran Jim Dickson stepped in on bass, a role he had probably quietly dreamt of since first witnessing them in 1976. By the Australian tour of May/June 2002, it was obvious the wave of Birdman mania hadn't dipped in the slightest.

They played three packed nights at the Metro in Sydney, with the re-formed Lipstick Killers opening two shows.

Minutes before the first Metro gig, yours truly was dispatched across the road to Utopia Records to grab a CD of the first Blue Oyster Cult record. The band's intro music for the night was to be BOC's 'Then Came the Last Days of May', but no one had brought a copy.

Rehearsals for the run of shows had been fiery, for more than the usual reasons.

Ron Keeley: 'Jim was pumping so much power through his amp that the speaker coils got red hot and set fire to the cones. Everyone ran about like headless chooks, but I spotted a CO_2 extinguisher by the door, picked it up and put out the flames. Navy damage-control training, I guess, plus North Sea survival skills!'

The following year, Radio Birdman finally hit Europe once more, this time far more successfully, and with much stronger media support, than had been the case in 1978.

But for Deniz, eight years after they'd reunited, it was time to recalibrate. In 2004, he announced to his colleagues he wanted to push the boundaries and make a fresh new album, rather than rest on the past.

Deniz Tek: 'I decided that we had to have new material. I told the others that I wasn't interested in being a tribute band to our seventies selves.'

Ron Keeley was still living in the UK and immediately flagged his concerns. He had professional commitments and couldn't take several months off to work up material, go into the studio and record, and then take a further leave of absence to go on tour. He decided to do the honourable thing and vacate his position, to allow the band to continue unfettered. A letter of resignation was prepared, but never formally tendered.

In July 2004, DKT/MC5, the surviving members of the MC5—Michael Davis, Wayne Kramer and Dennis Thompson—hit Australia. Rob Younger and Deniz Tek were the local guests, among a rotating line-up, to celebrate the legacy of the Motor City Five.

The Birdmen and the DKT/MC5 project would meet up again in September, with both acts appearing at Spain's Azkena Festival, a major event before a large crowd, where they shared the bill with the reunited New York Dolls, the Flamin' Groovies and others. For the Australian act, the gig was a one-off, making it something of a poisoned chalice for Ron Keeley, who despite a week of rehearsal had no chance to build up full match fitness—drummers being the athletes of rock and roll—with a string of strenuous gigs prior.

For some reason, the Birdmen didn't take the festival stage until around two in the morning. It wasn't a good omen.

Ron Keeley: 'I don't rate it [Azkena] as my worst ever, but it was pretty bad, mostly because I had a mechanical problem with my kick pedal, which threw my timing right off. To this day, I don't know why I didn't call a roadie to sort out the problem, whatever it was.

'Later, Deniz accused me of yelling, "Next [song]!". Actually, I was yelling "Stop!" but one number followed another in a rush.'

Much as they had 24 hours earlier.

Ron Keeley: 'The night before, Rob insisted on a full run-through of the set. It was one of the best we ever played. The rehearsal room had whitewashed walls, which was just as well. Paint would have blistered.

'The problem with such a full-on rehearsal is that it is hard to muster the same level of physical and emotional commitment the next day. So even if my kick-pedal had been working properly, I would have been struggling'.

Keeley—a member of the Rats, with Rob Younger and Warwick Gilbert, as far back as 1974, and the most senior figure in Birdman's original scene—was shown the door the following day. What should have been a dignified earlier exit on his own terms was lost.

Deniz Tek: 'In retrospect, there was no reason to sack Ron when we did. I think that in a short time he would have declared that he was leaving, anyway, because of the pending recording. That would have been kinder, face-saving for him, and saved a lot of grief.'

Ron's departure saw the end of one internal personality clash, but there remained other civil wars to be fought.

In the outside world, the ground had expanded further.

Mambo founder Dare Jennings launched Deus Ex Machina, a brand that would also soon establish an international reputation.

Hollywood celebrities were donning New York Dolls T-shirts, with Jennifer Aniston of *Friends* wearing an MC5 number in one episode, while the character of Linda in *Becker* appeared with a banner for the documentary on the Detroit act, 'A True Testimonial', across her chest.

The Stooges were in semi-vogue globally as well. They reunited, with Ron Asheton on guitar, and toured Australia for the first time in 2006 as part of the Big Day Out. At each stop, more than 30,000 bodies went nuts for a band almost totally unknown in Oz in their initial lifetime.

The allure of the 'Detroit sound' had become an almost tunnel vision religion for some, worshipping anything musically connected to Michigan and all on the back of Radio Birdman. A mention of the Stooges or MC5 at every opportunity was now a hip ritual although there was no similar name dropping of John Lee Hooker or Jimmy Reed by AC/DC fans when the Youngs were storming through the late seventies.

There were other shifts in the culture.

In January 2007, Lou Reed brought his once-room-clearingly bleak *Berlin* to life at the ornate State Theatre in Sydney for several nights. Two months later, the surviving members of the New York Dolls—boy prince Johnny Thunders had died in 1991—finally visited Australia, only for ticket sales to the band's sole Sydney appearance at the Metro to be so slow, they were offered as two for one. And it still didn't sell out.

Radio Birdman's star, however, was on the rise on the back of a fresh-ground-breaking new album, *Zeno Beach*, with drummer Russell 'Rusty' Hopkinson from You Am I after an alliance with the MC5's Dennis Thompson fell through. The recording was more of a collaborative effort in terms of songwriting with a note of 'special thanks' to Ron Keeley and a dedication to the memory of Rats' and original Radios' bassist Carl Rorke, who passed away in 2006, on the sleeve.

Part of the subsequent touring schedule was their first dates in America, almost thirty years after originally being planned.

By that point the ongoing decibel roar on stage was in full ear-bleeding cry.

Deniz Tek: 'I didn't turn up to match [Masuak's] volume, because I needed to hear the drums, primarily, and the singing.

Often, I even turned down a bit, so I could hear something of what was going on above the crushing volume from Chris's side of the stage.

'We had sound guys quit because of it. And we had many people walk out halfway through shows, because the [sound] balance was so bad.'

After the final date in Denver, the Radios flew to Melbourne in July 2007 to be inducted into the ARIA Hall of Fame at the Regent Hotel, by silverchair's Daniel Johns.

Deniz Tek: 'We had been invited to be inducted before. Maybe twice. Both times, we politely declined. We had no interest in getting an industry award from an establishment that had rejected us from the start. The third time, we decided to accept, mainly because our families found out.'

Rob Younger: 'I still think we should have refused it. I think our legacy would have been more strongly reflected by continuing to stand outside the so-called industry. We took a certain pride, maybe even delight, in being seen as outsiders. That felt like an accomplishment.

'Suddenly you're in favour and you're supposed to graciously accept? I wasn't feeling that way. I was a bit surprised everyone [in the band] really wanted that award.'

But what should have been a 'Fuck you!' celebration was displaced by grief, with word of the tragic passing of Pip Hoyle's son Will just prior to the event. Pip immediately flew to Sydney, while the remainder of the band blew the roof off the ARIAs room with fiery versions of 'Aloha Steve & Danno' and 'New Race'. With the departure of Rusty Hopkinson who remained in the US with You Am I, Murray Shepherd [the Hitmen] sat in, going almost full circle from his days in rabid Birdman fans the Fun Things.

Ron Keeley: 'Warwick and I were invited on the basis that we wouldn't cause any fuss. A "no bile clause", it was called.'

Warwick Gilbert: 'For me and Ron sitting in the audience, it was really insulting. They had an excuse that they didn't have time to rehearse us. For fuck's sake! I had to talk Ron out of not standing up and booing them! But I was very pleased to be accepted in that forum by my peers. I think personally it was an achievement.'

Arriving back in Sydney and collecting his bag at the airport, Rob Younger saw an upside.

Rob Younger: 'The award, being so sharp, had punched its way through my bag. There was this big spike sticking out when it came around on the carousel at Sydney Airport. It looked great! I thought, "That's almost worth accepting the thing."'

With Rusty back on drums, the band—less a grieving Pip Hoyle—returned to America and Europe. The home stretch of the tour would be a disaster, with visa issues, the subsequent rejigging of travel arrangements, the dumping of a London date that had already sold out, and the departure of their drummer leaving the Radios without a beat keeper for the final dates in Greece.

Russell 'Rusty' Hopkinson: 'If I had my time again, I would handle things differently. The fact is being a part of delivering some of those tunes was as alluring as any drug. Playing a song like 'Do the Pop' with Rob just dancing like a dervish whilst everyone locked in was an honour. But at the same time, it was a hard band to be in. There were a lot of internal dynamics and conflict you had to take on board and constantly traverse, and I'd had my fill.'

A member of the band's road crew, Joel Perdue, thankfully stepped up to the kit. However, the die was cast and the morning following the final date in Athens, Rob Younger handed in his notice.

Rob Younger: 'The reason I left mainly relates to two things, musical and interpersonal. The latter was all to do with Masuak, who was intolerable.

'His guitar tone had become so fucking shrill. Totally inappropriate in the context of the band's desired musical style. And the ridiculous volume he played at, in defiance of reasonable requests to turn it down, so it wasn't deafening Pip and Rusty, and drowning out my monitors. The band's music was turning to shit.'

The issues stretched further and deeper than ampage. Nonetheless, with Younger's departure, added to their other personnel losses, the Birdvan drove off into the sunset in October 2007.

Deniz Tek: 'The situation with Chris, both personally and musically, had reached breaking point. It had been increasingly miserable for years. Rob said he was done, we had lost the drummer, Pip was out, and it looked like the band was finished, anyway, so we just let it go.'

Dig It Up

It was February 2014 and one of Bruce Springsteen's minders approached Deniz Tek and Rob Younger, minutes before one of a string of dates by 'the Boss' in Sydney.

'I think you're going to be very pleasantly surprised tonight!' Springsteen's representative announced. The 'New Jersey Devil' had a habit of playing a song by a well-known local act on his global tour stops. Was he about to perform 'Aloha Steve & Danno'? Maybe 'New Race'? Or the hit that wasn't, 'More Fun'? The Birdmen took their seats in the arena, the lights went down, and the E Street Band kicked into . . . 'Just Like Fire Would' by the Saints.

They had bigger fish to fry that year, after manager John Needham was contacted by Alberts, the home of the Easybeats, Rose Tattoo, the Angels and AC/DC, regarding a wealth of recorded material they had discovered in their archives. The contents of those boxes would see a way forward for Radio Birdman, while bringing a long-standing internal issue to a brutal close.

Iggy Pop, who knew about rebirth and loss, had returned to Australia in 2011, again in Stooge mode and once more as part of the Big Day Out festival, this time with *Raw Power*–era axeman James Williamson, after the passing of Ron Asheton in 2009.

In April, Deniz Tek was invited to take part in a memorial concert for Asheton at the Michigan Theater in Ann Arbor.

It was already something of a hallowed site for the Radios' man as it was where he'd seen movies and spilt his popcorn as a kid.

Hosted by Henry Rollins, the event saw Tek join the Stooges on guitar—while Williamson took a break—for 'T.V. Eye', 'Loose', 'Dirt' and 'Real Cool Time', and then with Williamson for an encore of 'No Fun'.

To cap off the pinching-himself moment, Iggy spoke glowingly of Tek in interviews around the occasion.

It was the reaching of both a personal and professional summit—albeit mournfully—for someone who had first seen the Stooges back in 1968.

Deniz Tek: 'It was very much a career highlight. I was able to honour my dear, departed friend, and play a set as a Stooges guitarist, all at once. It was an immensely powerful experience.'

The moment also paved the way for Deniz's later collaboration with James Williamson on *Acoustic K.O.*—a rendering of four Stooges' songs unplugged with the title punning on their chaotic final curtain—and the *Two to One* album.

In the interim, Tek was involved in another pairing. In 2012, Feel Presents staged 'Dig It Up! The Hoodoo Gurus Invitational', a national event devised and co-curated by Feel, along with the Gurus, as a celebration of the band's 30th anniversary. In Sydney, the bill featured Died Pretty, the not-so-secret re-emergence of the Sunnyboys as Kids in Dust, as well as Seattle's sixties punk kings the Sonics plus the Fleshtones and Redd Kross—and one other act, titled simply Tek and Younger.

Tim Pittman (Feel Presents): 'Brad Shepherd had asked for Birdman to play "Dig It Up". Their future was unknown, so I suggested something more casual: a party band playing a mix of covers and originals under another name, to lessen the expectation and pressure. I spoke to Deniz about the concept, and when he asked what it [would] be called, I suggested Tek and Younger. That gave an idea of what to expect, but also kept it open to surprise. I think it worked.'

The line-up for the one-off appearance was Deniz and Rob, plus Jim Dickson, Dave Kettley and Calvin Welch.

The following year, the second Dig It Up! Gurus Invitational, again via Feel Presents, featured the Flamin' Groovies, the Buzzcocks and the Blue Oyster Cult, in what was BOC's first-ever trip to Australia.

Brad Shepherd: 'I have a very strong memory of playing "Kick Out the Jams" in Melbourne at the Forum. The Blue Oyster Cult, Hoodoo Gurus and Rob singing, and then everyone else joining in. You know the inside [sleeve] of [the Blue Oyster Cult's] *On Your Feet or on Your Knees*, with the five guitar players? We had about twenty!'

That was roughly the same number of boxes of Radio Birdman recordings that were found at Alberts.

Deniz Tek: 'It was odd, because we were never there [at Alberts] to record, but they had all the Trafalgar sessions, including demos and outtakes, plus the entire Paddington Town Hall gig from December 1977. John [Needham, Birdman manager] and I retrieved the tapes and had them restored. I listened to everything and selected the best.'

A boxed set of that unearthed material, along with the original albums, was released in 2014 on Needham's Citadel label—a package of eight discs, including a DVD—by which time Deniz had tied up some loose ends regarding the song 'Insane Alive', which had been based on 'Wild in the Streets' by Garland Jeffreys.

Deniz Tek: 'I referenced Garland Jeffreys in the song "I-94", and many years later he contacted me about it. He thought it was great and put a link on his website. We met up in New York and got acquainted. "Insane Alive" was recorded by both TV Jones and Radio Birdman, but neither version was ever finished or released, until the box set. By then, I was in touch with Garland, and he approved it.'

The most obvious way to promote the project was with a reunion, but that, of course, was problematic.

Rob Younger: 'I was asked by John and Deniz if I would consider reforming with the others for some shows, if Masuak wasn't invited back. Pip, I was told, had stipulated that Chris's exclusion was paramount. I said I would, adding that I'd be more keen if we had a European tour built into that idea. At the time I made the comment that Chris would be completely gutted by all this, as obviously he'd take the news badly, and be considerably hurt, so I was empathetic to a degree. But I also knew he'd be the same old problem as previously.'

Deniz Tek: 'Neither Pip nor Rob would consider playing in the band with Chris again, so the choice was to reunite without Chris, or not at all. Finally, Pip, Rob, Jim and I agreed to carry on with a new drummer and new guitarist.

'I got stuck with the unenviable task of informing Chris that we were getting back together without him. He hasn't spoken to me since. It was the right call, but I still have nightmares about it.'

Chris Masuak: 'I was excluded because Younger has had his sights on me for decades—working at me, trying to hurt me, trying to get under my skin. I allowed it to continue for so long, because of my incredible stupid loyalty to the band and the music, and, in fact, to those people in the band who were clearly no longer my friends.

'I at one time had tremendous admiration of the band and the things it stood for and the people. I hoped against hope that somehow these things could be recovered. Well, they couldn't be and were never going to be. There was a constant search for excuses and reasons for me to be not okay.

'All the narrative from that side of the fence has been that I have a problem with Rob. I don't have a problem with Rob. Rob has a problem with me. And I acknowledged [in emails] that there was a problem, and I said that for the sake of the band I would keep clear of that, sit in the back of the bus and do my job.

'So I have an [email] undertaking to Tek that there'll be no problems from my side. The next thing is the announcement that they'll be going ahead, he's so sorry, blah blah blah.

'The thing is . . . the band was really my calling and there was nothing they could do or say to me, no harassment or insult or humiliation really mattered, because that band was the most important thing. I was loyal to the band. And it just got worse and worse and worse, and intensely personal. In the end, they won.

'It [his tenure] ended with an email.'

The new Radio Birdman line-up emerged in November 2014, with Rob Younger, Deniz Tek, Pip Hoyle and Jim Dickson joined by Nik Rieth on drums and Dave Kettley on guitar.

Deniz Tek: 'We went back to being a functional team again, for the first time in decades.'

The Golden Age of Leather

'My wife and I had to move from down the front,' volunteered the gentleman in line at the bar inside Sydney's Enmore Theatre. 'I felt something on the back of my legs and I turned and this bloke was pissing on me!'

The occasion could have been any time, anywhere in the golden-shower era of Australian pub rock of the early eighties.

The packed Enmore included some physically large, more than slightly intimidating bodies, the sort of punter that once comprised the Angels' 'Mr Damage' legions. Some were happily slamming into others, and then, for no apparent reason, suddenly charging their way through the audience like battering rams. There was even the throwing of the metal 'horns' finger salute.

It was June 2017 and this was Radio Birdman's audience, in part at least. In fact, the capacity at modern-day Radios' gigs had for some time been rethought accordingly, with rooms that typically held 1000 people only able to accommodate, say, 800 Birdman fans. Size mattered.

The great migration had begun with the New Race tour in 1981, was given steroids at the 1996 reunification, and now had set up camp in the car park.

The demographic the band had risked life and limb to address in the suburbs during the mid-seventies had, in the end, come to them. And they came not to heckle nor launch projectiles, but to worship, and as such there was a distinct warmth in the room, as there had been for some time.

Rob Younger: 'People are actually singing along on choruses, for Christ's sake! In the old days, not everyone was in the room to enjoy the band, and there were more confrontational aspects to it. It used to be just me throwing myself around. Now I'm trying to sing and throw myself around. Not as insecure as I used to be, I suppose.'

There was other movement. The Radios then made it onto the big screen, through Jonathan Sequeira's 2017 movie *Descent into the Maelstrom*. After the sold-out Sydney premiere at the Event Cinemas, the author, at the request of Deniz Tek, facilitated a Q&A session with Deniz, Pip Hoyle and Sequeira.

The doco had already been given a more private unveiling for band and friends in the Chauvel Cinema at the revamped Paddington Town Hall, the site of the bloodied glory performance in late December 1977, just a few blocks from the Oxford Hotel.

★

Ron S. Peno, the elfin figure on the bow of the eternally ethereal Died Pretty, had scaled the stairs of the Oxford on countless occasions in 1976 and 1977.

Tragically, the true original believer in Radio Birdman was diagnosed with cancer in January 2019 and was deeply touched to receive calls from both Rob Younger and Deniz Tek the night before his first stint in hospital.

With his condition in mind, each time I had questions for Ron for this book, I opted for text messages in the first instance, in the belief that a few words on a screen to be read at leisure might be a less intrusive form of communication than blunt cold calls. He usually rang me back anyway.

For a time, there seemed to be some hope in his battle but in April 2021, just days after a national tour with Died Pretty, it was confirmed the beast had circled back, this time fastening its talons tightly.

On 3 July 2023, just after nine in the morning, I again needed to activate the text-first approach with some further points for discussion and clarification. And once more, Ron opted to speak directly in reply rather than tap out a response.

But this time, judging from the background noise, he wasn't sitting quietly at home. Instead, he was speaking from under the endless fluorescent white stare of hospital lighting and minutes from another round of treatment.

Precisely the scenario I had long been at pains to avoid.

The near child-like thrill in his voice from our previous discussions was now buried under a lead weight of cold yet calm resignation.

I made several attempts at wishing him well—an entirely shithouse endeavour under the circumstances—and excusing myself, allowing the singer space and time to focus on the procedure that approached.

Ron wouldn't hear of it—after all, he had made the effort to call—so we spoke for about five minutes. After quickly dispensing with the questions I had sent to him earlier, he had a far more pressing concern.

A matter of reverence.

'I want to make sure I've fully expressed to you my enormous respect and admiration for Radio Birdman,' he said solemnly.

We didn't speak again. Ron passed on 11 August 2023.

Maybe he was five foot one. Doesn't matter.

Ron S. Peno was always, and will forever be, our Iggy.

He missed the reissue, late in the year, of the overseas version of the *Radios Appear* LP, a copy of which was given to major fan Prime Minister Anthony Albanese, who also receives each new T-shirt design.

The record was no doubt blasted through the Lodge in Canberra on the $12,000 record player that President Biden had presented to the PM at the White House in October 2023—complete with POTUS seal on the turntable mat.

Radio Birdman have not always soared in such distinguished surrounds, making the announcement of their 50th anniversary tour in June and July 2024—snappily titled Birdman Five-0—and possibly their farewell all the more remarkable.

The celebrations were tempered just days after the half-century declaration by the death of the MC5's Wayne Kramer. Then came news that Charlie Georgees, the much-loved guitarist primarily in the Hellcats with Ron S. Peno and then the Other Side alongside Rob Younger, had also passed.

Sadly, it didn't end there. Radio Birdman lifer Alley Brereton then died suddenly, a loss publicly acknowledged online by the band.

Warm, strong and worldly, Alley—a nickname bestowed by James Griffin reflecting her habit of moving about Sydney via the back alleys of Darlinghurst, Paddington and Surry Hills—was the heartbeat behind Birdman even before day one as well as a marvellous, deeply expressive singer too few knew about. Within her was a string of unwritten books, yet-to-be recorded albums and movies still to move into production.

She was thrilled at the prospect of seeing her favourite band mark their half century later in the year but will undoubtedly be there in spirit, dancing joyously from a position considerably more elevated than the alcoves of Paddington Town Hall.

★

It was a torturous, heroic path initially for Radio Birdman, but after their early local aping of Alice Cooper's achievement of clearing the Cheetah Room in LA and darkly shadowing the Stones at Altamont, the Radios now rightly claim a revered position on the global stage.

Their logo is etched several layers of skin deep on a multitude of devotees around the world and displayed on their cars, surfboards and any other flat surface of worth.

It might be a stretch to rejig John Lennon's famous ground-zero statement, regarding the impact of Elvis Presley, that—in Australia—before Birdman there was nothing.

Still, while sixties' acts such as the Easybeats and the Masters Apprentices had a considerable impact, they didn't provide the path to transcendence the Radios summoned up nor open a channel for change.

To be touched by Birdman in the mid to late seventies, even if only via a sense of them, an awareness, was to be transformed. Being smitten by the band didn't just make for a private badge of honour but a level of personal elevation. Senses were heightened, expectations sharpened and internal wiring rerouted, forever changed. Every new enlistee since has had much the same experience.

Radio Birdman took on a cultural landscape in Sydney and a seemingly intractable seventies' conservatism and won, shaping a new future at a time some were howling none existed.

Their gig beats your entire festival.

Alley Brereton making her mark in the UK. Photo: Penny Cullen.

Acknowledgements

These things take time, for me at least. I first discussed a book such as this with Deniz Tek back in the late eighties during an interview for the *Under the Ashes* boxed set.

What seems like months of interviews, certainly countless phone calls, emails, texts and conversations later, here we are.

The team at Allen & Unwin made it all possible; Jane Palfreyman, my publisher, was enthusiastic from day one. Genevieve Buzo provided both oversight and insight, while Samantha Kent went above and beyond, calmly and expertly charting a comfortable editorial course to the finishing line. I'm hugely grateful.

Patrick Mangan, the neurosurgeon of editing, lifted and sharpened the manuscript into its best possible form.

My wife, Tracey, quietly kept everything else ticking over, which allowed me to be locked in a room for years writing and researching. I'm eternally thankful.

A major part of this tale revolves around a cast of original followers of Radio Birdman in Sydney who made up a mosaic, a veritable force field, around the band. I was constantly mindful of delving into much more than old memories but rather venturing onto highly personal ground, with many never having gone public prior to this. So my heartfelt thanks go to Abby Beaumont, the late Alley Brereton, Angie Pepper, Anny Douglass, Andrew Thomas, Andy 'Mort' Bradley, Barry James,

Bob Short, Brad Franks, Bruce Tindale, Catherine Kingsmill, the late Charlie Georgees, Clyde Bramley, Colleen Giles, Damien Minton, Dan McAloon, Dare Jennings, Doug Lonsdale, Duncan Taylor, Frank Cotterell, George Munoz, Glenn Rafferty, Gregg Masuak, Jeff Sullivan, Jim Flowers, John Needham, Johnny Kannis, Joan Cootes, Jules R.B. Normington, Julie Mostyn, Kath 'Good Vibes' Kendall, Lee Taylor, Mark Sisto, Mark Taylor, Michael Charles, Mick Lyne, Patrick Bingham-Hall, Paul Gearside, Penny Ward, Ria Lyne, Richard Burgman, Rick Grossman, Roger Grierson, Roger Roland Di Lernia, the late Ron S. Peno, Sarah Bishop, Shelley Kay, Steve Harris, Stephen Vineburg, Tara Anderson, Tim Johnson, Toby Creswell and Tracey Burgess.

Thanks also to the following for their recollections, views and assistance: Albert Bouchard, Andy Newman, Andy Turner, Arnaud Durieux, Biba Charity Peno, Bill Holdship, Bob King, Bob Spencer, Bob Yates, Brad Shepherd, Bruce Griffiths, Bruce Milne, Carol Jamison, Charles Fisher, Chris Jones, Chris Pepperell, Clare Moore, Craig Barman/Regan, Christie Eliezer, the late Damien Lovelock, David Laing, David N. Pepperell, David Nichols, David Williams, David Wilson, Dennis 'Machinegun' Thompson, Desley Hatfield, Frank Brunetti, Freddie Brookes, Garry Gray, Glenn A. Baker, Glenn Terry, Greg Morris, the Grey Brothers, Harry Butler, Henry Rollins, Henry Weld, Ian Hartley, Irish John, James Anfuso, James Williamson, Jeff Jarema, Jen Jewel Brown, Jim Manzie, Joe Camilleri, Jo Knight, John Brewster, John Cotter, John Dowler, Jon Schofield, Jonathan Sequeira, Keith Glass, Kent Steedman, Kevin Blyth, Keith Walker, Larry McGrath, Leigh Stephens, Marcus Schintler, Maree Robertson, Mark Corbett, Mark Gable, Michael Gethen, the late Michael McMartin,

Mick Harvey, Mike Hurst, Monte Connor, Murray Shepherd, Paul Trynka, Peter Garrett, Peter Rix, Phill Calvert, Philip Mortlock, Pete O'Doherty, Ray Ahn, Ricky Brunaccioli, Richard Guilliatt, Rob Hastie, Robin Wills, Rod Willis, Robert Grieve, Roger Gold, Roger Miller, Ronald Clayton, Rusty Hopkinson, Ruth Corbett, Scot Smith, Simon Tatz, Stuart Coupe, Scott Morgan, Seymour Stein, Scott Henthorn, Stephen Cummings, Steve Abrahall, Steve Kambly, Steve Lorkin, Steve 'Mac' McLennan, Suellen Dainty, Suzy Ramone, Steve Long, Sam Cutler, Tim Pittman and his ongoing grounding skills, Tim Rogers, Tony Robertson, Toby Mamis, Tracey Shorter Davies, Wiktor Zubenko, Warren Nunn and Wyatt.

Thanks also to those who wished their contributions to remain anonymous.

As for the Birdmen themselves, I'm hugely grateful for their trust, patience and frankness. I scratched far deeper than some were comfortable with but the vast majority of my inquiries—and there were more than a few over the course of this project—were met with candour and understanding. Seventeen-year-old me still can't believe I was in any way involved in such a process.

As far as other sources go, I've of course drawn from *RAM* magazine as well as *Juke*, Steve Gardner's *Noise for Heroes* and *Another Tuneless Racket*, *Australian Rolling Stone*, *Roadrunner*, *B Side*, Harry Butler's *DNA*, Craig Regan/Barman's I-94 Bar, Ian McFarlane's *Prehistoric Sounds* and countless articles I've read over the decades, along with a large number of online posts.

Vivien Johnson's book *Radio Birdman* was a major guide and I also tapped Paul Trynka's *Iggy Pop: Open Up and Bleed*, Iggy Pop's *I Need More*, Joel Selvin's *Altamont*, George Munoz's

When the Birdmen Flew: An Illustrated History, Roger Grierson's *Lobrow*, Chris Masuak's *Faith and Practice in Bedlam* and many more.

Thanks to Ron Keeley for offering me his in-progress autobiography as a background resource and Deniz Tek for allowing me access to several draft chapters of his life and times.

Movies? Primarily, *Gimme Shelter* and Jonathan Sequeira's *Descent into the Maelstrom*.

I'd like also to shine a light on a few individuals. Anny Douglass for the ice-breaking and the High Priest, Jim Dickson, provided spiritual guidance, calm direction and chocolate digestives.

Angie Pepper placed her trust in me and this project. She also undertook the herculean task of digging through a wealth of archival material and personal items and then drove for much of a day to deliver the treasure trove to me in Sydney. Angie's detective work was also invaluable in identifying photos, times and places. A true light in the dark. I lack sufficient grasp of the language to fully express my appreciation to her.

Last, but no means least, Bob Short, King of Punk, generously fielded countless painstaking questions about minor details and is deserving of a national monument for services to the culture. He still plays regularly, and true to his DIY punk roots, has his own label, Full On Noise Records. And he can write. His first book, *Trash Can*, is still hopefully available through Lulu books while the second, *Filth*, might require some digging. Both are well worth seeking out, as are his comics.

All quotations are from interviews conducted by the author, unless otherwise stated.

Photo: Lee Taylor